Tibetan Astrology

By
Michael Erlewine

Tibetan Astrology

An ebook from

Startypes.com
315 Marion Avenue
Big Rapids, Michigan 49307

First published 2007

© 2006 Michael Erlewine / StarTypes.com

ISBN 978-0-9794970-6-3

Graphic designs by Michael Erlewine

Some image elements © 2007 JupiterImages Corp.

This book is dedicated to
Sange Wangchuk

Who translated and patiently taught me the
fundamentals

Tibetan Astrology

Table of Contents

Tibetan Astrology

Tibetan Astrology

An Introduction

The Spiritual Roof of the World

Tibet, often called the spiritual and physical "roof of the world," has been the source of great inspiration to Westerners for over two centuries. Part of this attraction may be due to the fact that Tibetan astrology is inextricably bound to Tibetan Buddhism. With few exceptions, the primary practicing astrologers in Tibet have for centuries always been and are today Buddhist monks. The word for astrology in Tibetan is "Tsi," and astrologers are called Tsi-Pa, those who practice "Tsi." In Tibet to learn something about astrology is to learn something about the dharma and Buddhism, and usually vice versa. Tibetan Buddhist monks all use astrology.

I found out early on that I could not just skim the astrology off the top of the Tibetan Buddhism. In order to understand Tibetan astrology, I had to learn something about the Buddhist psychology in which it is embedded. I doubt that I am alone in this.

In other words, it is impossible to separate Tibetan astrology from Tibetan Buddhism, so it is important for readers to understand at least something about the Dharma and how it relates to the astrology of Tibet.

To best prepare for what follows, here are several concepts that you may need to better understand this material, so please bear with me. First, let's examine what it is to learn any astrological technique, Tibetan or otherwise.

Tibetan Astrology

What is Astrological Technique?

Most traditional astrological techniques are originally the residue of a particular insight or astrological realization that someone, somewhere, had. After the initial fire of the original insight is gone (the realization passes), what remains is what we can remember that led to the experience, whatever caused us to have the realization in the first place. This is what ritual is all about, trying to recreate a sacred experience – to realize it again.

Therefore, most astrological technique amounts to a method to capture or recreate that realization experience, a method or technique to realize an experience or insight again, if possible. In our day-to-day work, many of us are given and use techniques for which we have never had realization and in which we have not been fully empowered. We are lucky if we get realization on even several of the many astrological techniques that we use. Unfortunately, that's just the way it is.

To realize a technique in the truest sense, we somehow have to do just that, make it real, re-member or actually recreate it. And to do that, ultimately, we must become empowered in that technique through having the actual experience that caused it to arise in the first place or through the guidance of someone who has that realization. This is why I like to study with master astrologers, if I can find them. They have the experience and therefore the capacity to empower us.

In short, many of us hope that with the help of a good book or a teacher (and a lot of concentration) we will sooner or later find our way to the experience itself and actually have that experience, the one that originally gave rise to the astrological technique in the first place.

Tibetan Astrology

If we can manage that, we can begin to use the technique in something more than a rote or mechanical fashion, for we have ourselves "realized" it. It has become part of us; we understand what it is about and how it works. This is even truer when it comes to a whole new kind of astrology such as that which the Tibetans use. We need a guide.

Don't worry; I am not suggesting that I am a teacher in this subject. I am just a fellow traveler, but I am pointing out here that the best guide to Tibetan astrology I know is learning something about its root, the dharma. In the end that is what I had to do. Since it may save you making some of the same mistakes I did, let me briefly tell you how I got into all of this.

The Swans and the Lake

In the 1970s the head of the Tibetan Karma Kagyu lineage, His Holines the 16th Gyalwa Karmapa, was asked why he had come to visit America. His answer was: "If there were a lake, the swans would go there." And so it has been, for the last 35 years or so. Many of the great Tibetan teachers have come to America to visit and to teach the dharma.

My interest in all of this stretches back to the 1950s and the beat movement -- Jack Kerouac, Allen Ginsburg, etc. These writers helped to introduce Buddhism to many of us at that time. Writers like Allan Watts and D.T. Suzuki (who wrote and spoke on Buddhism) educated a whole generation on the subject, but back then it was mostly theoretical. In the late 50s and very early 60s, Buddhism appeared to me as one interesting philosophical view among many others such as Existentialism and the Beat movement itself.

Buddhism at that time (of the Allan Watts variety) was necessarily very intellectual and philosophical --

something to think about and have words over. After all, we were just hearing about it. We would sit up until late at night, smoke cigarettes (I am sorry to say), drink lots of coffee, and talk about such things until the sun came up. It was all very "heady."

Few of us made the connection that Buddhist thought was not just something else to think or philosophize about, but rather a path or dharma, a method, something to do – a way of action. We knew little of methods. This came much later.

It is important to make clear that (as I understand it) Buddhism is not a religion in the ordinary sense of that word. Although I have worked with it for many years, I have never considered myself as particularly religious. Going to church once a week, as most Americans do, is not going to solve many of my problems. I need something I can do all week long.

What I was interested in back then was psychology -- the human psyche and the mind itself. In fact, my interest in astrology itself can be traced to an interest in the psyche -- how the mind and all of its experiences work. How does the mind work?

In the early 70s, Buddhism took the next step to being understood as a practical path when the work of a young Tibetan lama Chogyam Trungpa Rinpoche became available. His book "Cutting through Spiritual Materialism" is perhaps the best example of what I am pointing toward, a practical Buddhism – mind practice.

With Trungpa came the end of Tibetan Buddhism of the through-a-glass-darkly and sit-and-talk-about-it variety. Previous to Trungpa's appearance, most insight into the inner or astrological side of the Buddhism of Tibet came through writers like Alexandra David-Neal, T. Lobsang Rampa, T. Evans-Wentz, and other early writers on what has been called "esoteric Buddhism," people like H.P. Blavatsky and C.W. Leadbeater. Even then, there was little or no mention of Tibetan astrology per se. These writers were Westerners who could not help but put their own spin on the subject of Buddhism. Trungpa ended that.

Chogyam Trungpa Rinpoche made it very clear to us that Buddhism was not only a philosophy to think about, but above all a life path to walk, something very practical to put into practice in day-to-day life. He pointed out that Buddhism was primarily a way of handling our experience in this world we live in -- a dharma path. I can remember that this came as almost total news to those of us brought up on the intellectual Buddhism of the late 50s and 60s.

I met Chogyam Trungpa early in 1974 when I helped to bring him to Ann Arbor, Michigan to speak. I designed the posters for his event and ended up as his chauffer for the weekend. From the moment I picked him up at the airport, suffice it to say that I quickly got a very different take on Buddhism, which leads me to the other main point that I must present before we can discuss Tibetan astrology, and that is meditation.

Prior to meeting Trungpa, I had the (quite common) idea that meditation was a method to relax around, a way to get away from the chaos of day-to-day life -- a form of stress management. I had never found the time nor interest for it. The whole idea was boring to me. I was way too active to sit still.

No sooner had I brought Trungpa Rinpoche back from the airport than he took me into a room with him, closed the door behind us, and proceeded to introduce me to my own mind. Looking back, I realize he was showing me how to meditate, although he didn't call it that. In fact, he never named it. And there was no prologue. He did not announce what he was about to do. He just jumped in.

At the time I don't believe I was able to grasp all of what was going on. It was only years later that I realized what really happened on that day. What I experienced through his instruction (and in his presence) were some real answers to questions that had always tortured me – big questions, questions about death, about letting go, about actually living life - things like that. Most of all, Trungpa pointed out and demonstrated what real awareness looked and acted like. My response was a simple: "Oh, now I get it."

I watched him enjoying and using his mind in a multitude of ways that I had never considered as possibilities. It was a pure case of monkey see, monkey do, and I wanted to be like he was being. Where I was used to sitting around, twiddling my thumbs, and waiting for the next thing to happen, Trungpa Rinpoche was all over the place, peering, poking at, questioning, and mostly enjoying and investigating every moment and every thing. I wanted to kick myself that I had never thought to make use of my own time like this.

Trungpa demonstrated before my eyes that the mind and our awareness could be worked with - practiced. Intuition or true insight could be developed. All you had to do was to try and do it. The mind could be trained. What a thought!

My original idea of meditation as at best a way to relax, and at worst a big bore was giving way to something much more active. I began to see that meditation had to do with my developing insight and intuition, learning to use my own mind to connect within myself and the taking possession or advantage of our current situation -- whatever it happens to be.

From that day in February 1974, I began to connect more with myself and to explore the so-called outer world in a somewhat different way. Once you see someone do something for real, you know that you can probably do that too. I had seen something done and I wanted to do that too.

What I am getting at here is that the primary tool for learning astrology in the Tibetan system is not a set of ephemerides, a series of calculations, and lots of research in books. Instead, it involves establishing this inner connectivity -- call it insight, intuition, meditation, mind practice, mind training, whatever you want to call it. When I first saw it, I had no words at the time, but I got the idea. It leapt inside me.

I had grown up here in the West where learning astrology is often centered on memorizing the various correspondences between terms, like: Aries relates to Mars, relates to the Ascendant, relates to the first house, and so on. If you can't get into learning about astrological correspondences, then you are going to have real difficulty grasping classic western astrology as it was taught in the 19th and 20th centuries.

In Tibetan astrology, the primary educational tool is your own mind and learning to use it and your intuition in a direct and practical way. Tibetans call this "mind practice" or most often just "meditation." Of course they have a dozen or so words for meditation. My point here is that if you approach the Tibetan lamas, you may not find easy access to their astrological teachings without some very basic mind training, not because they won't share it with you, but because your mind (and probably your life) is a little too chaotic and rushed to get a handle on it. You don't have time for insight. You have to make time. Time is also something we make.

And this lack of access to the teachings is not because these matters are in any way secret, but rather because we may lack the one essential tool for grasping them – mental awareness and an active intuition. In this sense, many of these astrological concepts are what have been termed 'self-secret'. The sheer simplicity, openness, and directness of the subject are closed to us because of our own inherent confusion and complexity – our internal white noise. What to do?

I can well remember my first meeting with a Tibetan lama at which I asked about the Tibetan astrological tradition. I was just after Christmas and we had driven 800 miles during the coldest day of that year, and with my entire family. As we reached the top of a mountain in upstate New York where the lama's monastery is located, we could only see out of the car by scraping a tiny spot on the frosted windshield. It was that cold.

Having arrived at the monastery in the dark of night, we were ushered into a small room for a very brief interview. We waited. In time, the rinpoche came in and welcomed us. He did not speak a word of English, but he did have a translator. I then explained through the translator my interest in astrology and the fact that I had worked for so very many years in this field and was even somewhat known for my astrological work. Secretly I was hoping somehow to be able to skip a few rungs, perhaps like that boring "Meditation 101," and enter one of the more interesting advanced practices that I had read about or imagined must exist.

The lama listened patiently to me and then began to speak very slowly. Very kindly, he said that although he could see that I had never harmed anyone with my astrology, still, in this area of working with the mind, it was best for me to start at the very beginning point with meditation. He explained what I should do. And then he was gone. I was deflated.

I left the monastery in somewhat of a daze and that night my family and I were sheltered nearby in a tiny motel room with one small wall heater. The night was bitter cold. We were 800 miles from home. And it was in that moment that I felt I had to decide to accept his advice and start at the very beginning or follow my pride and refuse to admit that, after all my years of spiritual work, I knew little to nothing about the mind and meditation, and would have to start at the beginning like anyone else.

I am forever grateful that I was able to admit to myself that I knew nothing about mind practice and would just have to begin at the beginning. When we got back home to Michigan, my wife and I went and got instruction on how to meditate properly and, very slowly, began to learn about mind practice. That has to be one of the key decisions made in my life.

My point is that here in the West we have so much going for us technically and educationally, with so many tools at our fingertips, but there is one topic that for the most part is not taught here and about which we know little to nothing, and that is about the nature of the mind itself. And I am not talking about philosophy or psychology. I am talking about our personal skill at looking at the mind itself. For example, look now at who is reading this page. Who is that? Where does that "who" reside? Is he or she in there somewhere? If so, just where? You get the idea. We seldom (if ever) inquire, much less set out to learn about the mind.

Tibetan Astrology

That is what mind training is all about and most of us in this culture have yet to begin that training. That being said, here is something a little more traditional on the topic of the astrology of Tibet.

This is not primarily a book about the history and culture of astrology in Tibet. My motivation for writing here is to share with you what I have learned on this subject over the last thirty years or so. Hopefully you will come away with at least some idea what Tibetan astrology is actually all about and how it compares to Western astrology. From there, you can decide if you would like to learn more. However, some brief comments on the origin of Tibetan astrology are warranted.

The Astrology of Tibet

Although Tibetan history is ancient, its records are largely symbolic before somewhere around 600 A.D. The tradition states that the Tibetan civilization started somewhere in the fertile Yarlung Valley along the great Tsangpo River in the south-central part of Tibet. Tibet's cultural relationship with China over their long history has always been fairly constant and mostly somewhat difficult. Even though Tibet was small compared to China, this did not mean that Tibet always had little influence.

During one of the better periods (around the Yuan dynasty in the 13th century), the Chinese rulers actually adopted Tibetan Buddhism and there ensued a period of great cultural exchange. In particular the 8th Tai Situ Rinpoche, Chökyi Jungne, traveled extensively in China and was very active as an astrologer.

It is speculated that the Chinese Princess Wen-Ch'eng's move from China to Tibet in 641 A.D. involved bringing with her the Yi-Ching and other philosophical and perhaps geomantic texts. This was probably a watershed event intellectually. It is written that she brought with her 360 works on divination, although that number itself seems symbolic. The point here is that the geomantic and astrological roots of China were transmitted and mixed into Tibetan culture somewhere around that time, if they were not already present.

In particular geomancy and astrology were important to the Bön-po, the pre-Buddhist religion of Tibet as part of their interest in the Lords of the Earth, the Sa-Dag, literally: Earth Lords. These same topics are spread throughout all the major lineages of Tibetan Buddhism today. Tibetan Buddhism, astrology, and the geomantic practices are intertwined, although distinct.

Along with the Yi-Ching came the the Lo-Shu or Magic square, and the eight Parkhas or trigrams. The Magic Square is a square made up of nine number arranged in a square, in which any three numbers add up to 15. More about this later.

Kar-Tsi and Jung-Tsi: The Two Streams

The astrology of the Tibetans stems largely from two sources, India and China, and this fact is clearly reflected in the Tibetan astrology system, by the words Kar-Tsi and Jung-Tsi, which translate to 'white astrology' and 'black astrology.' Kar-Tsi (white astrology) comes from India and represents the dharma, the actual teachings of the Buddha, and things mostly having to do with the calculation of ephemerides, and so forth, while Jung-Tsi (black astrology) comes from China, and includes the geomantic and divinatory aspects of the Tibetan tradition, the trigrams, the five elements, and so forth. Black and white here refers to colors only, and carries no suggestion of good and evil.

The Chinese divinatory sciences, astrology in particular, are said to have arisen in an area in China called Wu-

Tibetan Astrology

Tai Shan, which consists of five sacred mountains, four mountains arranged in the form of a square with a central mountain in the middle. From the area of these five mountains (so it is written) arose an emanation of the Buddhist bodhisattva Manjushri, the deity especially connected to astrology. Manjushri arose as a youth and from his head issued a golden tortoise, from which emanated a vast number of teachings (84,000) that relate to astrology.

Humankind, so it is written, soon took to the astrology, even to the point of ignoring the actual dharma teachings of Lord Buddha. Manjushri, who was displeased by this, is said to have then hidden the astrology teachings on the eastern side of the Wu-Tai Shan mountains as what is called terma or hidden dharma, and from that point astrology was lost to humankind. Without astrology, mankind was unable to guide itself through the obstacles of life, and so suffered greatly.

However, after a time (and at the suggestion of the bodhisattva Avalokiteshvara, who pitied mankind's suffering) Guru Rinpoche (perhaps the greatest Tibetan saint) petitioned Manjushri to please restore the astrological teachings and to teach him the tradition, so that he could share them once again with the Tibetan people.

In his petition to Manjushri, Guru Rinpoche made it clear that although astrology and the divinatory practices are not a part of the dharma as taught by Buddha, nevertheless they are of great importance to mankind on a relative, if not an absolute, basis. I can testify to this view myself. When I approached by own teacher, a Tibetan rinpoche, as to the validity of astrology, he affirmed its usefulness, but said this: "Astrology is one of the limbs of the yoga, but not the root." The dharma teachings of Buddha are the root.

My point here is that until such time as we can develop full awareness, astrology can be useful to us *on a relative basis* in guiding us through life's obstacles. In other words, in the confused world we often find ourselves in, bewildered by our own ignorance of what is real, and stumbling around, astrology and the other divinatory practices can help to point the way through the confusion to greater clarity. Beyond that, as I understand it, astrology has no particular merit.

Astrology is one of the relative truths, but not the absolute truth. This explanation made immediate sense to me and is typical of the kind of wisdom I have come to expect from Tibetan dharma teachers.

In 2004 I was fortunate enough to travel to Mt. Wu-Tai-Shan in China with my teacher Khenpo Karthar Rinpoche and spent a week there. We traveled to the top of all five of the sacred mountains. It was quite a trip.

Summary

The Tibetan system of astrology is a combination of Indian and Chinese methods, the greater and most essential (meaning) part being taken from the Chinese, and with the technical (calculation) element tending to come from the Indian system. Of course, the Buddhist dharma itself came from India. The Indian or technical part (ephemerides, lunar tables, etc.) is called Kar-Tsi and the Chinese or spiritual part, is called Jung-Tsi.

The Tibetans, who were short on calculation ability, originally borrowed whatever planetary tables they use from the Indians, and don't depend upon these planetary ephemerides for much of their system. They make great use of the 12-year cycle of the animal signs plus the five-fold element sequence as used in the various forms of Chinese astrology (Jung-Tsi). The Kar-Tsi came from the Indian system along with the dharma and the Kalachakra Tantra. The quintessential portion of the Indian system of value to the Tibetans is the division of the lunar month into 30 equal parts, called "tithis" in the Indian system.

Tibetan astrology is lunar-based, with the Sun (and all the planets) taking a secondary position to the Moon. As proof of this, witness the fact that your Tibetan birthday is not your solar birthday (or yearly return), but the lunar phase-angle day on which you were born. Thus you would celebrate your birthday on that 25th (or whatever) day of the lunar month you were born in. Note: not the 25th calendar date (which is solar), but the 25th lunar day as measured from the previous New Moon.

Astrologers in general seem to love to manipulate cycles and numbers. The Tibetans (even lacking planetary calculations) make up for it with the manipulation of the various cycles they do use. In

Tibetan Astrology

Tibetan astrology, numbers are counted forward, backward, and around in many different combinations. It is just complicated enough so that not everyone can do it. It requires an astrologer, a Tsi-Pa. In fact, it is ironic that astrology, East and West, seems to be just complex enough that the average person can't do it for themselves and requires some expert to do it for them. I guess that is how we make a living.

Although my experience with the system is not that great, it is enough to assure me that the net result of the Tibetan calculation methods is quite similar in effect or portent to Western methods. After all, the point of any kind of astrology is to provide some kind of personal direction, perhaps to establish a dialogue between the individual and the cosmos – an oracle. Astrology is a complex oracle. In other words, the amount of information or life direction (if you will) is of the same caliber (and quantity) as similar material here in the West.

The chief exception to this generalization is the use of the lunar cycle in day-to-day life. It is here that the Tibetan system excels and has a great deal to offer Westerners. Here in the West the awareness of the lunar cycle has been lost or trivialized. It is interesting to note that although few high lamas that I have met make that much use of the cycle of the animal signs, elements, Parkhas and Mewas that I shall present (some do), they all seem to depend upon the cycle of the lunar days for creating their practice and teaching calendars. In other words, much of Tibetan astrology is considered non-essential or of secondary (lesser) importance to the formal Buddhist practitioner. However, this opinion does not extend to the lunar cycle, which is accorded much attention.

Tibetan Astrology

To sum up this very, very brief discussion of how Tibetan astrology as we know it today originated, Tibet took from both India and China, but primarily (aside from the dharma teachings), in its heart essence, it is the Chinese influence that governs the meaning of Tibetan astrology, the Jung-Tsi.

In other words, concepts like the Parkha (eight trigrams), Mewa (Lo-Shu numbers), animal zodiac, and so forth, were taken from China and are precious to Tibetans. Vedic (Indian) astrology and its meanings did not take root, outside of the 30-day lunar cycle, which cycle is crucial to the Tibetan approach. Of course the dharma and the Kalachakra Tantra came from India. Remember that the dharma is the root or heart of the astrology.

These two streams of influence mixed together historically and the Tibetans assimilated them, changing, modifying, and above all incorporating them. They made them their own, and in many cases re-wrote history as if they originated these concepts. In some cases, perhaps they did. In particular, as a matter of course, Manjushri was considered the origin of all the astrological teachings, whether or not they originally came from China. Manjushri is the deity from whom these kinds of concepts are in essence born.

It is clear from writings from the 18th century onward that Tibetans were skilled in all manner of the divinatory arts, not just astrology. This included divinations based on mirrors, dreams, casting lots, arrows, malas (prayer beads), yantras, lamps, stones, drums, bones, bowls of water, cards, medical examination, and of course, mediumistic oracles, to name a few.

Astrology and most of the other forms of divination were performed by Buddhist monks rather than lay people, although it seems that all lay people follow at least some of the indicators, such as the various element combinations. For the most part, monks handle not only the dharma rituals, but also astrology and the other forms of divination. Even the highest rinpoches often practice what is called "Mo," a form of divination, and it is common practice to approach a Tibetan lama with a burning question and ask them to do a "Mo" on that question.

Some lamas don't do divination, and the Nyingma lineage (as a whole) is probably the most oriented to these forms of divination. When asked to do a Mo, a lama may do it on the spot for you or ask you to come back later or the next day to receive the answer. And the answers to Mo questions are seldom very mysterious, but usually very matter of fact, like: "Yes, do go back to school," or "No, don't travel there."

As mentioned earlier, astrologers are called "Tsi-Pa" in Tibetan and every monastery has a Tsi-Pa, almost by default, just as here in the West there is almost always someone who knows a little astrology, and astrological questions inevitably fall to that person. It is the same in Tibet, although monasteries always require some astrology to set up their schedule for group practice, since it is based on the lunation cycle.

Tibetan Astrology

Where I Came In

My own background in learning about Tibetan astrology started around 1974 when I met the Ven. Chogyam Trungpa Rinpoche and the 16th Gyalwa Karma, Rigpe Dorje, and with my asking just about every rinpoche I encountered about astrology. Surprisingly, most of them knew (or claimed they knew) very little, and often their only interest seemed to be reading the small Tibetan practice-calendar books, looking for dates for this or that kind of practice.

As an student who was trying to studying Buddhist psychology and also learning about mind training, I continued to be fascinated by Tibetan astrology. My reasoning went something along the lines of: if their psychology is so powerful (which it indeed is), their astrology must also reflect this as well. I read through the various Buddhist scholarly works in which astrology was even mentioned, finding only an occasional few words and the odd diagram here or there. There was no sense of any comprehensive understanding.

I then met John Reynolds, an American who was studying Tibetan Buddhism and who also had an interest in Tibetan Astrology. He spoke and read Tibetan, fluently. I set up a workshop here in Big Rapids, Michigan and John came and gave a seminar on Tibetan astrology. This was in the early 1980s. I learned a lot from meeting Reynolds, but most of all I remember these words of John's to me. He said that in order to learn Tibetan astrology, you have to learn the Buddhist psychology around which it was based. He confided to me that the Buddhist psychology was much more interesting to him than the astrology, and that he had become fascinated with that, leaving the astrology somewhat unfinished. "Interesting," said I.

Sange Wangchuk

My next step was to invite Nepalese Sange Wangchuk and his wife Tseten to come and reside at our center here in Michigan in 1985. Wangchuk, a former monk, skilled calligrapher, and artist was fluent in seven languages, including Tibetan, Nepalese, Bhutanese, Hindi, Pali, and Sanskrit. Today Wangchuk is director of the National Library of Bhutan. Sange Wangchuk spent 2 1/2 years with us and, during that time, we translated a lot of Tibetan astrology from the original manuscripts, mostly the works of the 3rd Gyalwa Karmapa, Rangjung Dorje. This really helped me fill in many of the blanks. I was finally learning. By now I was also working on learning what meditation practice was all about.

But like John Reynolds, I was becoming increasingly seduced by the Buddhist psychology at the expense of the astrology. There is no doubt about the fact that if it is personal results you are interested in, the Tibetan Buddhist psychological teachings are the very essence of that of which astrologers dream. Or, as mentioned earlier: astrology is one of the limbs of the yoga, but not the root or trunk itself. Sooner or later you want to learn about the root.

The Buddhist psychological or dharma teachings themselves are the root, and these profound teachings are deserving of the respect they inspire. They have value because they help an individual orient him or herself within their current situation and provide a method for them to take action of a clarifying and creative nature.

By this time, our center here in Big Rapids had become one of the primary centers in North America for the translation, transcription, and publication of Buddhist texts of the Karma Kagyu tradition. We had become the Heart Center KTC (Karma thedsum Choling), and affiliate of KTD (Karma Triyana Dharmachakra) Monastery in Woodstock, New York. For many years, we maintained a full-time publication staff, starting in 1986.

During our time together, I worked with Sange Wangchuk translating from a number of astrology texts (he did the translating), and we put together an outline for Tibetan astrology, some of which was published by

Tibetan Astrology

Wieser in a book on Eastern astrology some years ago. Among other things as mentioned, Wangchuk translated some of the astrology teachings of the 3rd Gyalwa Karmapa, Rangjung Dorje. I also programmed most of the Tibetan astrological techniques,and released a program in May of 1998. A new and expanded version of that program has been released in 2007 and is available at StarTypes.com.

In the summer of 1997 our center brought Dr. Drubgyud Tendar to our complex, the Heart Center KTC here in Big Rapids. Dr. Tendar was an accomplished Tibetan astrologer and Tibetan doctor, who had been trained at Rumtek Monastery in Sikkim in the Tsurphu tradition (the astrological methods used by the Karma Kagyu Lineage), originating from His Holiness, the 3rd Karmapa, Rangjung Dorje. Together we worked to reconstruct the calculations for the traditional Tsurphu calendar and thus try to preserve its integrity.

In the late summer of 1997 my family and I traveled to Tibet and we were able to present our preliminary results to the head of the Karma Kagyu Lineage, His Holiness Urgyen Trinley Dorje, the 17th Karmapa. The Karmapa is the actual "Golden Child" after which the Eddie Murphy movie was based.

I also traveled to Rumtek Monastery in Sikkim, the seat of His Holiness, Rigpe Dorje, the 16th Karmapa, where I met with one of the main astrologers at that monastery. While traveling in the East, I was also able to present our work to the Venerable Bokar Rinpoche and His Eminence, Gyaltsap Rinpoche. I continued to work with Dr. Drubjud Tendar through the fall of 1997 to complete the calculations we had been working on.

In the spring of 2006, I met Khenpo Ugyen Tenzin, who was Senior Abbot at Nalanda Institute of Rumtek,

Tibetan Astrology

Sikkim. Lama Ugyen had been thoroughly trained in the Tsurphu method of astrology and he was able to clear up some questions that had been troubling me. And lately I have been getting some help from Edward Henning, a translator of Tibetan and a scholar of Tibetan astrology. Henning, who in my opinion is doing the most important work in this field helped to translate much of the material about the Tibetan Earth Lords, the Sa-Dak found in this book.

I should also mention my main dharma teacher, the Ven. Khenpo Karthar Rinpoche, who has worked with me since 1983. Khenpo Rinpoche has been of invaluable help, far beyond any words I could possible write. In addition, Ven. Bardor Tulku Rinpoche has also been very helpful in many ways, including providing the verbal reading or instructions (Tibetan: Lung) for the Tibetan Mo form of divination.

Lamas and rinpoches that have been helpful in my journey to learn something about Tibetan astrology are many, and they include Lama Karma Duldul, Lama Yeshe Gyamtso, Ven. Thrangu Rinpoche, Ven. Bokar Rinpoche, His Eminence Gyaltsap Rinpoche, His Eminence Jamgon Rinpoche, His Eminence Shamar Rinpoche, His Eminence Tai Situ Rinpoche, and of course His Holiness the 16th Karmapa, Rigpe Dorje, and His Holiness the 17th Gyalwa Karmapa, Ogyen Trinley Dorje.

You would think that with all this help I would know a lot by now, but I am still just learning the essentials. Much of this is due to the fact that to learn the Tibetan astrology system, you have to first learn and practice the dharma, and that has been much more difficult to learn and do than the astrology part of it. I am still working on that.

Tibetan Astrology

Astrology is Astrology is ...

Tibetan astrological methods are in some ways less complex than the computer-generated technology that most of us here in the West currently use. Much of it involve the manipulation of the various animal signs, elements, Parkhas, mewas, etc., and take considerable skill (great care) in calculation and, as might be expected, even more expertise when it comes to interpretation. The net result is that the Tibetan system of astrology is a somewhat complex system that, like its Western counterpart, allows so much interpretation that hard and fast conclusions can seldom be drawn. As far as I can determine, one can't predict the stock market with either Tibetan or Western astrology, at least I can't. If I could, our center here would be much larger.

When all is said and done, astrology East or West is essentially an oracle, and like all oracles, its purpose is to allow the universe to speak to us. For it to be any use to us, we must be able to listen.

Tibetan Astrology

Astrology as an Oracle

We probably can agree that astrology is a somewhat complex and intricate oracle. There is another factor in Eastern astrology that deserves general comment. It has been the view of Western observers that the East has a tendency toward fatalism and resignation to whatever fate has delivered to them.

I was always somewhat surprised that most of the Tibetan lamas and teachers that I met (outside of using the lunar cycle to plan and time events) were not all that interested in the astrology. Perhaps astrology may have a number of more secret uses in Tibetan Buddhism, which are not presented to the general public, and of which I am not aware of. One thing I can report is that Tibetans are not interested in the kind of astrology of personality so popular here in the West.

To the Buddhist mind, our personality makeup is not really all that important. Unlike Western astrology,

Tibetan Astrology

Tibetan astrology is not an astrology of personality. For, no matter what our personal makeup, good or bad, the remedy remains the same from the Buddhist point of view: mind practice of one form or another.

In fact, throughout the East, you do not find the interest in personality psychology that we have here in the West. The reason is clear to anyone who has studied Eastern philosophy. They have no need to flirt with the deeper areas of the mind, but have long ago been introduced to matters of psychology, and assume them as a matter of course, rather than as a novelty. Here in the West we are just beginning to learn about the training of the mind. Psychology here is still new to us.

Remember that reincarnation is the accepted belief system in both India and Tibet and, for that matter (in sheer numbers of people), the greater part of the world. They have, as a standing belief, what we have as yet to accept -- the continuity of consciousness beyond death. They are the majority, we the minority.

Here in the West, this awareness of cycles or life beyond physical death is not self-evident to most of us. As astrologers, we may attempt to bring it to the public's attention. Yet as a society, we have yet to come to such a conclusion, much less push toward making this a part of our day-to-day beliefs.

Buddhist countries, long trained in the analysis of emotions and desires, have little interest in re-examining emotional and personality issues, which have already been clarified in ancient times. Instead, the interest in expanding the awareness of the person (happy or sad) beyond such personal issues and focusing on the actual root of our problems and sufferings is assumed. Everyone over there in Asia knows this from childhood.

Tibetan Astrology

Any Western astrologer can easily check this out for himself by doing an astrological reading for an East Indian. They are not remotely interested in our psychological observations. Concepts that fascinate us here in the West like: soul, spirit, unity, are already their old friends.

Their response to our psychological pap is "Yes, yes, yes... please get on to something of importance, like exactly how many children will I have, and what will their sexes be." Or, "How much money will I make this year and when."

There is no point in hinting to a Tibetan or Hindu that consciousness may extend beyond this life or that he or she is somehow "one" with the creative forces. That is for them already a given, a fact upon which they have depended all of their lives. The psychological crib out of which we Westerners are just learning to climb (when it comes to the mind), the continuity of consciousness, and all that these thoughts suggest, is old news in China, India, Tibet, and most of Asia for that matter..

The fact that the whole world is, in reality, our personal mandala and that everything that appears to us is a sign from the cosmos may be a revelation to a New Yorker, but not so for a resident of Katmandu or Delhi. While here in this country we continue to explore our psychological infancy, this holds little interest for those from the East. With this said, let us look at some of the main elements of Tibetan astrology.

How to Use This Book

From this point forward, we are ready to begin looking at the actual nuts and bolts of Tibetan astrology. I have introduced you about all I can. It is time to work with the actual content itself.

There is no right or wrong order in how to approach this material. I have tried to arrange it so that some of the main concepts and techniques are presented first, but it is really up to you. Of course, everyone knows about the twelve animal signs, and you may want to know what the element-animal combination for the year you were born is, like: "Year of the ??"

While it can be read sequentially and this works pretty well that way, a better approach might be to browse the table of contents for something that interests you and check that out.

Some sections are very general, while others offer step-by-step calculation methods. If you are just browsing, you may want to skip over the more technical stuff.

Where possible, I have included Astro*Image cards and illustrations to make things more visible. Many of the designs are based on age-old descriptions, while others are modern interpretations of whatever verbal descriptions I could find.

I am not a practicing Tibetan astrologer. Rather, I am someone trained in Western astrology who is studying the Tibetan methods and trying to make sense out of them. Although I have learned to read the Tibetan script, I am not fluent (or confident) enough to do my own translations. There is very little written in English on this topic, and unfortunately one of the main published books on the subject is filled with errors. At this very beginning stage of bring Tibetan astrological methods to

Tibetan Astrology

the West, I guess errors and misunderstandings should be expected. We are all learning. It is my wish that this book be of some use and help to make this fascinating subject sensible to more readers.

In a book this large, there are bound to be typos and errors. I would very much like to hear about them.

Michael Erlewine
June 2007
Michael@Erlewine.net

The Tibetan Calendar

The heart of Tibetan astrology is the annual almanac or Tibetan calendar. Every lama and monk has one. Here we will go over what you might expect to find in the average almanac, but t.This is not the place (and I am not the expert) on all the subtleties of the Tibetan calendar system. I refer readers to the very excellent book by Edward Henning "Kalachakra And the Tibetan Calendar," which should be available by the time your read this. Here it will have to suffice to lay out the general characteristics, point out some of the problems involved, and mention how some students of the subject are dealing with them.

I don't know how many lamas and rinpoches I have approached with questions I have about the Tibetan calendar system, but it seems that most of them are not concerned with this kind of detail. They tend to use the Tibetan astrological calendar as it is handed to them, with no questions asked.

The problem is that these small practice calendars (and there are quite a few of them) for the most part don't even state what time zone the calendar refers to and, as any astrologer here in the West knows, you can't list the time of the New Moon, without declaring the time zone it refers to. Is it India or New York? You need to know.

Before getting too much deeper into this, it is crucial that you understand why this type of astrological calendar is produced in the first place, and that has to do with group dharma practice, for these are primarily practice calendars.

If one is coordinating the practice schedule at a large monastery with perhaps several hundred monks, everyone has to agree on what calendar day and time any group practice should convene. The various astrological indicators like the moment of the New Moon, the moment when the Moon changes lunar mansions, and so on are not so considerate. The natural astronomical phenomena change when they change and that's that. That's a given.

If the Full Moon occurs at 3 o'clock in the morning, this is not a time when just everyone at a monastery is likely to be up and ready for practice. So, as a hedge against the natural order of things, the communal practice calendar was drawn up. It really is a compromise and goes against the grain of how one might imagine this astrological information ideally might be used. In other words, in some ways almanacs are counter-intuitive, trying to pigeonhole natural events, but it is easy to understand why these compromises are made.

What the Tibetans have done with the practice calendar (in most cases) is to declare sunrise for a given day as the point to take the surrounding astrological temperature, so to speak. Somewhere around 5 A.M. is the time when Tibetan almanacss sample indicators like which lunar day it is, what Nakshatra (lunar mansion) is in play, which Karana, and so on. These indicators are listed in the astrological almanac for sunrise, even through the actual time most of these indicators actually began could be as far off as much as almost 24 hours. In other words, these calendars indicate where a given astrological factor is at 5 A.M., which says nothing about when it started.

For example: If at sunrise on a given day, it is the 10th lunar day, that day could change to the 11th lunar day five minutes later, and so literally the entire calendar day would be in the 11th lunar day, but still be listed as the 10th day. You get the idea. Whenever we make up rules like this, there is compromise and some information is lost. In this case, the information can be (in my opinion) quite important.

It is understandable that for group practice, decisions have to be made that cut through the niceties of monitoring the actual changes that the sky offers us. However, something valuable is lost. Today, more and more dharma students (who are not engaged in group practice) are beginning to use astrological calendars in which the exact time of various astrological changes are listed. Instead of following the group listings for sunrise, these students note when the actual change from one lunar day (or whatever indicator they are using) changes and time their practice based on that. This only makes sense.

If you use an astrological almanac or calendar, be sure to keep these thoughts in mind and to ask at least what time zone whatever time listings give are calculated in.

Zodiacs: Tropical or Sidereal?

As to which zodiac to use: this is an even thornier problem and I will not get into the long history of Tibetan zodiacs. Please consult Edward Henning's book for more details. Let me just be very general here:

There are two main kinds of zodiacs used by astrologers, the tropical and the sidereal.

The tropical zodiac can be defined as one where the zero-degrees Aries) can be characterized as the point in the heavens when the transiting Sun reaches the vernal equinox. In the sidereal zodiac, the first point of Aries is measured not in reference to equinoxes or solstices, but from some key point or star out there in the heavens – nothing to do with the equinox or Earth.

Tibetan Astrology

While there can be no argument as to the definition of the tropical zodiac, as you might imagine, sidereal astrologers have seldom agreed which star should be the starting point for their zodiac, although they do more or less agree on the general area of the heavens where this point should be found, somewhere in the constellations Aries to Pisces. This dispute has gone on for centuries and will not be elaborated on here.

The tropical zodiac (the earth's general frame of reference) is very gradually shifting, and this very slow shift is called precession, with the result that the zero-degree Aries point is drifting backward in the zodiac something just less than a minute of arc a year – some 50 seconds.

A long time ago, around 1,500 years, the two zodiacs (tropical and sidereal) matched up, but since that time they have slowly drifted apart until today they are something like 30 degrees apart, thus the confusion. I will not go into more detail about the phenomenon of precession or the history and practice of these two zodiacs (tropical and sidereal) in the astrological tradition. There are many good books out there that handle this. What we want to know here is what system is used in Tibetan astrology?

The main treatise on astrology in India is the Kalachakra Tantra, which came from India and literally translates as the "Wheel of Time." The Kalachakra clearly uses the tropical zodiac, as Tibetan scholar Edward Henning points out in his book on that topic. However, most Indian astrology today is sidereal, so many assume that the Kalachakra would share this quality. It does not. The Kalachakra depends on the moment the Sun reaches the winter solstice, and this by definition is the tropical zodiac.

Tibetan Astrology

The long and the short of all this, and it is bad news too, is that most Tibetan astrologers today use a zodiac that is neither tropical nor sidereal. It is somewhere in between. As Edward Henning so aptly puts it, it is "simply wrong," a product of misunderstandings technically.

As a student who has great respect for the lamas and the Tibetan dharma tradition, I found it very difficult to confront these few areas of knowledge which are not particularly enlightened, and where errors have been compounded and passed on for so long that they become hard to challenge or question. This is one of those areas. The upshot is that the Tibetans intended to use the tropical zodiac as indicated by the Kalachakra, but due perhaps to confusion when bringing the system into Tibet from India, something was lost along the way and they were left with a zodiac that is neither fish nor fowl, neither tropical or strictly sidereal. It is something of a red herring.

Modern astrologers are simply tiptoeing around this problem. The Tibetans, in general, are deep into the concept of not throwing the baby out with the bathwater, and it is difficult to change anything, especially in the chaos that has threatened the entire system since Tibet has been in political upheaval.

The Lunar Months

We have a similar problem with the definition of the twelve lunar months as defined by the Chinese, the Phugpa tradition (Dalai Lama and Gelugpa Lineage) and the Tsurphu tradition (the Karmapa and Kagyu Lineage.) These three systems do not always agree on Losar, the Tibetan New Year, which marks the first month of any year. The one thing they all agree on is that the point of the New Moon marks the start of the year, but which New Moon? These three systems can be off from one another by an entire month, and sometimes are.

The Phugpa system is the most divergent from the other two, with the Tsurphu system generally agreeing with the Chinese New Year, but not always. You and I are not going to solve this for the Tibetans and the Chinese, so the most we can do is note it and not be surprised if we discover that two different astrological calendars for the same year have the start of the New Year on different dates. Since so much depends on when the year starts, you can imagine the problems.

The Lunar Days: Double and Omitted

I have described the lunar month of 30 days elsewhere in this book. What I want to point out here is the existence of what are called double and omitted days in Tibetan astrological calendars. This concept is actually quite simple, and depends on the length of the solar or calendar day, which is measured from mean sunrise of one calendar day to mean sunrise of the next calendar day, approximately 24 hours.

Since lunar days depend on the relation of the Moon to the Sun and the Moon goes faster in one part of its orbit and slower in another, the following takes place: It can happen that the Moon is in a particular lunar day at sunrise of one calendar day, and the Moon is moving so fast that it reaches the start of the next lunar day (not calendar day) BEFORE the next calendar day's sunrise. In this case that short lunar day is not noted on either the first or second calendar day, but is simply omitted from the calendar.

The reverse situation also holds. When the Moon is moving very slowly in its orbit, it can happen that the same lunar day is noted at the sunrise of two contiguous calendar dates, thus effectively doubling that lunar date on the calendar.

Please keep in mind that omitted or doubled days are only an artifice of the solar calendar. No lunar day is actually lost or doubled. They are all there.

The Intercalary: Lunar and Solar Months

We have mostly been describing the lunar months in this book, which are measured from the moment of New Moon to the succeeding New Moon. These months, as we have pointed out, do not neatly match up with the standard solar calendar month.

We should differentiate between lunar months and the solar month or what are called the 'solar terms." Solar months have to do with the passage of the Sun through the tropical zodiac, and the first solar term or solar month is called by the Chinese the "Beginning of Spring." In Chinese and Tibetan astrology, it begins the moment the Sun reaches 15 degrees of the tropical zodiac sign Aquarius (15° Aquarius), which takes place somewhere around February 4th or 5th each year. From the Chinese point of view, the familiar vernal equinox (0° Aries) is the middle of spring, not the beginning.

As mentioned, lunar and solar months do not neatly match, and the number of lunar months in a solar calendar year (Gregorian calendar) are more than the standard twelve calendar months we all know. The net result is that every 32.5 lunar months, these extra lunar days accumulate to the point that an extra (intercalary) month has to be added to that year's calendar. Just as we occasionally add an extra day at the end of February in the solar, an extra month is added every few years.

Another point to keep in mind is that the Tibetans use the mean longitude of the Sun for their calculations, and not the true longitude that astronomers would use.

This has been a quick overview. I have tried here to point out a few of the calendar concepts that concern the Tibetan astrologer – some of the problems. It would take most of a book just to define what these problems are and how best to view them. Luckily that book exists in Edward Hennings "Kalachakra And the Tibetan Calendar." Please see that book for a very thorough explanation of these matters.

Solar Calendar Data

Included in some Tibetan astrological calendars (often listed last) is what has been called the "solar data," which term has nothing to do with the movement of the sun or any other astronomical calculations. Here, the term "solar" refers the solar calendar, which the entire world uses, where each year is divided into months and days, and we count through our calendar, day by day, just as we cycle through the days of the week in strict order (Sunday, Monday, Tuesday, etc.), although any connection to the planet for each weekday (Monday = Moon, etc.) is purely symbolic at this point.

In the same way, the Tibetans cycle through a number of the principle astrological factors, including the twelve animals, the ten yogas (element combinations), the eight trigrams, and the nine Mewa.

Each of these cycles is based on an epoch or starting day and continued forward. Edward Henning in his excellent book "Kalachakra and the Tibetan Calendar," lists these positions for the New Moon on March 1, 1995 as:

Ten Elements   6   Iron

Tibetan Astrology

12 Animals	0	Hare
Eight Trigrams	4	Khen
Nine Mewas	6	4 Green
Lunar Mansion		Uttarabhadrapada (#25)

Tibetan Astrology

The above are based on:

10 Elements
Fire	1, 2
Earth	3, 4
Iron (Metal)	5, 6
Water	7, 8
Wood	9, 0

12 Animals
Hare	0
Dragon	1
Etc. …	
Tiger	11

8 Trigrams
Li	1
Khon	2
Etc.	

9 Mewa
With the nine Mewa, the incremented number is divided by 9 and the result is subtracted from 10. If the result is "0," then that is registered as a "1."

Both the Phugpa (Gelugpa Lineage) and the Tsurphu (Karma Kagyu Lineage) calculation results agree on these cycles.

As for the Lunar Mansion, this is not used in the Phugpa calendar, but is part of the Tsurphu calculations. In the above 1995 date, the lunar mansion is Uttarabhadrapada, the 25th mansion, if you are numbering from 0 to 26).

Tibetan Astrology

This solar data is not based on any astronomical principles, per se, but is derived, much like our day of the week (Monday, Tuesday, etc.) from a simple counting through the cycle. This is true for daily elements, animals, lunar mansions, trigrams, and Mewa. This solar data is most used by dharma practitioners using the Tsurphu calendar, in particular the lineage known as the Karma Kagyu.

The Twelve Animal Signs

The wheel of the animal zodiac is ancient, arising somewhere in central Asia and later incorporated by the Chinese. The calendar used by the Chinese is said to have entered Tibet in the year 642 AD by the Chinese Princess Kong-jo, who married the first Buddhist King of Tibet.

The Tibetan wheel of twelve animals, with its twelve-fold division, reminds us of its Western counterpart, the familiar zodiac. Unlike the West, where your astrological Sun sign is determined by the solar calendar, in the East your sign is determined according to which year you are born in. The cycle of twelve animals rotates in strict succession from year to year. The order of the animals is Mouse, Ox, Tiger, Hare, Dragon, Snake, Horse, Sheep, Monkey, Bird, Dog, and Pig. Each animal sign has its own qualities, which are well-known to the general Asian public, just like most folks know something about Sun Sign astrology here in the West. What sign are you?

However, please note that these years are not measured from either your birthday or from January 1st of any year. Instead, they are measured from the beginning of the Tibetan New Year, a fluctuating point that (in general) marks the New Moon that is nearest to the beginning of February. It is important to note that on occasion, the start of the Tibetan and Chinese New Years can differ by an entire month! Even the two Tibetan-style calendars covered here, the Tsurphu (Karma Kagyu Lineage) and the Phugpa (Gelugpa Lineage) can, on occasion, differ by one month!

The animal of one's birth year is central to both the Tibetan and Chinese systems of calculation, and is the most common form of counting time. The twelve-year animal cycle repeats itself from year to year. Just as we might inquire about a person's Sun sign, in the East they want to know what element and animal sign were you born under. There is also an element-animal combination for each month, each day, and each double-hour.

Tibetan Astrology

Your Animal Year

It will be important for you to know the animal year you were born in. For most, it will be as simple as looking at the charts on the following pages, finding the year of your birth and noting which Element-Animal combination you were born under. For example, I was born in July of 1941. Looking at the charts, I can see that I was born in the year of the Iron-Snake.

The Tibetan year is measured from Tibetan New Year to Tibetan New Year, and the date of the New Year depends on when a particular New Moon occurs somewhere between January and March. So, if you were born in those months, you will need to take an additional step and consult the Year-Change Charts on the pages following the first three diagrams to determne which Tibetan year you belong to.

On these additional pages, you will find a list of years from 1900 to 2050. Look up the year you were born and on that row or line is the month, day, and time of the New Moon which marks the exact beginning of that Tibetan year. The time is given in Greenwich Mean Time, which is five hours ahead of New York, which is on Eastern Standard Time. You may have to adjust for your time particular zone. When that is done, if you were born at or after that date and time, then use the element-animal combination for that year.

If you were born BEFORE that date and time, use the element-animal combination for the previous year.

Also note that two calendar systems are listed, the Tsurphu system, which is that of Karma Kagyu lineage (The Karmapa) and the Phugpa system, which is that of the Gelugpa lineage (Dalai Lama). The last column in each list tells whether there was an eclipse on that day,

Annular, Total, or Partial. As to which system to use, this depends upon the Tibetan Buddhist lineage you are affiliated with. Most use the Phugpa system, since that belongs to the Gelugpa Lineages and His Holiness the Dalai Lama. I use the Tsurphu system, since that belongs to the Karma Kagyu lineage and His Holiness the Gyalwa Karmapa.

Animal Year Tables

Sixty-Year Cycle (1-20)

1) Wood-Mouse:	4	2	(1924, 1984)
2) Wood-Ox:	3	3	(1925, 1985)
3) Fire-Tiger:	2	4	(1926, 1986)
4) Fire-Rabbit:	1	8	(1927, 1987)
5) Earth-Dragon:	9	6	(1928, 1988)
6) Earth-Snake:	8	7	(1929, 1989)
7) Iron-Horse:	7	8	(1930, 1990)
8) Iron-Sheep:	6	9	(1931, 1991)
9) Water-Monkey:	2	1	(1932, 1992)
10) Water-Bird:	4	2	(1933, 1993)
11) Wood-Dog:	3	3	(1934, 1994)
12) Wood-Pig:	2	4	(1935, 1995)
13) Fire Mouse:	1	9	(1936, 1996)
14) Fire-Ox:	9	6	(1937, 1997)
15) Earth-Tiger:	8	7	(1938, 1998)
16) Earth-Rabbit:	7	8	(1939, 1999)
17) Iron-Dragon:	6	9	(1940, 2000)
18) Iron-Snake:	2	1	(1941, 2001)
19) Water-Horse:	4	2	(1942, 2002)
20) Water-Sheep:	3	3	(1943, 2003)

Tibetan Astrology

Sixty-Year Cycle (21-40)

```
21) Wood-Monkey:     2 4 (1944, 2004)
22) Wood-Bird:       1 9 (1945, 2005)
23) Fire-Dog:        9 6 (1946, 2006)
24) Fire-Pig:        8 7 (1947, 2007)
25) Earth-Mouse:     7 8 (1948, 2008)
26) Earth Ox:        6 9 (1949, 2009)
27) Iron-Tiger:      2 1 (1950, 2010)
28) Iron-Rabbit:     4 2 (1951, 2011)
29) Water-Dragon:    3 3 (1952, 2012)
30) Water-Snake:     2 4 (1953, 2013)
31) Wood-Horse:      1 8 (1954, 2014)
32) Wood-Sheep:      9 6 (1955, 2015)
33) Fire-Monkey:     8 7 (1956, 2016)
34) Fire-Bird:       7 8 (1957, 2017)
35) Earth-Dog:       6 9 (1958, 2018)
36) Earth-Pig:       2 1 (1959, 2019)
37) Iron-Mouse:      4 2 (1900, 1960, 2020)
38) Iron-Ox:         3 3 (1901, 1961, 2021)
39) Water-Tiger:     2 4 (1902, 1962, 2022)
40) Water-Rabbit:    1 8 (1903, 1963, 2023)
```

Sixty-Year Cycle (41-60)

```
41) Wood-Dragon:     9 6 (1904, 1964, 2024)
42) Wood-Snake:      8 7 (1905, 1965, 2025)
43) Fire-Horse:      7 8 (1906, 1966, 2026)
44) Fire-Sheep:      6 9 (1907, 1967, 2027)
45) Earth Monkey:    2 1 (1908, 1968, 2028)
46) Earth-Bird:      4 2 (1909, 1969, 2029)
47) Iron-Dog:        3 3 (1910, 1970, 2030)
48) Iron-Pig:        2 4 (1911, 1971, 2031)
49) Water-Mouse:     1 8 (1912, 1972, 2032)
50) Water-Ox:        9 6 (1913, 1973, 2033)
51) Wood-Tiger:      8 7 (1914, 1974, 2034)
52) Wood-Rabbit:     7 8 (1915, 1975, 2035)
53) Fire-Dragon:     6 9 (1916, 1976, 2036)
54) Fire-Snake:      2 1 (1917, 1977, 2037)
55) Earth-Horse:     4 2 (1918, 1978, 2038)
56) Earth-Sheep:     3 3 (1919, 1979, 2039)
57) Iron-Monkey:     2 4 (1920, 1980, 2040)
58) Iron-Bird:       1 8 (1921, 1981, 2041)
59) Water-Dog:       9 6 (1922, 1982, 2042)
60) Water-Pig:       8 7 (1923, 1983, 2043)
```

Year-Change Charts

```
Tsurphu Tradition        Phugpa Tradition
We|1900-01-31  1:22:49|  |Th|1900-03-01 11:24:57|  |
Tu|1901-02-19  2:44:60|  |Tu|1901-02-19  2:44:60|  |
Sa|1902-02-08 13:21:08|  |Sa|1902-02-08 13:21:08|  |
We|1903-01-28 16:38:45|  |We|1903-01-28 16:38:45|  |
Tu|1904-02-16 11:04:05|  |Tu|1904-02-16 11:04:05|  |
Sa|1905-02-04 11:05:47|  |Sa|1905-02-04 11:05:47|  |
Fr|1906-02-23  7:57:36|P |Fr|1906-02-23  7:57:36|P |
Tu|1907-02-12 17:42:25|  |Tu|1907-02-12 17:42:25|  |
Su|1908-02-02  8:36:41|  |Mo|1908-03-02 18:56:34|  |
Sa|1909-02-20 10:52:11|  |Sa|1909-02-20 10:52:11|  |
Th|1910-02-10  1:12:22|  |Th|1910-02-10  1:12:22|  |
Mo|1911-01-30  9:45:01|  |We|1911-03-01  0:30:52|  |
Su|1912-02-18  5:43:55|  |Su|1912-02-18  5:43:55|  |
Th|1913-02-06  5:21:19|  |Th|1913-02-06  5:21:19|  |
We|1914-02-25  0:01:58|A |We|1914-02-25  0:01:58|A |
Su|1915-02-14  4:30:25|A |Su|1915-02-14  4:30:25|A |
Th|1916-02-03 16:05:32|T |Th|1916-02-03 16:05:32|T |
We|1917-02-21 18:09:08|  |We|1917-02-21 18:09:08|  |
Mo|1918-02-11 10:04:00|  |Mo|1918-02-11 10:04:00|  |
Fr|1919-01-31 23:07:07|  |Su|1919-03-02 11:10:59|  |
Th|1920-02-19 21:34:54|  |Th|1920-02-19 21:34:54|  |
Tu|1921-02-08  0:36:09|  |Tu|1921-02-08  0:36:09|  |
Fr|1922-01-27 23:48:14|  |Fr|1922-01-27 23:48:14|  |
Th|1923-02-15 19:06:44|  |Th|1923-02-15 19:06:44|  |
Tu|1924-02-05  1:38:20|  |Tu|1924-02-05  1:38:20|  |
Mo|1925-02-23  2:12:24|  |Mo|1925-02-23  2:12:24|  |
Fr|1926-02-12 17:20:09|  |Fr|1926-02-12 17:20:09|  |
We|1927-02-02  8:54:40|  |Th|1927-03-03 19:24:26|  |
Tu|1928-02-21  9:41:13|  |Tu|1928-02-21  9:41:13|  |
Sa|1929-02-09 17:54:51|  |Sa|1929-02-09 17:54:51|  |
We|1930-01-29 19:08:02|  |Fr|1930-02-28 13:32:29|  |
Tu|1931-02-17 13:10:59|  |Tu|1931-02-17 13:10:59|  |
Sa|1932-02-06 14:44:48|  |Sa|1932-02-06 14:44:48|  |
Fr|1933-02-24 12:44:17|A |Fr|1933-02-24 12:44:17|A |
We|1934-02-14  0:43:28|T |We|1934-02-14  0:43:28|T |
Su|1935-02-03 16:27:32|P |Su|1935-02-03 16:27:32|P |
Sa|1936-02-22 18:42:39|  |Sa|1936-02-22 18:42:39|  |
Th|1937-02-11  7:34:09|  |Th|1937-02-11  7:34:09|  |
Mo|1938-01-31 13:35:41|  |We|1938-03-02  5:39:45|  |
Su|1939-02-19  8:28:50|  |Su|1939-02-19  8:28:50|  |
Th|1940-02-08  7:44:32|  |Th|1940-02-08  7:44:32|  |
Mo|1941-01-27 11:03:22|  |We|1941-02-26  3:01:53|  |
Su|1942-02-15 10:03:00|  |Su|1942-02-15 10:03:00|  |
Th|1943-02-04 23:28:60|T |Th|1943-02-04 23:28:60|T |
Th|1944-02-24  1:59:25|  |Th|1944-02-24  1:59:25|  |
Mo|1945-02-12 17:33:29|  |Mo|1945-02-12 17:33:29|  |
Sa|1946-02-02  4:43:36|  |Su|1946-03-03 18:01:16|  |
Fr|1947-02-21  2:00:55|  |Fr|1947-02-21  2:00:55|  |
Tu|1948-02-10  3:01:46|  |Tu|1948-02-10  3:01:46|  |
Sa|1949-01-29  2:42:49|  |Sa|1949-01-29  2:42:49|  |
Th|1950-02-16 22:53:30|  |Th|1950-02-16 22:53:30|  |
```

Tibetan Astrology

```
Tu|1951-02-06  7:53:49|  |Tu|1951-02-06  7:53:49|  |
Mo|1952-02-25  9:16:22|T |Mo|1952-02-25  9:16:22|T |
Sa|1953-02-14  1:10:51|P |Sa|1953-02-14  1:10:51|P |
We|1954-02-03 15:55:38|  |We|1954-02-03 15:55:38|  |
Tu|1955-02-22 15:54:54|  |Tu|1955-02-22 15:54:54|  |
Sa|1956-02-11 21:38:04|  |Sa|1956-02-11 21:38:04|  |
We|1957-01-30 21:25:21|  |Fr|1957-03-01 16:12:10|  |
Tu|1958-02-18 15:38:60|  |Tu|1958-02-18 15:38:60|  |
Sa|1959-02-07 19:22:03|  |Sa|1959-02-07 19:22:03|  |
Fr|1960-02-26 18:23:41|  |Fr|1960-02-26 18:23:41|  |
We|1961-02-15  8:10:60|T |We|1961-02-15  8:10:60|T |
Mo|1962-02-05  0:10:07|T |Mo|1962-02-05  0:10:07|T |
Su|1963-02-24  2:06:10|  |Su|1963-02-24  2:06:10|  |
Th|1964-02-13 13:01:50|  |Th|1964-02-13 13:01:50|  |
Mo|1965-02-01 16:36:03|  |We|1965-03-03  9:55:56|  |
Su|1966-02-20 10:49:57|  |Su|1966-02-20 10:49:57|  |
Sa|1967-03-11  4:30:35|  |Th|1967-02-09 10:43:56|  |
Mo|1968-01-29 16:30:05|  |Mo|1968-01-29 16:30:05|  |
Su|1969-02-16 16:26:08|  |Su|1969-02-16 16:26:08|  |
Fr|1970-02-06  7:12:46|  |Fr|1970-02-06  7:12:46|  |
Th|1971-02-25  9:48:47|P |Th|1971-02-25  9:48:47|P |
Tu|1972-02-15  0:29:33|  |Tu|1972-02-15  0:29:33|  |
Sa|1973-02-03  9:23:03|  |Mo|1973-03-05  0:07:43|  |
Fr|1974-02-22  5:34:31|  |Fr|1974-02-22  5:34:31|  |
Tu|1975-02-11  5:17:33|  |Tu|1975-02-11  5:17:33|  |
Th|1976-01-01 14:41:02|  |Su|1976-02-29 23:24:48|  |
Fr|1977-02-18  3:37:52|  |Fr|1977-02-18  3:37:52|  |
Tu|1978-02-07 14:54:13|  |Tu|1978-02-07 14:54:13|  |
Mo|1979-02-26 16:45:18|T |Mo|1979-02-26 16:45:18|T |
Sa|1980-02-16  8:51:55|T |Sa|1980-02-16  8:51:55|T |
We|1981-02-04 22:13:53|A |We|1981-02-04 22:13:53|A |
Tu|1982-02-23 21:13:30|  |Tu|1982-02-23 21:13:30|  |
Su|1983-02-13  0:32:54|  |Su|1983-02-13  0:32:54|  |
We|1984-02-01 23:46:38|  |Fr|1984-03-02 18:31:06|  |
Tu|1985-02-19 18:43:20|  |Tu|1985-02-19 18:43:20|  |
Su|1986-02-09  0:55:49|  |Su|1986-02-09  0:55:49|  |
Th|1987-01-29 13:45:02|  |Th|1987-01-29 13:45:02|  |
We|1988-02-17 15:55:03|  |We|1988-02-17 15:55:03|  |
Mo|1989-02-06  7:37:04|  |Mo|1989-02-06  7:37:04|  |
Su|1990-02-25  8:54:33|  |Su|1990-02-25  8:54:33|  |
Th|1991-02-14 17:32:44|  |Th|1991-02-14 17:32:44|  |
Mo|1992-02-03 19:59:40|  |We|1992-03-04 13:22:44|  |
Su|1993-02-21 13:05:32|  |Su|1993-02-21 13:05:32|  |
Th|1994-02-10 14:30:24|  |Th|1994-02-10 14:30:24|  |
Mo|1995-01-30 22:47:60|  |We|1995-03-01 11:47:55|  |
Su|1996-02-18 23:30:50|  |Su|1996-02-18 23:30:50|  |
Fr|1997-02-07 15:06:27|  |Fr|1997-02-07 15:06:27|  |
Th|1998-02-26 17:25:58|T |Th|1998-02-26 17:25:58|T |
Tu|1999-02-16  6:39:37|A |Tu|1999-02-16  6:39:37|A |
Sa|2000-02-05 13:03:19|P |Sa|2000-02-05 13:03:19|P |
Fr|2001-02-23  8:21:11|  |Fr|2001-02-23  8:21:11|  |
Tu|2002-02-12  7:41:47|  |Tu|2002-02-12  7:41:47|  |
Sa|2003-02-01 10:48:17|  |Mo|2003-03-03  2:35:09|  |
Fr|2004-02-20  9:18:17|  |Fr|2004-02-20  9:18:17|  |
Tu|2005-02-08 22:28:43|  |Tu|2005-02-08 22:28:43|  |
```

```
Su|2006-01-29 14:15:02|   |Su|2006-01-29 14:15:02|   |
Sa|2007-02-17 16:15:12|   |Sa|2007-02-17 16:15:12|   |
Th|2008-02-07  3:44:53|A  |Th|2008-02-07  3:44:53|A  |
We|2009-02-25  1:35:18|   |We|2009-02-25  1:35:18|   |
Su|2010-02-14  2:52:42|   |Su|2010-02-14  2:52:42|   |
Th|2011-02-03  2:30:44|   |Fr|2011-03-04 20:46:55|   |
Tu|2012-02-21 22:35:06|   |Tu|2012-02-21 22:35:06|   |
Su|2013-02-10  7:21:21|   |Su|2013-02-10  7:21:21|   |
Th|2014-01-30 21:38:54|   |Sa|2014-03-01  8:00:22|   |
We|2015-02-18 23:48:05|   |We|2015-02-18 23:48:05|   |
Mo|2016-02-08 14:39:43|   |Mo|2016-02-08 14:39:43|   |
Su|2017-02-26 14:58:50|A  |Su|2017-02-26 14:58:50|A  |
Th|2018-02-15 21:06:31|P  |Th|2018-02-15 21:06:31|P  |
Mo|2019-02-04 21:04:11|   |Mo|2019-02-04 21:04:11|   |
Su|2020-02-23 15:32:28|   |Su|2020-02-23 15:32:28|   |
Th|2021-02-11 19:07:05|   |Th|2021-02-11 19:07:05|   |
Tu|2022-02-01  5:46:36|   |We|2022-03-02 17:36:01|   |
Mo|2023-02-20  7:06:37|   |Mo|2023-02-20  7:06:37|   |
Fr|2024-02-09 23:00:17|   |Fr|2024-02-09 23:00:17|   |
Fr|2025-02-28  0:45:36|   |Fr|2025-02-28  0:45:36|   |
Tu|2026-02-17 12:02:16|A  |Tu|2026-02-17 12:02:16|A  |
Sa|2027-02-06 15:57:03|A  |Sa|2027-02-06 15:57:03|A  |
Fr|2028-02-25 10:38:02|   |Fr|2028-02-25 10:38:02|   |
Tu|2029-02-13 10:32:56|   |Tu|2029-02-13 10:32:56|   |
Sa|2030-02-02 16:08:05|   |Mo|2030-03-04  6:36:01|   |
Fr|2031-02-21 15:49:36|   |Fr|2031-02-21 15:49:36|   |
We|2032-02-11  6:25:28|   |We|2032-02-11  6:25:28|   |
Su|2033-01-30 22:00:31|   |Tu|2033-03-01  8:24:41|   |
Sa|2034-02-18 23:11:12|   |Sa|2034-02-18 23:11:12|   |
Th|2035-02-08  8:23:34|   |Th|2035-02-08  8:23:34|   |
We|2036-02-27  5:00:10|P  |We|2036-02-27  5:00:10|P  |
Su|2037-02-15  4:55:28|   |Su|2037-02-15  4:55:28|   |
Th|2038-02-04  5:52:58|   |Fr|2038-03-05 23:16:41|   |
We|2039-02-23  3:18:14|   |We|2039-02-23  3:18:14|   |
Su|2040-02-12 14:26:09|   |Su|2040-02-12 14:26:09|   |
Fr|2041-02-01  5:43:38|   |Sa|2041-03-02 15:40:51|   |
Th|2042-02-20  7:39:40|   |Th|2042-02-20  7:39:40|   |
Mo|2043-02-09 21:09:07|   |Mo|2043-02-09 21:09:07|   |
Su|2044-02-28 20:13:32|A  |Su|2044-02-28 20:13:32|A  |
Th|2045-02-16 23:52:02|A  |Th|2045-02-16 23:52:02|A  |
Mo|2046-02-05 23:10:50|A  |Mo|2046-02-05 23:10:50|A  |
Su|2047-02-24 18:26:42|   |Su|2047-02-24 18:26:42|   |
Fr|2048-02-14  0:33:10|   |Fr|2048-02-14  0:33:10|   |
Tu|2049-02-02 13:16:49|   |Th|2049-03-04  0:13:27|   |
Mo|2050-02-21 15:04:14|   |Mo|2050-02-21 15:04:14|   |
```

On the following pages, you will find a description of each of the animal signs.

The Twelve Animals

Mouse

The mouse is quiet. He is not friendly or outgoing and tends to be stable. He is not rough. Even though he does good things for others, others don't seem to respond. On the outside, he is open and relaxed in appearance, but inside he is very strong and critical. Very open-mouthed, he says what he thinks. He is kind, but not generous. He misses the big opportunities, and takes the small ones. He is always searching.

Current Day: This a good day for getting married, making forward progress, business of any kind, finding valuable things, and for a son be born. On this day, you should avoid eating meat, divination of all kinds, and travel.

Tibetan Astrology

Ox

The ox is a difficult person. He is hard to get to work, and is not obedient. He likes to sleep. He often exhibits bad behavior. While it is hard to change him, he is most often an agreeable person. However his slogan is "Don't mess with me!" He is very slow and doesn't care much if things are satisfactory or not. He postpones everything. He is good-tempered. He likes to eat and sleep like a bull.

Current Day: This is a good day for taking care of whatever has piled up, starting projects, laying the foundation for things, resolving important issues, and taking it to your enemies. This is a good day for travel. This is not a good day for business of any kind, religious vows and ceremonies, spirituality in general, and defaming others.

Tibetan Astrology

Tiger

The tiger is brave, active and bright. Always proud and loyal to close relatives, he tends to have rough behavior and speech. He does a lot of thinking. He likes gambling and makes a good businessman.

Current Day: This is a good day for travel to the West and East, for taking steps to get wealth, building things, and artistic projects, in general. Not a good day for getting married, for any public ceremony, and for theft.

Tibetan Astrology

Hare

"I am just for myself." The hare is independent, and does not need or ask others for their help. "I can survive. There is much opportunity in the world to be enjoyed. I am satisfied with that." He tends to be indirect, devious and possibly dishonest, but always skillful. He is stingy, but smiles and is generous on the surface. Possible diseases include those of the stomach and gall bladder.

Current Day: This is a good day for funerals, cemeteries, and conferring honor of any kind, also purchasing or selling animals. This is not a good day for making money, parties and celebrations, projects involving water, becoming prosperous, or pursuing your adversaries.

Dragon

The dragon is neither brave nor active, but is good. He never does "bad." "I am not very powerful, but nobody harms me." He does not make much effort, but also does not procrastinate or put things off. When the time comes, he does his duty. He has a short temper, but is good minded. He is talkative. He listens to others talk. He has trouble containing himself. He has less disease than some of the other signs but if he gets sick, it can be serious.

Current Day: A good day for religious ceremonies, ordination, and spiritual practice of any kind. Also good for removing obstacles and negativity. Not good for working with the land, any kind of navigation, surgery, and attacking your enemies.

Tibetan Astrology

Snake

The snake has a bad temper and is always burning his own mind-stream. However, he has a good heart and is very optimistic or forward minded. Even if others are jealous of him, no one has the power to put him down. He can, however, destroy himself. He may have a somewhat rough character and can be mean. Once his mind is made up, he won't change it. He tends to diseases of the stomach and liver.

Current Day: This is a good day for giving or loaning things to others, traveling toward the South, and making offerings to the nagas - nature spirits. Not a good day for working with trees or any work with water or land. Also bad for funerals, doctors, and medical care, commerce of any kind, and travel to the East, West, or North.

Tibetan Astrology

Horse

The horse is said to have miraculous power and is capable of great effort. Even though 1000 enemies chase him, he cannot be defeated. His older life will be better than his youth. He listens to others. He likes horses. He is a fast walker and enjoys play. He has a self-sacrificing character and always helps others. He needs little sleep. His life has a lot of ups and downs.

Current Day: This is a good day for undertaking projects, celebrating, and going to festivals, legal and judicial matters, attacking your enemies, and high-level relations. Not good for holding funerals, marriage, petitioning for anything, and making weapons. Avoid touching blood on this day.

Sheep

The sheep does not talk much and tends not to be not too bright. He can be a rough character. He likes to eat. He causes others no harm, but does not sacrifice himself for them either. He is generally good tempered and good hearted. Always relaxed, he does not rush. He is not lazy, but can't get things done on time. He does not show either like or dislike. He is a good provider

Current Day: A good day for high-level ceremonies, marriage, any work on the land, and work around the house. Not a good day for medicine and medical operations, ordination, important issues, petitioning, and attacking your enemies.

Tibetan Astrology

Monkey

Monkeys are very smart, not very talkative and tend to have bad tempers. They have lightweight, weak bodies. They are not always open minded and are said to have "small" mind power. Not noted for their sense of responsibility, they like to play and enjoy themselves. Their words are not to be trusted and they talk, gossip and lie too much – are surface oriented. They look clean but tend to eat dirty things. Very ambitious, they always have great plans. They like to praise themselves.

Current Day: A good day for having fun, entertaining, going to festivals, taking in sports, gambling, music, and the arts. Also good for both marriage and funerals and removing obstacles. Travel to the East or North is favored. Not good for taking on additional responsibilities.

Tibetan Astrology

Bird

It is easy for the bird to lose his possessions, legacy, inheritance, what-have-you? They are always advising others, but seldom take their own advice. Possessing a very strong sexual desire, they always need company. They like to be neat and clean, and don't require much sleep. They are prone to blindness. They love style, dressing up, and tend to smile a lot. They enjoy walking and stylish movement. Good with friends.

Current Day: A good day for healing and the preparation of medicines, agriculture, helping others, business, and making requests. Not a good day for festivities, celebrations, making gifts, good acts, or any rituals for removing negativity.

Dog

The dog is proud, mean, and somewhat wrathful. He can't seem to get kindness from others no matter how hard he tries. He is self-interested, does only for himself, and never for others. His mind is always filled with lots of thoughts. He tries to do things right, but they tend turn to out bad or wrong. He likes meat. He is a fast walker. Very sexual. A traveler. He is high or good minded, and elegant people tend to like him

Current Day: A good day for becoming more prosperous, business, making things, and offering up criticism. Not a good day for marriage, planting, violent acts, making war, making serious requests, and work around the house.

Tibetan Astrology

Pig

The pig is not bright. He likes to eat but is not concerned with what type of food. He eats everything. He likes yoga. He has good self-discipline. Can be greedy and often takes advantage of others. He does not benefit himself. He lies. He has a big stomach. He is good with the good people, and bad with the bad people. He seldom smiles and is often mean. He can be a rough character.

Current Day: A good day for ceremonies and transferring power. Not a good day for working with the earth, beginning school of studies, painting, and any rituals to remove obstacles.

The above twelve descriptions are pretty much direct translations from the Tibetan.

Tibetan Astrology

Animal Days: Electional

Day of Mouse

Favorable Action for Astrology (calc, not reading)
Favorable Action for Petitions
Favorable for making rain
Favorable for Trading
Not Favorable for Journeys
Not Favorable for Banishing Negativity

Day of Ox

Favorable for Building
Favorable for Starting a Fight
Favorable for Irrigation/water
Favorable for Journeys
Not Favorable for Banishing Negativity

Day of Tiger

Favorable for Fire rituals
Favorable for Building
Favorable for wealth (Jzambhalla)
Favorable for Journeys East and West
Not Favorable for Marriage
Not Favorable (Purification)
Not Favorable for Feast Days, Offerings
Not Favorable for Starting a Fight
Not Favorable for Hair Cutting
Not Favorable for Medicine (giving remedies)

Day of Hare

Favorable for Funeral
Favorable for Trade
Not Favorable for Agricultural
Not Favorable for Banishing Negativity
Not Favorable for Starting a Fight

Tibetan Astrology

Not Favorable for Irrigation/water
Not Favorable Wealth (Dzambhala)

Day of Dragon

Favorable for Banishing Negativity
Favorable for Building
Favorable for Taking on Responsibility
Not Favorable Agricultural Work
Not Favorable for Funeral
Not Favorable for Starting a Fight
Not Favorable for Irrigation/water
Not Favorable for Medicine (Surgery)

Day of Snake

Favorable for Local Deities
Favorable for Journeys to South
Not Favorable for Journeys North, West, East
Not Favorable for Marriage
Not Favorable for Agricultural
Not Favorable for Banishing Negativity
Not Favorable for Felling Trees
Not Favorable for Funeral
Not Favorable for Irrigation/water
Not Favorable for Medicine

Day of Horse

Favorable for Feast Days, Offerings
Favorable for Taking on Responsibility
Favorable for Trade in Day of Horse
Not Favorable for Marriage
Not Favorable for Funeral
Not Favorable for Hair Cutting

Tibetan Astrology

Day of Sheep

Favorable for Agricultural
Favorable for Marriage
Not Favorable for Starting a Fight

Day of Monkey

Favorable Action, Petitions
Favorable for Funeral
Favorable, making rain
Favorable for planting Trees
Favorable for Journeys to North and East
Favorable for Marriage
Not Favorable for Taking on Responsibility

Day of Bird

Favorable Action, Petitions
Favorable for Fire rituals
Favorable, making rain
Favorable for Medicine (making remedies)
Favorable for Trade (selling)
Not Favorable for Banishing Negativity

Day of the Dog

Favorable for Trade (buying)
Not Favorable for Marriage
Not Favorable for Agricultural
Not Favorable for Starting a Fight
Not Favorable for Hair Cutting

Day of the Pig

Favorable for Hair Cutting
Favorable for Making Rain
Not Favorable for Agricultural
Not Favorable for Banishing Negativity

The Sixty Year Cycle

The Sexagenary Table

The sexagenary or sixty-year animal-element cycle is a cornerstone of Tibetan astrology and is part of Jung-Tsi, Tibet's astrological heritage from China. This sixty-year cycle combines two cycles within itself, the 12-year cycle of animals (Mouse, Ox, Tiger, Hare, Dragon, Snake, Horse, Sheep, Monkey, Bird, Dog, and Pig) and the cycle of the five elements (Wood, Fire, Earth, Metal, and Water). This cycle is also called the Great Cycle of Jupiter.

In this cycle the 12 animal signs follow one another in strict sequence, with each animal sign taking one year, and these are paired with the five elements, but the elements are repeated twice, so that one element is the same for two successive years. It may be easier to just look at the list as shown below.

Tibetan Astrology

	M/F	Ele. Animal	Vital	Body	Power	Wind	La
4	Female	Fire-Hare	Wood	Fire	Fire	Fire	Water
5	Male	Earth-Dragon	Earth	Water	Earth	Water	Fire
6	Female	Earth-Snake	Fire	Wood	Earth	Water	Wood
7	Male	Iron-Horse	Fire	Earth	Iron	Iron	Wood
8	Female	Iron-Sheep	Earth	Earth	Iron	Fire	Fire
9	Male	Water-Monkey	Iron	Iron	Water	Wood	Earth
10	Female	Water-Bird	Iron	Iron	Water	Water	Earth
11	Male	Wood-Dog	Earth	Fire	Wood	Iron	Fire
12	Female	Wood-Pig	Water	Fire	Wood	Fire	Iron
13	Male	Fire-Mouse	Water	Water	Fire	Wood	Iron
14	Female	Fire-Ox	Earth	Water	Fire	Water	Fire
15	Male	Earth-Tiger	Wood	Wood	Earth	Earth	Iron
16	Female	Earth-Hare	Wood	Earth	Earth	Fire	Water
17	Male	Iron-Dragon	Earth	Iron	Iron	Wood	Fire
18	Female	Iron-Snake	Fire	Iron	Iron	Water	Wood
19	Male	Water-Horse	Fire	Wood	Water	Iron	Wood
20	Female	Water-Sheep	Earth	Wood	Water	Fire	Fire
21	Male	Wood-Monkey	Iron	Water	Wood	Wood	Earth
22	Female	Wood-Bird	Iron	Water	Wood	Water	Earth
23	Male	Fire-Dog	Earth	Earth	Fire	Iron	Fire
24	Female	Fire-Pig	Water	Earth	Fire	Fire	Iron
25	Male	Earth-Mouse	Water	Fire	Earth	Wood	Iron
26	Female	Earth-Ox	Earth	Fire	Earth	Water	Fire
27	Male	Iron-Tiger	Wood	Wood	Iron	Iron	Water
28	Female	Iron-Hare	Wood	Wood	Iron	Fire	Water
29	Male	Water-Dragon	Earth	Water	Water	Wood	Fire
30	Female	Water-Snake	Fire	Water	Water	Water	Wood
31	Male	Wood-Horse	Fire	Iron	Wood	Iron	Wood
32	Female	Wood-Sheep	Earth	Iron	Wood	Fire	Fire
33	Male	Fire-Monkey	Iron	Fire	Fire	Wood	Earth
34	Female	Fire-Bird	Iron	Fire	Fire	Water	Earth
35	Male	Earth-Dog	Earth	Wood	Earth	Iron	Fire
36	Female	Earth-Pig	Water	Wood	Earth	Fire	Iron
37	Male	Iron-Mouse	Water	Earth	Iron	Wood	Iron
38	Female	Iron-Ox	Earth	Earth	Iron	Water	Fire
39	Male	Water-Tiger	Wood	Iron	Water	Iron	Water
40	Female	Water-Hare	Wood	Iron	Water	Fire	Water
41	Male	Wood-Dragon	Earth	Fire	Wood	Wood	Fire
42	Female	Wood-Snake	Fire	Fire	Wood	Water	Wood
43	Male	Fire-Horse	Fire	Water	Fire	Iron	Wood
44	Female	Fire-Sheep	Earth	Water	Fire	Fire	Fire
45	Male	Earth-Monkey	Iron	Earth	Earth	Wood	Earth
46	Female	Earth-Bird	Iron	Earth	Earth	Water	Earth
47	Male	Iron-Dog	Earth	Iron	Iron	Iron	Fire
48	Female	Iron-Pig	Water	Iron	Iron	Fire	Iron
49	Male	Water-Mouse	Water	Wood	Water	Wood	Iron
50	Female	Water-Ox	Earth	Wood	Water	Water	Fire
51	Male	Wood-Tiger	Wood	Water	Wood	Iron	Fire
52	Female	Wood-Hare	Wood	Water	Wood	Fire	Water
53	Male	Fire-Dragon	Earth	Earth	Fire	Wood	Water
54	Female	Fire-Snake	Fire	Earth	Fire	Water	Wood
55	Male	Earth-Horse	Fire	Fire	Earth	Iron	Wood
56	Female	Earth-Sheep	Earth	Fire	Earth	Fire	Fire
57	Male	Iron-Monkey	Iron	Wood	Iron	Wood	Fire
58	Female	Iron-Bird	Iron	Wood	Iron	Water	Earth
59	Male	Water-Dog	Earth	Water	Water	Iron	Fire
60	Female	Water-Pig	Water	Water	Water	Fire	Iron
01	Male	Wood-Mouse	Water	Iron	Wood	Wood	Iron
02	Female	Wood-Ox	Earth	Iron	Wood	Water	Fire
03	Male	Fire-Tiger	Wood	Fire	Fire	Iron	Water

Sixty Element-Animal Combinations

As you can see each year the male and female polarity alternates. The 12 animals rotate in strict sequence, while each of the five elements persists for two years, and then rotate to the next in the element series.

These 60-year Tibetan cycles are measured from the year 1027, the year that the Kalachakra teachings are said to have come to Tibet, although the similar cycle from the Chinese version of this cycle marks the year 1024 as the start. The difference is three years and that is why the list above starts with the year of the Female Fire-Hare, rather than the Male Wood Mouse. In any case, the difference in starting points does not change what animal-element combination goes with which year.

At the close of each sixty-year cycle, the entire cycle begins again. Below are all sixty animal-element combinations along with an Astro*Image and interpretive text.

These are translations directly from the Tibetan. Please not that some of the statements appear very matter of fact, like that you will live 75 years, etc. Tibetans take these with a grain of salt and understand them to be general statements that give a flavor of what this combination is all about.

#01 Male Wood Mouse

The Wood Mouse is an expert at lying and deceiving others, and at this they have great skill. They possess good skills in arts and crafts and are very bright. Their wealth will be average, children three or five in number, and their lifespan is 75 years. There will be seven obstacles.

#02 Female Wood Ox

The Wood Ox will have more than average wealth and prosperity and tend toward jealousy. They are very intelligent. Their lifespan is said to be 60 years and they will face six obstacles. They will have many enemies, and their life spirit (La) will be attacked by various Earth Lords, as punishment for having disturbed tombs in the past.

#03 Male Fire Tiger

The Fire Tiger is very strong, physically, quite fierce, and very prideful. They will harm those who refuse to assist them, have short tempers, and little faith. They will suffer from internal ailments. The lifespan is 79 years, and they will face five obstacles. They are very educated and upper middle class.

#04 Female Fire Hare

The Fire Hare enjoys rough speech, can be deceitful and not speak the truth, and likes to criticize others, while singing their own virtues. They love the opposite sex, and like to be well educated. Their lifespan is 75 years and they will face seven obstacles. The Earth Lords will attack them, and their parents may suffer as a result. They will suffer from diseases of the heart and wind disorders. They will be wealthy.

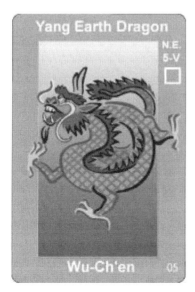

#05 Male Earth Dragon

The Earth Dragon has many faults, not the least of which is their tendency not to speak the truth. They will be light hearted, very healthy, and generally joyful. They will be lazy, love alcohol, and enjoy many partners. Their lifespan is 55 years and there will be six obstacles. They will be well-to-do, educated, and have much wealth.

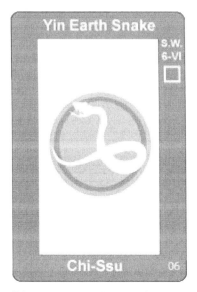

Yin Earth Snake

S.W.
6-VI

Chi-Ssu 06

#06 Female Earth Snake

The Earth Snake will be very wealthy and have many resources. Their wealth may decline in time and be slowly lost. They are very skillful and have strong minds. Having great pride, it is said that they are black-hearted, dark-complexioned, and both passionate and jealous.

They enjoy the company of lazy and bad-intentioned friends. Their average lifespan is 79 years and they will face four obstacles. There will be six children. They are easily injured, and may commit suicide. Males may die overseas.

#07 Male Metal Horse

The Iron Horse is lazy, and enjoys the company of family and close relatives. They love their spouse, and will have four children, which they will have trouble raising. They love to find faults in others, while ignoring their own. Their average lifespan is 57 and they will face nine obstacles. They will be attacked by the Earth Lords, and will be susceptible to wind and cold disorders.

Tibetan Astrology

#08 Female Metal Sheep

The Iron Sheep tend to be overweight and subject to diseases of the eye. They are slow to react and have poor memories. Their average lifespan is 81 years and they will face four obstacles, not to mention more than their share of enemies and disputes. Very few children.

Tibetan Astrology

Yang Water Monkey
North
9-IX

Jen-Shin   09

#09 Male Water Monkey

The Water Monkey is very bright, highly motivated, sensitive, and possesses great skills. They will have great wealth and own much property. Their average lifespan is 57 years and they will face seven obstacles. There are three children. They may succumb to muggings and family feuds. They have the protection of the Earth Lords.

Tibetan Astrology

Yin Water Cock

North
10-X

Kuei-Yu   10

#10 Female Water Bird

The Water Bird loves to travel and has many friends, but they tend to be lazy and easily distracted. They have poor memories and are considered somewhat unreliable, and very impressionable. They enjoy deceiving others. Their average lifespan is 60 years and they will face nine obstacles. They may have disputes with neighbors and friends. Two children.

Yang Wood Dog

East
1-XI

Chia-Hsu   11

#11 Male Wood Dog

The Wood Dog is handsome, very skilled, quite sensitive, and have excellent memories. They may become elected officials. They have considerable wealth in the short term, but may suffer long-term losses. Their average lifespan is 79 years and there are five obstacles which they will face. There may be family feuds. Three children.

#12 Female Wood Pig

The Wood Pig is heavy, but strong, and, in generally, quite fierce, and more than a little thoughtless. They are easily deceived by both lovers and friends, and suffer from too much food and sex. Their average lifespan is 64 years and they will face five obstacles. They will accumulate wealth, but have few or no children.

#13 Male Fire Mouse

The Fire Mouse loves both food and wealth, and excess in general, but exercise self-control nevertheless. They have good memories, like to think, and are not above revealing the faults of others. They may steal and kill. Their average lifespan is 68 years and they will face five obstacles. They are garrulous.

Tibetan Astrology

#14 Female Fire Ox

The Fire Ox is strong, very well built, somewhat lazy, and fond of sleep. Poor eyesight. They will have moderate wealth and well-furnished homes. Their average lifespan is 71 years and they will face eight obstacles. They will have one son and two daughters. There will be some slight harm from enemies.

Tibetan Astrology

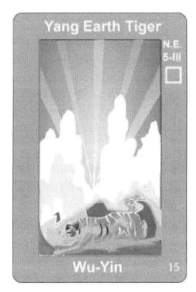

#15 Male Earth Tiger

The Earth Tiger may be fat, easily angered, and enjoy harming others. They love food and are very skilled as writers and speakers, not always telling the truth. They will have little harm from enemies. Their average lifespan is 72 years and there will be seven obstacles. Two children.

Tibetan Astrology

#16 Female Earth Hare

The Earth Hare loves to talk and is quite intelligent, easily mastering philosophy and other texts. They will have few material resources, and enjoy gambling, adultery, and the like, possibly affecting their relatives. Their average lifespan will be 50 years and they will face six obstacles. One child.

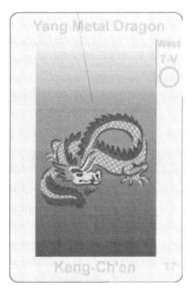

#17 Male Iron Dragon

The Iron Dragon is large, strong, and has great pride. They love to eat, and actually enjoy lying and dwelling on the faults of others. They will be very wealthy. Very skilled as speakers, they like to put off doing the right thing, and act negatively. Through this, they will suffer great losses of wealth, and still not reform. Their gentle words betray darker intentions. Their average lifespan is 80 years and they will face three obstacles. There will be one or five children.

Tibetan Astrology

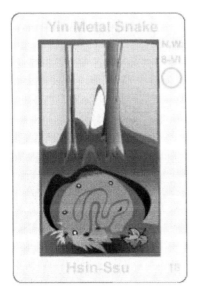

#18 Female Iron Snake

The Iron Snake are very sharp and skilled in all the arts. They are very critical of others and can incite theft and create enemies due to association with bad friends. They will have more wealth later in life, than when they are young. Their average lifespan is 78 years and they will face six obstacles. They will be three children.

#19 Male Water Horse

The Water Horse is very bright, and they are skilled in the area of arts and crafts. Quite naturally aware, they don't stoop to pointing out the faults of others, and are for the most part virtuous. They have very little anger and no guile, and like to be independent. They will have considerable wealth. Their average lifespan is 57 or 77 years and they will have three or four children.

Tibetan Astrology

#20 Female Water Sheep

The Water Sheep loves to travel and tends to be very wealthy, although their wealth may decline in time. They are said to have small intelligence and many cravings. Their average lifespan is 73 years and they will face five obstacles. They fear thieves and their enemies. Very few children, if any.

#21 Male Wood Monkey

The Wood Monkey tends to be big and have many cravings. They are very bright and mentally very adept. They are of average wealth, and may have two homes. They enjoy bad companions and could have many ailments. Their average lifespan is 78 years and they will have many enemies. There are one or five children.

Tibetan Astrology

Yin Wood Cock
S.E.
2-X

Yi-Yu 22

#22 Female Wood Bird

The Wood Bird will have many physical ailments, and friends and relatives may end up as enemies. There may be many disputes. The average lifespan is 60 years and they will have one or three children.

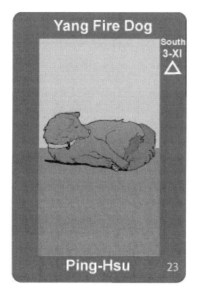

#23 Male Fire Dog

The Fire Dog show great patience and has many virtues, but also may ailments. There is danger of fevers and bile disorders, and their house may burn down. The average lifespan is 68 years and they will face seven obstacles. There will be three children.

Tibetan Astrology

#24 Female Fire Pig

The Fire Pig has a body that is frail and subject to many ailments. There is danger of superiors becoming antagonistic and also of their home burning. The average lifespan is 68 years and they will face seven obstacles. One child.

Tibetan Astrology

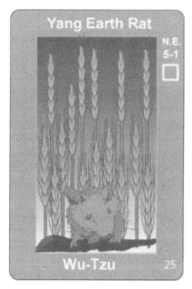

#25 Male Earth Mouse

The Earth Mouse tends to be short, rather than tall, lazy, and has a number of serous faults, not the least of which is that they enjoy killing. They are very soft spoken, but never lose track of their own advantage. The average lifespan is 68 years and there will be seven obstacles. One child.

#26 Female Earth Ox

The Earth Ox has great pride, and tends to be quarrelsome, brusque, and somewhat fierce. They will have few resources and little wealth. Mentally, they are ponderous. Their average lifespan is 50 years and they will face seven obstacles. There is one child.

#27 Male Iron Tiger

The Iron Tiger is simultaneously very generous and very fierce, enjoying killing. They are brusque in speech, love food and alcohol, and are generally of a fair complexion. They have an average lifespan of 60 years and will face five obstacles. Their wealth will be somewhat unstable, and they will have two or four children.

#28 Female Iron Hare

The Iron Hare tends to by lazy, but very open minded, with a sharp mind, a love of education, and strong ambitions. Despite more than their share of suffering, nevertheless, they are kind and generous to others. Their average lifespan is 61 years and they will face five obstacles. They will have an average amount of wealth and five children. There may be family feuds.

#29 Male Water Dragon

The Water Dragon moves around a lot, living in many homes. They love sports and tend to be very wealthy, although they will manage to lose most of it to relatives. Their average lifespan is 62 and they will face six obstacles. There are one or five children.

Tibetan Astrology

#30 Female Water Snake

The Water Snake is easily angered and not soon to forget a slight. They chose their friends more for their wealth than for their friendships, and are not above slander. They have an average lifespan of 68 years and may have to struggle to sustain the family line. They will have few children.

Tibetan Astrology

#31 Male Wood Horse

The Wood Horse is rather dull minded, very talkative, have considerable anger, and little motivation or faith. Yet, they have great strength and require little. They do not make friends easily, but love the few friends that they have. They have an average lifespan of 60 years and face threeobstacles. One child.

#32 Female Wood Sheep

The Wood Sheep is very keen minded, love over-eating, and all kinds of foolishness. Their average lifespan is 60 years and they will face two obstacles. Two children.

Tibetan Astrology

#33 Male Fire Monkey

The Fire Monkey loves good things and will be wealthy and socially prominent, although somewhat rough in nature. Their average lifespan is about 67 years and they will face five obstacles. Five children.

#34 Female Fire Bird

The Fire Bird has a short memory and many desires, managing to excel when it comes to lying and killing. They have many ideas, and delight in promiscuity. They fear being harmed. Their average lifespan is 65 years and they will face six obstacles.

#35 Male Earth Dog

The Earth Dog is very competitive, even aggressive, and will probably not accumulate much wealth. Passionate. Their average lifespan is 70 years and they will face seven obstacles. Several children.

#36 Female Earth Pig

The Earth Pig will be quite wealthy, but also have many problems and enemies. Possessing little knowledge, they will bring little good to their friends and relatives. Their average lifespan is 77 years and they will face six obstacles. Two children.

Tibetan Astrology

#37 Male Iron Mouse

The Iron Mouse tends to be heavy bodied, but also possesses considerable elegance and beauty. They love playing games and being the darling of the social scene. They have plenty of material wealth, but they like to cause arguments and the ensuing fights will deplete their wealth. Others respect them and they respect others, putting their own ambitions to the side. The average lifespan is 57 years and they will face six obstacles. There will be five children.

Tibetan Astrology

#38 Female Iron Ox

The Iron Ox is physically small, somewhat lazy, and very skilled when it comes to arts and crafts. They have generally good health and are ethical in their behavior. They are ever stubborn, even to the point of fierceness. They like their sleep and the company of superiors. The average lifespan is 55 years and there will be seven obstacles. Two children.

#39 Male Water Tiger

The Water Tiger is very energetic, fun-loving, and somewhat self-involved, in particular when it comes to their own virtues. They completely ignore their own faults. Quite promiscuous, they are gifted speakers, but their intentions are not good. The average lifespan is 71 years and they will face seven obstacles. Divorce is likely, and there will be one child. They tend to squander their wealth.

#40 Female Water Hare

The Water Hare loves business and all that it involves, although they are very slow to trust others. Their co-workers tend to distrust them. They tend to be stingy, and easily forget what they should remember. Their paternal home may be taken from them. The average lifespan is 72 and their children may be destined for great things.

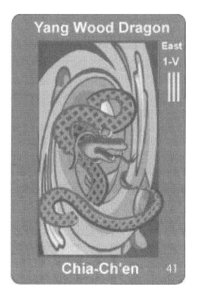

#41 Male Wood Dragon

The Wood Dragon is a skilled artisan, highly educated, and very eloquent. They are easy to get to know. They will have above average wealth, and be envied by others. Their average lifespan is 66 years and they will face six obstacles. Few children.

#42 Female Wood Snake

The Wood Snake will be very wealthy, loved by superiors, and hated by inferiors. They are said to be physically tall, mentally small. Very healthy. They are very talkative, always self-involved, and mostly narrow minded. The average lifespan is 77 years and they will face four obstacles. They will have sons.

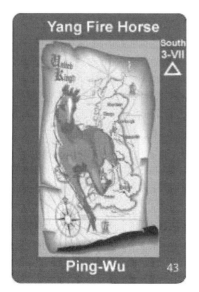

#43 Male Fire Horse

The Fire Horse is fierce, even wrathful, very stubborn, and loves to fight. They love animals, especially horses and dogs, but may have trouble making friends, since they are rough with people. They tend to lose their wealth over time. They love their partners. Their average lifespan is 78 years and they will face seven obstacles. Two children.

Tibetan Astrology

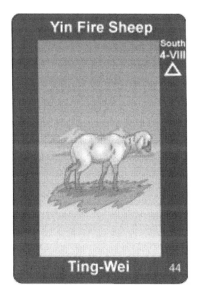

#44 Female Fire Sheep

The Fire Sheep love wealth and well-being, tend to corpulence, and make very stable friends. They are strong willed and able to achieve whatever it is they set their minds to. They are pleasant spoken and mentally pleasing. Their average lifespan is 77 years, love to accumulate wealth, and will face many obstacles. Many children and grandchildren.

#45 Male Earth Monkey

The Earth Monkey has little self-pride and is respected by all. They are refined in their conduct and skillful in speech and make friends easily. They have considerable wealth and are very deliberate in their actions toward goals. Their average lifespan is 78 and they will face nine obstacles, some life threatening. Three children.

Tibetan Astrology

#46 Female Earth Bird

The Earth Bird is friendly and light-hearted to all, but very perceptive. However, they have a short temper and tend toward jealousy, pride, and too many desires. Their average lifespan is 70 years and they will face seven obstacles. Six children.

#47 Male Iron Dog

The Iron Dog is very modest, soft-spoken, even to the point of shyness. They say little. Their hearts are pure and they indulge in virtuous actions. They love to sleep and they tend to be wealthy and to prosper. It is said that they are very deluded when it comes to worldly things. Their average lifespan is 77 years and they will face seven obstacles. Three or four children.

#48 Female Iron Pig

The Iron Pig is very refined and keen of mind. They may become priests or high officials, worthy of respect. They tend to have two partners. Their average lifespan is 70 years and they will have seven obstacles. Two or four children.

#49 Male Water Mouse

The Water Mouse will have to work hard for their wealth, and may lose it easily. They appear very refined - cool, calm, and collected. They have many desires, tend to promiscuity, and are easily led astray into deceit. Their average lifespan is 72 years and they will face seven obstacles. Two or five children.

#50 Female Water Ox

The Water Ox is very self-involved and tends to selfishness. They tend to foolishness, are lazy, and love their sleep. They speak gently, but engage in many deceitful actions, have evil intent, and this results in harsh language. Their average lifespan is 70 years and they will meet seven obstacles.

#51 Male Wood Tiger

The Wood Tiger loves fighting, being fierce, and is generally quite wrathful. They will have abundant wealth. They have very strong desires, are forever stingy, and they are jealous, selfish, and stone-faced when dealing with others. They tend to marry toward the latter part of life and may have many illegitimate children. They love promiscuity and staying out all night. Their average lifespan is 66 years and they will face five obstacles.

Tibetan Astrology

#52 Female Wood Hare

The Wood Hare love the opposite sex, and are not above committing adultery. They love to play, sing, and dance. Their minds are crafty and they fear both ill-health and many enemies. Their average lifespan is 67 years and they will meet six obstacles. They will have children both early and late in life.

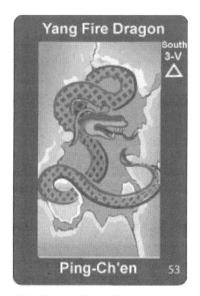

#53 Male Fire Dragon

The Fire Dragon is generally wealthy and of generous proportions. They have great appetites and manage to acquire great wealth and resources. They tend to be combative with their relations, and will suffer much from thieves and enemies. They may marry a widow. They are very skillful. Their average age is 71 years and they will meet seven obstacles. Two children.

#54 Female Fire Snake

The Fire Snake tends to corpulence, but are generally healthy and suffer few illnesses. They will be very wealthy, perhaps becoming an elected official, provide support for many others, and will be well respected. They may take five or seven spouses. The average lifespan is 71 years and they will meet seven obstacles. Two children.

#55 Male Earth Horse

The Earth Horse is courageous, but has a very short fuse. They don't always tell the truth, and tend to develop a bad reputation. Others will put their hope and trust in them, but little will come of it. They have many obstacles and will be picked apart by enemies and illness. The average lifespan is 75 years and they will meet seven obstacles. Two children.

#56 Female Earth Sheep

The Earth Sheep tends to carelessness in speech, extreme selfishness, and pride. Their reputation is generally poor. While outsiders will respect them, those closest to them will not. There may be great loses, but one descendant, and other bad luck. They have a great fear of their enemies, and are subject to many illnesses. Males will be drawn to their daughters, and females to their sons. The average lifespan is 60 years and they will face four obstacles.

#57 Male Iron Monkey

The Iron Monkey is dearly loved by all, for they are beautiful in appearance and naturally attractive. They will have a great amount of wealth and resources. They are naturally ambitious, but may suffer losses or get involved in family feuds. If they work hard for success, it is said that they will be happy in old age. Their average lifespan is 70 years and they will meet eight obstacles. One of five children.

#58 Female Iron Bird

The Iron Bird enjoys great wealth and abundance in all things. They are natural leaders, have strong attachments, but can even love their enemies. They may be afflicted by family feuds. Their average lifespan is 70 years and they will meet seven obstacles. Four children.

Yang Water Dog
North
9-XI
Jen-Hsu   59

#59 Male Water Dog

The Water Dog tends to be miserly and to live in fear of illness and enemies. They don't give up performing negative actions. Their wealth is little and they tend to be ignored by both friends and family. It is said that they have ugly marks on their body and succumb easily to injury and ill health. Their average lifespan is 73 years and they will meet many obstacles. Few children.

Tibetan Astrology

#60 Female Water Pig

The Water Pig is intellectually very bright, even gifted. They will have a generous amount of wealth and property, and they like to expose the pride and jealousy in others. There is a risk of suicide or fatal falls. Their average lifespan is 60 years and they will meet five obstacles. There are four children.

The Twelve Lunar Months

Tibetan astrology is primarily lunar based, rather than solar based as is our astrology here in the West. In the West we ask questions like: "What is your Sun Sigh?" or "What is your birthday?" Our calendar is solar or Sun based.

In Tibet and many other Asian countries, although the Sun is also important, it is the Moon that rules and the cycles of the Moon. In Tibet they don't celebrate birthdays as we do here. However, Tibetans might want to know what lunar day you were born in.

In other words, Tibetan months should not be confused with months as we have them in calendars here in the West (January, February, etc.). In Tibet, a month means a lunar month, and a lunar month is measured from New Moon to New Moon. Tibetans have a year of twelve or thirteen lunar months, and the starting and ending times and dates for these lunar months (their New Year) is not fixed. They vary. As mentioned earlier on, Tibetans have special lunar almanacs to keep track of this.

The Tibetan New Year (which is called "Losar") does not start on January 1st as does the Western calendar year. Instead, the beginning of the year in Tibet is a fluctuating point that (in general) starts with the day after the New Moon that is nearest to the beginning of February. But even that is not written in stone.

For example, the Tibetan and Chinese New Year celebrations can differ by an entire month! Even the two Tibetan-style calendars covered here, the Tsurphu (Karma Kagyu Lineage) and the Phugpa (Gelugpa Lineage) can, on occasion, differ by one whole month! It can only differ by an exact lunar month because no matter which system you use, the Asian year begins on the day following a New Moon.

For those of us used to calendars being absolute, this can be very confusing. How can New Year be off by an entire month?

Months and Elements

Each of the twelve or thirteen Tibetan lunar months is assigned one of the sixty element-animal combinations, such as, for example, a month might be called the "Water-Tiger" month. Here again I must point out that there is not complete agreement among Tibetans as to just how this should be done. In fact, there are several schemes for assigning elements and animals, and the differences are much too complicated to go into here. I suggest anyone who wishes to study these differences see the book "Kalachakra and the Tibetan Calendar" by Edward Henning.

One established method of naming the Tibetan months is where the animal for the first month of the year is always the Tiger, and the rest of the months follow in the standard order of the Tibetan animal cycle (Tiger, Hare, Dragon, etc.).

As for determining the element that goes with the animal or branch for each month, again there are differences. The Phugpa tradition states that the element that goes with the first month is always the son of the element of the year. For example, using the sexagenary cycle, I was born in 1941, the year of the Iron-Snake, so Iron (metal) is the element for the year 1941, and the son or child or Earth is the element Water.

In this method the son of the element of the year is the element of the first month, the son of the element of any month gives the element of the first day of the month, and the son of the element of that first day gives the element of the first double-hour.

Each element holds for two months, and the order of the element is in the standard order: iron (metal), water, wood, fire, and earth.

To recap: the son of the element of the year is the element of the first two months (Tiger and Hare). Then, the son of the element used in the first two months becomes the element used in the third and fourth months, and the son of that element (third and fourth months) becomes the element for the fifth and sixth month, and so on for the rest of the year.

However, according to Edward Henning, the above-described method is not that much used in almanacs. What is used is the following method, based on the animal-gender combination (the stem) for the current year.

Year Stem	First Month Element
Wood (male)	Fire-Tiger (male)
Earth (female)	Fire-Tiger (male)
Wood (Female)	Earth-Tiger (male)
Iron (male)	Earth-Tiger (male)
Fire (male)	Iron-Tiger (male)
Iron (female)	Iron-Tiger (male)
Earth (male)	Wood-Tiger (male)
Water (female)	Wood-Tiger (male)
Fire (female)	Water-Tiger (male)
Water (male)	Water-Tiger (male)

For example, I was born in 1941, the year of the Iron-Snake (female), so the animal-element combination for the first lunar month of 1941 would be the Iron-Tiger, and therefore the second month would be Iron-hare.

148

Remember that the animal signs go in order, one for each month, but the elements are doubled.

After these first two, we follow the rule given earlier that the son of the element used in the first two months becomes the element used in the third and fourth months, and so on. For 1941, the third month would be the Water-Dragon, and the fourth the Water-Snake, since Water is the son of Iron. And so it goes.

The Lunar Month

For starters, as mentioned, it is important to understand that Tibetan astrology is lunar based (the Moon), rather than solar based like the calendar we are used to here in the West. What is of interest to Tibetans is the lunar month, which is (on average) 29.5 days in length. The lunar month is based on the solunar angle, which is the ever increasing (or decreasing) angle between the Sun and the Moon, as the Moon makes its monthly journey around the earth from New Moon to the next New Moon.

Tibetans divide the 360-dgree lunar cycle into 30 days, each day lasting for the time it takes for the solunar angle to increase by 12 degrees of arc. Because the Moon moves in an ellipse (going faster or slower at different parts of its orbit), some lunar days take less time to cover those 12 degrees, while others take more. They do not measure an even 24 hours, like conventional clock time. This varying speed of the Moon allows for the double and omitted lunar days in the Tibetan almanac or calendar.

The Phases of the Moon

The phases of the Moon have been observed for ages. The Moon, from a Sanskrit term for measure, is still the primary means by which the majority of the people in the world (even in this 21st century!) measure time and the events in their own lives. I am referring here to the Asian countries, where astrology is an accepted part of society.

Although measuring time and life by the Moon is ancient, it is not just some primitive sort of clock. The very sophisticated concept of lunar gaps springs from centuries of painstaking psychological observation by the lamas of Tibet, and the Hindu sages. They practice it today with the same vigor and intensity as they did a thousand years ago. Unlike many other traditions, where the line of successors (lineage) has been broken due to various events, the dharma and astrological tradition of Tibet remains pure and unbroken to this day.

Although much of the Tibetan dharma tradition requires dedication and intense practice, learning to use the Moon's phases and the concept of lunar gaps is easy to get into. The theory is simple.

It involves the ongoing relationship between the Sun, the Moon, and the Earth -- the monthly cycle of the phases of the Moon. We already know about the Moon cycle, and can even walk outside at night and see which lunar phase we are in. We are always in the middle of the lunar cycle.

This is not the place (and I am not the expert) to describe to you either the very complicated astronomical motions these three heavenly bodies produce, or the profound theories of what all of this motion means in a philosophical sense. What is quite accessible is the concept of lunar gaps.

As we know, the Moon cycle goes through its phases from New Moon to Full Moon, back to New Moon in a cycle of about one month, some 30 days. This is seen as an ongoing cycle of activity -- endless in extent. It goes on forever.

However, although the Moon cycle is unending, it does have distinct phases, such as the Full Moon, New Moon, the quarters, and so on. In Tibet and India, the monthly lunar cycle is divided into 30 parts called lunar days. There are thirty lunar days (cumulative 12-degree angular separations of the Sun and Moon) starting from the New Moon (considered the 1st day), counting through the waxing half of the Moon cycle to the Full Moon (start of the 16th day) and on around through the waning cycle, back to the New Moon again.

What is interesting about the Tibetan view of this 30-day cycle is that the 30 lunar days are not considered all of equal importance. Here in the West, we note difference between New Moon and Full Moon, at least some folks do, but not much else.

To the Tibetans, the monthly lunar cycle has many more event points within it other than those of the Full and New Moons. These lunar gaps or openings that occur in each 30-day moon cycle are opportunities waiting to be observed and perhaps taken advantage ot.

It is at these lunar gaps or openings in this endless cycle that it is often possible get a glimpse or some insight into various areas of our own life or to have certain kinds of experiences. In fact, the Tibetans take full advantage of these very regular lunar gaps to perform very specific practices. In other words: certain of the lunar days have proven themselves to be auspicious for particular kinds of activities and others perhaps should be avoided.

In the East, they speak of mental obscurations that tend to cloud our minds, but that can sometimes clear up, just as the Sun comes out from behind the clouds. These moments of clarity are the gaps in the clouds. From a reading of the Eastern literature on this subject, one gets the sense that (in general) life is perceived as being filled with the noise of our own problems (obscurations), making clear insight often difficult for us. These obscurations can be many and their accumulation amounts to the sum total of our ignorance -- that which we at present ignore.

Therefore, in Eastern countries, these articulation points or lunar gaps (windows in time/space) are very much to be valued. They amount to opportunities for change. In fact, the Eastern approach is to analyze the lunar cycle in minute detail in order to isolate these moments (gaps in time/space) where insight into our larger life situation can be gained. Much of the day-to-day practice in Eastern religions amounts to a scheduling of precise times for personal practice or activity around the natural cycle of the moon – lunar days. In its own way, this is a very scientific approach. In the East, they have been astute observers of the mind for many centuries.

Here in the West, we are no stranger to clear days in our mind. We have those too! The only difference, is that we tend to believe that these so-called clear days appear randomly -- every now and then. The more sophisticated (and ancient) psychological analysis of the East has found that these clear days are (for the most part) anything but random events. They have their own internal ordering, and often times this ordering can be associated with the phases of the Moon.

Tibetan Astrology

In summary, there are times each month when it is more auspicious or appropriate to perform or be involved in one kind (or another) of activity. There come gaps in the general obscuration or cloudiness of our mind when we can see through the clouds -- when penetrating insight into our own life is possible. Most of us could benefit from that insight. I know I need it.

As noted, the times when one can see without obscuration (see clearly) are very much valued in the Tibetan dharma tradition. These are viewed as real opportunities for insight and the subsequent development such insight generates. Knowing when and where to look for these insight gaps has been the subject of study and research in Tibet and Asia for centuries. Before studying Tibetan astrology, I didn't even understand these lunar gaps existed. It gives a whole new meaning to the British phrase "Mind the gap."

And this is not just academic research. Lunar gaps are used to plan a wide variety of events in the Tibetan calendar, everything from finding a time to perform a simple healing ceremony to full scale life empowerments.

Aside from knowing when these lunar gaps can be experienced, the other major thing to know about this subject is what to do when the gaps occur. As you might imagine, there are a wide range of practices, depending on the particular lunar gap (phase) and the personal needs of the practitioner.

However, in general, these lunar gaps are times to be set aside for special observation. Tibetans observe these days with great attention and care. In fact, in many Eastern countries they don't have Saturday and Sunday off. Instead, New and Full Moon days are considered holy days (holidays), and normal routines are suspended at these times. These are days that are set aside for observation of our own mind. In the Western tradition, holidays are observed, but not astronomical moments.

This word "observation" is worth mentioning, for this is what takes place at these times. In the West, we might use the catch-all word meditation. In Tibet there are many words that come under the general concept of meditation. The word "observe" is a lot closer to what happens during these lunar gaps. Observe the nature of the day. Observe your mind at these times. Be alert, present, and set that bit of time aside just to examine yourself, your mind, the time -- what-have-you? It is while being present -- observing these seed times -- that the so-called lunar gap can present itself, that we can glimpse or see through that window in time. Many great dharma teachers have pointed out the existence of gaps in our life, moments when clarity and real insight is possible.

And lest we get too far afield, sitting there waiting for a gap in time or space to occur, let me restate: The gap that appears is a gap in our particular set of obscurations, our own personal cloudiness. When such a gap takes place, there can be an intense insight into some particular aspect of our life situation, the effects of which may stay with us for a long time. One moment of real insight or vision can take weeks or months to examine in retrospect. Each time we bring such an insight experience to mind, its richness is such that it continues to be a source of inspiration. This is what lunar gaps are all about.

At this point, it is hoped that you have some general idea of what lunar gaps are and how you might go about taking advantage of them. It remains to give you a schedule of when they will occur.

The solunar angle between the Sun and Moon is the basis for much of Tibetan astrology and the key to measuring the start and end of each of the 30 lunar days. The Tibetan month begins at the moment New Moon, which is the start of the 1st lunar day. When the angle between the Sun and the Moon reaches 12 degrees, it is the start of the 2nd lunar day and so on. Each successive 12-degree arc of angular separation marks succeeding lunar days… on to the end of the 30th day, which is the next New Moon. However, the celebration or listing of the event may occur on the following day.

One source of possible confusion to keep in mind (mentioned earlier in this text) is that Tibetan practice calendars are geared for group practice, which means that if the moment of the New Moon is at 2 A.M., the group will most likely be asleep and not able to gather. For convenience purposes, the lunar day of the month at sunrise (about 5 A.M.) is usually listed as the lunar day for that calendar date, even if the beginning of it occurred many hours earlier on the preceding day.

For example, Losar, the Tibetan New Year is celebrated on the day *following* the day on which the actual New Moon occurs. In contrast, the Chinese celebrate the New Year on the actual calendar date on which the New Moon occurs. The point here is that most Tibetan almanac or calendars are geared for group practice. Here in the West, many solitary practitioners keep to the lunar calendar and observe the time when the actual lunar day changes.

Tibetan Astrology

Below you will find a list of the major lunar days in the Tibetan practice calendar and what they are about. There are still further divisions that we have not included here, to keep this simple. These are the days observed by most Tibetan lamas in one form or another.

These lunar opportunities are sometimes referred to as gaps or openings in the otherwise continuous stream of our lives – windows in time. The Tibetans conceive of these gaps as articulation points, much like an elbow is where the arm is articulated. They are natural joints or gaps in time/space upon which time and space turn and through which it is sometimes possible to gain access to information about the larger, dynamic life process that already encapsulates us. In other words, we can see beyond our personal obscurations at these times.

These lunar opportunities are sometimes referred to as gaps or openings in the otherwise continuous stream of our lives -- windows. These can be conceived as articulation points, much like an elbow is where the arm is articulated. These are natural joints or gaps in time/space upon which time and space turn, and through which it is sometimes possible to gain access to information about the larger, dynamic life process that already encapsulates us.

The idea here is that we are each in the midst of our lives, surrounded by the cloud of our own personal obscurations. As one Tibetan rinpoche put it to me: those of us living today are the ones who through all this time have never managed to get enlightened, the hard cases. Surrounding us, but ignored by us until now, are all the hints, teachings, suggestions, pointers, etc. on how to clear up our mind and become more enlightened. We have managed to ignore almost every opportunity for insight.

Therefore, the fact that these lunar gaps or openings exist should be welcome news to us, opportunities for us to see more deeply into our condition and get a better handle on things.

Major Practice Days

Let's go over briefly some of the more important lunar days that are observed give some idea as to the kind of practices performed on those days.

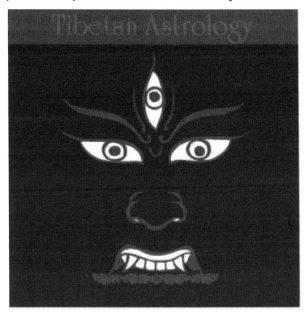

Dharma Protector Days

Both East and West lunar traditions agree that the two or three days preceding the moment of the New Moon can be difficult ones, days which require special observation and care. In the West these days have been called the dark of the Moon, or devil's days -- days when the so-called darker forces are said to have power. Both traditions affirm that we sort of survive these final three days each month. We wait them out.

Check it out for yourself. The three days before New Moon can be a hard time.

The East is in total agreement on this point, and the days prior to New Moon are set aside for invoking the fierce dharma protectors, those energies that ward off harm and protect us during the worst of times. In particular, the 29th day (the day before New Moon) is called Dharma Protector Day. It is a time given over to purification and preparation for the moment of New Moon. Ritual fasting, confession of errors, and the like are common practices.

Purification Days

In a similar vein, the days just prior to the Full Moon (the 13th and 14th) are also days of purification, days in which the various guardian and protector deities are again invoked, but in a somewhat more restrained way. For example, the 14th day is often given over to fire puja -- a ritual purification. In summary, during days prior to Full and New Moons, there is usually some attempt at purification, both physical and mental, in preparation for those auspicious events.

The Full and New Moons

It is clear from the Tibetan literature that the times of the New and Full Moon are considered of great importance. In fact, these days are set aside for special rituals and worship. As pointed out, Full and New Moon (Full more than New) are times of collective worship and public confession. In many traditions, the monks and priests assemble for a day of special observance. In the East, the Full Moon celebration and the entire waxing lunar fortnight are oriented to the masculine element in consciousness, what are called the Father-Line Deities. The New Moon and the waning fortnight are given over to the Mother-Line Deities and the feminine element. The Full Moon completes the masculine, or active, waxing phase of the cycle, and the New Moon completes the feminine, waning phase of the month. To my knowledge, this kind of analysis does not exist in the West to any real extent.

It is quite clear from the Eastern teachings that the moments of Full and New Moon are times when the various channels in the psycho-physical body are somehow aligned. This is not to say the New or Full Moon days are days of peace and quiet. It is taught in the East that, although a New or Full Moon day may tend to be wild or hectic, any patience or forbearance we can muster at that time will be much rewarded. In other words, there can be deep insights available to us at these times. That is why they are set aside for observation; they are observed.

Tibetan Astrology

Solar and Lunar Eclipses

According to these same teachings, an eclipse at the Full or New Moon is even more auspicious. In the teachings it is said that during these very special events that the winds and the drops, both male and female energies (the inner channels), are in simultaneous alignment -- the ultimate opportunity for observation. As you can gagther, the lunar cycle and its effects and opportunities have been analyzed in great detail in the Eastern teaching.

Tsok: Feast Days

Aside from the New and Full Moons, the two most auspicious lunar days in the East are the 10th and the 25th lunar days. The 10th day (120° of angular separation), called Daka Day, is considered auspicious for invoking the Father-Line Deities -- the masculine. The 25th day (300° of angular separation), called Dakini Day, is given over to the feminine principle and the Mother-Line Deities, in general. These two days, the 10th and the 25th, are formal feast days, days of observation when extra offerings are made and increased attention is given to what is happening. There is some sense of celebration at these points in the month, thus the feat or Tsok. In many respects, these two days even rival the New and Full Moon days in importance. The fact is that these four days (New, Full, 10th, 25th) are the primary auspicious days as practiced in many Eastern rituals. They are observed religiously.

Tibetan Astrology

Healing Days

There are many other days of lesser importance which might also interest Western astrologers. Health and healing are important in Eastern ritual, and the 8th and 23rd days of the lunar month are auspicious for this purpose. It is these days that straddle the first and last lunar quarters. The 8th day (96° of separation) is often called Medicine Buddha Day. Again this occurs in the male, or father-line, half of the month. The 23rd day (276° of separation), occurring in the feminine half of the month, is dedicated to Tara practice. Tara is the female deity connected to health, long life, and healing in general.

More Protector Days

Earlier we mentioned the days given over to purification, are most prominently the 13th and the 29th. In addition, on a lesser scale, the 9th and the 19th days are also noted as days when the protector deities should be invoked and kept in mind. These, too, are days of purification. And there are more, still finer, subdivisions that are made.

This brief overview should give you a general idea of how the monthly lunar cycle is broken up into days during which certain kinds of activities or observances are appropriate.

Lunar Practice Days

Below you will find a list of some of the major lunar days in the Tibetan practice calendar for each month, followed by activities for specific lunar months. There are still further divisions that we have not included here, in order to keep this simple.

In the first column is the number of the lunar month, and in the second column the lunar day of the month. Note that "00" means this happens each month.

M |D | Observance
00|03|Yoga Tantra -- All Seeing
00|03|Dharmapala Tsiu Marpo
00|03|Five Dakinis Practice (afternoon)
00|03|White Tara Practice (morning)
00|05|Dakini Day (minor)
00|08|Guru Rinpoche Day (minor)
00|08|Medicine Buddha Day
00|08|Tara Puja
00|08|Shri Hevajra
00|08|Gyalwa Gyatso - Red Chenrezig (morning)
00|08|Milarepa Guru Yoga (afternoon)
00|09|All Dharmapalas (dharma protectors) (minor)
00|10|Daka/Heruka Day (Male Deities) Feast Day
00|10|Heart Yoga Practice
00|10|Vajrayogini
00|10|Guru Rinpoche (afternoon)
00|13|12 Guardian Deity Offerings
00|13|Purification (minor) Prayer-Flag day
00|13|Fire Puja - Purification
00|14|Shri Hevajra
00|14|The 1002 Buddhas (Kshitagarbha Sutra)
00|14|Dharmapala Magzor Gyalmo, Shri Devi
00|14|Sojung (confession practice) (3 a.m.)
00|15|Amitabha Buddha Day/Full Moon Day

Tibetan Astrology

00|15|Chakrasamvara Practice (morning)
00|15|Full Moon Assembly
00|15|All Peaceful Deities
00|15|Amitabha Buddha
00|15|Drikung Phowa Practice
00|15|Chakrasmvara (morning)
00|15|Thang Lha (local deity) Afternoon
00|18|One of the Four Guardian Kings
00|18|Mahakala
00|19|Medicine Buddha
00|19|All Dharmapalas (protectors) (minor)
00|21|Chenresik
00|23|Tara/Healing (major)
00|23|Vajravarahi Practice
00|23|Shri Hevajra
00|23|Vairochana Buddha
00|23|Green Tara (long form) (morning)
00|23|Vajrayogini (short form) (afternoon)
00|24|Kshitagarbha Sutra
00|25|Dakini Day (Female Deities) Feast Day
00|25|Heart Yoga Practice
00|25|Vajrayogini
00|25|Guru Rinpoche (morning)
00|25|Vajrayogini (long form) (afternoon)
00|27|Purification
00|28|Purification
00|28|Amitabha Buddha
00|29|Dharma Protector Day (major)
00|29|Medicine Buddha
00|29|Shri Hevajra
00|29|All Dharmapalas (protectors)
00|29|Sojung (confession practice)
00|29|Dharmapala Day
00|29|Mahakala (all day)
00|29|Kunrik (purification practice) (3 a.m.)
00|30|30th Lunar Day New Moon

00|30|Buddha Day, Reading of Sutras
00|30|Vairochana Practice
00|30|Shakyamuni Buddha (100-fold merit)
00|30|Sojung (confession practice)
00|30|Drikung Phowa Practice

The above listt represents only some of the ways these 30 lunar days each month are observed. These are the days observed by Tibetan lamas of one lineage or another.

What follows is a somewhat extensive list of Buddhist practices for specific months. Note: "(B)" stands for standard Western-style birth day and "(A)" stands for "anniversary," which is the Tibetan way of saying the day they passed into nirvana. This list contains many saints and lamas from different lineages. It would take an entire book to describe who these saints are. Those of you in a particular lineage will recognize the teachers in your lineage. Otherwise, a web search may help.

01|01|Losar, Tibetan New Year
01|03|Dragshul Tinley Rinchen (A)
01|04|Monlam, 3 wks. Festival
01|05|Drikung Konchok Ratna
01|05|Rigdzin Kunzang Sherab
01|08|Rangjung Dorje, 3rd Karmapa (B)
01|08|H.E. Tai Situ Rinpoche (B)
01|08|9th Karmapa, Wangchuk Dorje (A)
01|08|6th Karmapa, Tongwa Donden
01|08|Change all House Prayer Flags
01|09|Karmapa Long Life (9th through the 15th day)
01|10|Cho Nga Chopa, 10th to 15th day
01|10|H.H. 12th Gyalwang Druchen (B)
01|13|7th Karmapa, Chodrak Gyatso (B)
01|13|Jikme Trinle Ozer, Dodrupchen
01|14|Milarepa's (A)

Tibetan Astrology

01|15|Chonga Chopa – Buddha's Miracles
01|15|7th Karmapa, Chodrak Gyatso (A)
01|15|Marpa (A)
01|15|Buddha's Incarnation
01|15|Garab Dorje (B)
01|15|Magha Puja (Theravadin)
01|21|14th Karmapa, Thekchog Dorje (1868) (A)
01|21|1st Jamyang Khyentse Wangpo, (A)
01|21|Gorampa Sonam Sengge (A)
01|23|Vajrayogini (23rd through 27th day)
01|24|13th Karmapa, Dudul Dorje (1797) (A)
01|24|Drukchen Dungse
01|25|Mon Lam Ends (studies begin)
01|26|Sakya Pandita Kunga Gyaltsen (A)
01|28|9th Karmapa, Wangchuk Dorje
01|28|Green Tara
02|02|Orgyen Terdak Lingpa
02|03|White Tara (3rd through 9th days) (morning)
02|03|Five Dakinis (afternnoon) (3rd through 9th day)
02|05|Jamyang Shepa
02|06|Chogyam Trungpa Rinpoche (A)
02|08|6th Karmapa, Thongwa Donden (1416) (B)
02|08|Sangye Yarjon
02|08|Yabje Kunga Rinchen of the Drolma Podrang (A)
02|12|1st Shamar, Trakpa Senge
02|12|Jetsun Dragpa Gyaltsen (A)
02|15|10th Karmapa, Choying Dorje (A)
02|15|Gyalton Rinpoche
02|20|Do Khyentse
02|22|Hevajra (22nd through 28th day)
02|23|5th Shamarpa, Konchok Yenlag (A)
02|24|3rd Jamgon Kontrul Rinpoche (1992) (A)
02|24|8th Tai Situ, Chokyi Jugne (1774) (A)
02|26|Khuwon Kunga Gyaltsen
02|26|Jetsun Taranata (A)
02|29|2nd Shamarpa, Kacho Wangpo (A)

168

Tibetan Astrology

02|29|Expulsion of scapegoat demon
02|30|Loter Wangpo (A)
02|30|Khangsar Jampa Sonam Zangpo (A)
02|30|Tinley Rinpoche of the Phuntsok Podrang (A)
03|01|Kalachakra New Year
03|02|Vajrakilaya (1st through 3rd day)
03|03|2nd Karmapa, Karma Pakshi
03|09|6th Karmapa, Thongwa Donden (B)
03|09|Kalachakra (9th through the 15th)
03|10|Tsechu: 8 Aspects of Guru Rinpoche
03|12|4th Karmapa, Rolpe Dorje (B)
03|15|Kalachakra Tantra Revealed by Buddha
03|15|Magha Puja Day (Sangha Day)
03|16|Terton Mingjur Dorje
03|18|Sazang Pagpa Shonnu Lodro (A)
03|18|Dezhung Rinpoche (A)
03|19|1st Shamarpa, Dragpa Senge
03|22|Tashi Paldrup
03|25|5th Dalai Lama (A)
03|26|15th Karmapa, Khakhyab Dorje (1922) (A)
03|26|Drikung Kyobpa Jigten Sumgon
03|28|10th Karmapa, Choying Dorje (B)
03|29|Tarlam Mahasiddha Kunga Namgyal (A)
03|29|L. K. Jamyang Tupten Lungtok Gyaltsen (A)
03|29|Jamgon Ngagwang Legpa (A)
03|30|Sangye Lingpa
04|04|Vajrakilaya (4th through 10th day) (main practice)
04|07|7th-15th day Sakya summer festival
04|07|Birth of the Buddha
04|08|Jamgon Kongtrul II, Khyentse Ozer (A)
04|08|Kalu Rinpoche, (A)
04|08|Khenchen Ngagwang Chodag (A)
04|11|Vajrakilaya Practice (concludes)
04|12|Khenchen Dampa Dorje Chang
04|12|Khangsar Khenchen Lama Dampa (A)
04|15|Sangyepa - Buddha attained Enlightenment (A)

Tibetan Astrology

04|15|Poson, Arhat Mahinda in Ceylon
04|15|Saga Dawa - Buddha Enlightened
04|15|Saga Dawa Dungdrup Puja (100 million mantras)
04|23|Mahasidda Virupa (A) (7-day celebration)
04|25|Ngorchen Kungpa Zangpo (A)
04|29|Mipham (A)
04|30|Nyala Pema Dudul
05|01|Chakrasamvara 7-days
05|01|Chogyur Lingpa
05|02|Sachen Kunga Lodro
05|04|3rd Shamarpa, Chokyi Lodro
05|05|Medical Buddhas
05|06|Khyentse Chokyi Lodro (A)
05|09|Chakrasamvara (9th through 15 day)
05|14|Khedrup Tenpa Dhargyey
05|15|Auspicious Fire-Puja Day
05|15|Dzam Ling Chi Sang - Local Deities Day
05|15|Theravadin 1st Buddha teaching
05|17|Lam Rim teaching (one month)
05|17|Nyoshul Lungtok
05|18|Khenpo Ngakchung
05|18|Shechen Gyaltsab Pema Namgyal
05|21|Jamyang Khyentse Wangchuk (A)
05|21|Magto Ludrop Gyatso (A)
05|23|Cho (23rd through 27th days)
05|24|Kungtok Shedrup Tenpe Nyima
06|04|Cho-Kor Duchen: Buddha Teaches Noble Truths
06|04|Deer Park Teaching
06|05|Chod - Practice 5 days
06|10|Guru Padmasambhava (A)
06|10|Sakya Lotsawa Kunga Sonam (A)
06|14|3rd Karmapa, Ranjung Dorje (1339) (A)
06|15|Gampopa (A)
06|15|Varsha: Rain Retreat (45 days)
06|15|Begin of Summer Retreat
06|18|5th Karmapa, Deshin Shegpa (1384) (B)

Tibetan Astrology

06|20|Buton Rinchen Drub (A)
06|20|Ngawang Tutop Wanchug (A)
06|23|Chos Cho (23rd-29th day)
06|25|Lama Sampa Sonam Gyaltsen (A)
06|29|Ngor Ponlop Jamyang Ngagwang Legdrub (A)
07|02|3rd Shamarpa, Konchok Yenlak
07|04|13th Karmapa, Dudul Dorje
07|05|Rigdzin Kumaradza
07|05|Panchen Shakya Shribhadra (A)
07|07|9th Karmapa, Wangchuk Dorje(1556) (B)
07|09|Rain of Wisdom Poetry (9th-15th day)
07|10|Jomo Menmo
07|12|11th Karmapa, Yeshe Dorje (1702) (A)
07|12|Sakyapa Ngag Chang Kunga Rinchen (A)
07|14|Ngag Chang Kunga Rinchen
07|15|4th Karmapa, Rolpe Dorje (1383) (A)
07|15|Dolpopa Sherab Gyaltsen (A)
07|15|Kunkhyen Pema Karpo
07|15|Sacrifice for the dead (India)
07|15|Trapa Ngonshe discovers 4 medical tantras
07|15|Tsarchen Losal Gyaltso (A)
07|15|Zhuchen Tsultrim Rinchen (A)
07|21|Red Chenrezik Mandala (7 days)
07|23|5th Shamarpa (1383) (A)
07|25|Pagmodrupa
07|29|2nd Shamarpa, Kha Chod Wangpo
08|01|5th Karmapa, Deshin Skekpa
08|03|H.E. 13th Shamarpa Rinpoche (1952) (B)
08|05|H.H. Sakya Trizin (B)
08|08|The Water Festival
08|08|Red Chenresik (8th-14th day)
08|10|15th Karmapa, Khakhyab Dorje (B)
08|10|5th Shamarpa, Konchok Yenlag (B)
08|15|5th Karmapa, Deshin Shegpa (1415) (A)
08|16|H.E. Gyaltshab Rinpoche (1954) (A)
08|19|Khyentse Rinpoche (1991) (A)

Tibetan Astrology

08|21|Khyabgon Sakya Trizin (A)
08|23|8th Karmapa, Mikyo Dorje (A)
08|25|Rigdzin Kumaradza
08|25|Rigdzin Tsewang Norbu
08|30|13th Karmapa, Dudul Dorje (1733) (A)
08|30|3rd Jamgon Kongtrul, Lodro Chokyi Senge (B)
09|03|Terton Karma Jigme Lingpa 5 days
09|03|2th Karmapa, Karma Pakshi (1282) (A)
09|04|Dagchen Lodro Gyaltsen (A)
09|04|Tartse Jampa Kungpa Tenpai Gyaltsen (A)
09|08|Beginning of Jigche Choto
09|09|Khyungpo Naljor (A)
09|09|16th Karmapa, Rigpe Dorje (A)
09|09|Shi Tro (Guru Rinpoche) (9th-13th day)
09|10|Terton Sogyal
09|14|Bokar Rinpoche (1940) (B)
09|14|Khyungpo Naljor
09|14|Khon Konchog Gyalpo (A)
09|14|Sachen Kungpa Nyingpo (A)
09|15|Katrina Puja
09|18|Gonma Jigdal Dagchen Sakya (A)
09|21|Jetsun Lorepa
09|21|Konchok Lhundrup
09|22|Founding of Karma Shri Nalanda, Rumtek
09|22|Lha Bab Duchen: Descent from Tushita Heaven
09|22|Exorcism Tor-Dok
09|25|Adzom Drukpa
09|25|Tsangpa Gyare Yeshe Dorje
09|28|6th Shamarpa, Chokyi Wangchug
10|03|Sangdu Choto (Gyume)
10|03|Vairochana (7 days)
10|04|8th Karmapa, Mikyo Dorje (B)
10|06|Dolpo Sangye
10|08|Muchen Sempa Chenpo (A)
10|10|Jamgon Kongtrul the Great, Lodro Thaye (B)
10|10|Khenchen Thrangu Rinpoche (B)

Tibetan Astrology

10|15|Doring Kungpang Chenpo (A)
10|16|Pawo Tsuklag Trengwa (A)
10|20|Gyalse Togme (A)
10|21|Ling Rinpoche
10|23|Kunrik (purificantion (23rd-27th day)
10|24|Chamchen Choje
10|25|Je Tsongkhpa (Ganden Ngamcho) (A)
10|30|12th Karmapa, Changchub Dorje (1732) (A)
10|30|Mitrukpa (purification) (30th-31st day)
11|01|Tibetan New Year (old style)
11|02|8th Shamarpa, Chokyi Tondrup
11|03|1st Karmapa, Dusem Khyenpa (A)
11|04|8th Karmapa, Mikyo Dorje (1507) (B)
11|06|Ngenpa Gu Dzom - 9 Bad Omens
11|09|14th Karmapa, Thekchog Dorje (B)
11|11|Lobpon Sonam Tsemo (A)
11|14|Panchen Sonam Drakpa
11|14|Sakya Pandita Kunga Gyaltsen (A)
11|15|10th Karmapa, Choying Dorje
11|16|8th Tai Situ, Chokyi Jungne (B)
11|17|Winter Doctrine Festival Month
11|18|H.H. Dudjom Rinpoche
11|19|Jetsun Chokyi Gyaltsen
11|19|Talung Thangpa
11|22|Dragon Chogyal Phagpa
11|22|Dorje Bernagchen (9 days)
11|22|Wrathful Dorje Drolod (9 days)
11|22|Drogon Chogyal Pagpa (A)
11|22|Dezhung Ajam Rinpoche (A)
11|26|Jamgon Kongtrul parinirvna the Great
11|29|Dharma Protector Offering Day (Gutor)
11|30|Night next year's deaths known
11|30|House Cleaning Day
12|01|Sonam Losar (Farmer's New Year)
12|02|Tormas begin to be made
12|03|3rd to 9th, Protector Worship

12|05|Beginning Demchok Choto
12|10|14th Karmapa, Thekchog Dorje (1799) (B)
12|14|Rongton Sheja Kunrig (A)
12|15|7th Shamarpa, Yeshe Nyingpo
12|15|Magha Puja, Sangha Day (Theravadin)
12|16|Phurbu Cycle Ritual
12|17|Lochen Rinchen Zangpo (A)
12|17|Tarlam Jamyang Losal (A)
12|18|Longchenpa (A) * *
12|18|Rigdzin Chokyi Drakpa
12|21|Phurbu ritual (upper action+)
12|22|Phurbu ritual,(upper action+)
12|23|Phurbu cycle ritual
12|23|Great Mahakala (23rd-29th day)
12|25|4th Shamarpa, Chokyi Trakpa
12|25|Phurbu cycle ritual
12|25|Khenchen Shonnu Lodro (A)
12|28|Phurbu ritual (lower action-)
12|29|Gutor (Exorcism)
12|29|Phurbu ritual, (lower action-)
12|29|Sacred Dances, followed by Losar
12|30|Festival of Good Omen begins
12|30|House Cleaning Day Tibet
12|30|Tashi (good luck ceremony) (in monasteries)

Tithies: The 30 Lunar Days

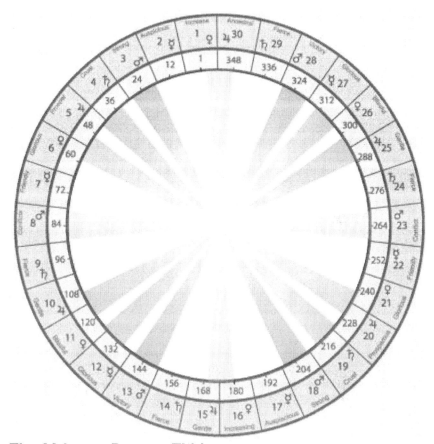

The 30 Lunar Days or Tithies

Tibetans operate on lunar days, rather than the solar days we use here in the West. Actually, they use both solar and lunar days, but the lunar day is usually considered the more important of the two. Tibetans, Chinese, Indians, and many other Asian countries divide the monthly lunar cycle into 30 parts, each 12-degrees of solunar angular separation, starting from the moment of the New Moon (lunar day one), and going around the cycle, ending in the 30th day, the day just

175

before the moment of the New Moon. Each lunar day has a distinct meaning, and most Asians plan events around the particular lunar day and its qualities.

Here is a brief description of all thirty lunar days, something about what they might be good for.

Lunar Day 1: Increase

This lunar is said to be favorable for most activities, including performing rituals and religious festivals, in general, and taking initiations. Travel is to be avoided

Favorable for Building
Favorable Marriage

Those born on this lunar day may have to be careful of the company they keep. Overall, they are very serious, and lacking in simple enjoyment. There may be some disgrace or scandal.

Lunar Day 2: Auspicious

This is a good lunar day for laying foundations and building things, in general. Also good for marriages, initiation, rituals, and religious ceremonies. This is good for giving and making offerings, resolutions, and spiritual practice of all kinds. But in all this, it is said that very little comes of any activity and the result is generally unproductive. However, there can be success from traveling on this day.

Those born on this lunar day may be lacking in friends, love, and in affection, and may like spouses other than their own. There is a lack of pure virtue and cleanliness.

Tibetan Astrology

Lunar Day 3: Powerful

This lunar day is good for cutting the hair and finger nails, and anything related to caring for the body, beauty, and health. Good for undertaking projects and building things. Favorable for Building

Those born on this lunar day may may lack motivation and be lazy and, in general, restless. Wealth is obtained and the direction north-east is favored.

Lunar Day 4: Cruelty

On these days, te favorable direction is the West, but travel is to be avoided, and, if taken, may bring the fear of death. This is not good for undertaking construction or new projects. Not Favorable for Hair Cutting

Those born on this lunar day may be very competitive and fierce about taking on a challenge and removing whatever obstructs them. Enjoyment of food, drink, and sex. Often rich, educated, and generous, but with a cruel streak. T

Tibetan Astrology

Lunar Day 5: Prosperity

A lunar day of excellent qualities, education, and obtaining wealth. Very good for helping and giving to others, but not likely to receive the same in return. A successful day for the vocation and victory, in general, and travel in any direction is favorable. Also favorable for the study of sacred texts, science, and philosophy.

Those born on this lunar day are kind hearted.

Tibetan Astrology

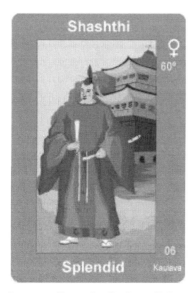

Lunar Day 6: Splendid

Efforts undertaken on this day, new projects, etc. will bring moderate success. This is not a day for travel, and doing so may bring losses.

Not Favorable for Journeys
Not Favorable for Marriage
Not Favorable for Hair Cutting

Those born on this lunar day are may be subject to some bombast, perhaps arguments, and egotism, in general, and a yearning to be in the spotlight.

Tibetan Astrology

Lunar Day 7: Friendliness

A very auspicious day for building and purchasing things, and undertaking new projects. Traveling on this day is also very favorable. Good for business and exchange of all kinds. Favorable for Journeys

Those born on this lunar day are good for obtaining wealth and especially fortunate with children. The favorable direction is South. Friendly nature. Likes to take charge.

Lunar Day 8: Conflicts

This is not a good lunar day to undertake new projects and for construction, in general. However, very good for obtaining wealth, increasing resources, health and healing, and honing expertise in the chosen field. The favorable direction is the South-East, but travel in any direction in this lunar day may bring illness.

Favorable for Hair Cutting
Not favorable for Marriage

Those born on this lunar day have love for marriage and family. Sensuality is strong. Interest in religion and truth.

Lunar Day 9: Fierce

Travel during this lunar day is not good,and it is said the person may not return. Good for all business and exchange, and taking charge and being the boss. Constructive efforts and new projects produce only moderate gains.

Favorable for Building
Favorable for Hair Cutting
Favorable for Marriage

In general, those born on this lunar day are aggressive and anger is never far. They enjoy children, the opposite sex, and education is favored. Also worship.

Lunar Day 10: Gentleness

This is an excellent day for travel and doing so may result in gains. In general, this lunar day is happy and good for relationships. Excellent for undertaking new projects and construction, in general. The favorable direction is the North-West and this day is good for speaking.

Favorable for Feast Days, Offerings
Favorable for Building
Favorable for Hair Cutting
Favorable for Journeys
Favorable for Marriage

Those born on this day have a good sense of right and wrong, although the tone may be somewhat serious.

Tibetan Astrology

Lunar Day 11: Bliss

A very auspicious day for travel, with good results. A day that produces fame and honor from society, but not good for undertaking new projects or construction. The direction North is favorable.

Favorable for Building
Favorable for Hair Cutting

For those born on this lunar day, wealth is very good and marriages and children are favored. Intelligent and pure of mind. Very good for religious practice.

Lunar Day 12: Splendid

A good lunar day to undertake new projects and for construction, in general. Not a good day for traveling, and doing so may result in the loss of wealth. Very favorable for study and learning.

Those born on this lunar day are somewhat restless, and the mind may wander.

Tibetan Astrology

Lunar Day 13: Victory

Travel on this lunar day is said to be favorable for making friends and creating alliances. A good day for undertaking new projects and beginning construction, as well as education.

A birth on this lunar day produces kindness, charity, and hospitality. Good for making friends, pleasures, and enjoyment of all kinds.

Tibetan Astrology

Lunar Day 14: Fierce

No travel is to be undertaken on this day. The direction East is favorable. Starting new projects and construction in general is not favored,and the day is somewhat aggressive, even bold and daring.

Not Favorable for Journey
Not Favorable for Hair Cutting

Those born on this day will receive honor from society. Wealth is favored and religious activities. Hot temper.

Tibetan Astrology

Lunar Day 15: Gentleness

Full Moon

Travel is forbidden on this lunar day. Good for invoking the ancestors and religious practice and ceremonies. Good for wealth and wisdom, and rightful actions. New projects and construction should not be undertaken.

Favorable for Action (Purification)
Not Favorable for Journeys
Not Favorable for Marriage
Not Favorable for Agriculture
Not Favorable for Hair Cutting

Those born on this lunar day have a fondness for food and the partners of others.

Tibetan Astrology

Lunar Day 16: Increase

This lunar is said to be favorable for most activities, including performing rituals and religious festivals, in general, and taking initiations. Travel is to be avoided.

Not Favorable for Hair Cutting

One born on this lunar day has to be careful of the company they keep. Overall, very serious, lacking simple enjoyment, and there may be some disgrace or scandal.

Lunar Day 17: Auspicious

This is a good lunar day for laying foundations and building things, in general. Also good for marriages, initiation, rituals, and religious ceremonies. This is good for giving and making offerings, resolutions, and spiritual practice of all kinds. But in all this, it is said that very little comes of any activity, and the result is generally unproductive. However, there is success from traveling on this day.

Not Favorable for Hair Cutting

A person born on this lunar day may be lacking in friends, love, and in affection, and may like spouses other than their own. There is a lack of pure virtue and cleanliness.

Tibetan Astrology

Lunar Day 18: Powerful

This lunar day is good for cutting the hair and finger nails, and anything related to caring for the body, beauty, and health. Good for undertaking projects and building things.

Persons born on this lunar day may lack motivation and be lazy and, in general, restless. Wealth is obtained and the direction north-east is favored.

Tibetan Astrology

Lunar Day 19: Cruelty

The favorable direction is the West, but travel is to be avoided, and, if taken, may bring the fear of death. This is not good for undertaking construction or new projects.

Favorable for Building
Favorable for Marriage

Persons born on this day are very competitive and fierce about taking on a challenge and removing whatever obstructs them. They enjoy food, drink, and sex. Often rich, educated, and generous, but with a cruel streak.

Lunar Day 20: Prosperity

A lunar day of excellent qualities, and good for education and obtaining wealth. A successful day for the vocation and victory, in general, and travel in any direction is favorable. Also favorable for the study of sacred texts, science, and philosophy.

Favorable for Building

A person born on this lunar day is very good for helping and giving to others, but not likely to receive the same in return. Kind hearted.

Tibetan Astrology

Lunar Day 21: Splendid

Efforts undertaken on this day, new projects, etc. will bring moderate success. This is not a day for travel, and doing so may bring losses

Not Favorable for Journeys

Persons born on this day will be prone to some bombast, perhaps arguments, and egotism, in general, and a yearning to be in the spotlight.

Lunar Day 22: Friendliness

A very auspicious day for building and purchasing things, and undertaking new projects. Traveling on this day is also very favorable. The favorable direction is South.

Favorable for Journeys

Persons born on this lunar day are good at obtaining wealth and especially fortunate with children. Also good for business and exchange of all kinds. Friendly nature. They like to take charge.

Tibetan Astrology

Lunar Day 23: Conflicts

This is not a good lunar day to undertake new projects and for construction, in general. However, very good for obtaining wealth, increasing resources, health and healing, and honing expertise in the chosen field. The favorable direction is the South-East, but travel in any direction in this lunar day may bring illness.

Favorable for Building
Not favorable for Agriculture

Those born on this lunar day will have love for marriage and family. Sensuality is strong. Also, an Interest in religion and truth.

Tibetan Astrology

Lunar Day 24: Fierce

Travel during this lunar day is not good and it is said the person may not return. Good for all business and exchange, and taking charge and being the boss. Constructive efforts and new projects produce only moderate gains.

Favorable for Building
Favorable for Journeys
Favorable for Marriage
Not Favorable for Agriculture

Those born on this lunar are generally aggressive, and anger is never far. Enjoyment of children, the opposite sex, and education is favored. Also worship.

Tibetan Astrology

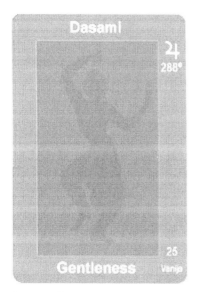

Lunar Day 25: Gentleness

This is an excellent day for travel and doing so may result in gains. In general, this lunar day is happy and good for relationships. Excellent for undertaking new projects and construction, in general. The favorable direction is the North-West and this day is good for speaking.

Favorable for Feast Days, Offerings
Favorable for Building
Favorable for Journeys

A person born on this lunar day has a good sense of right and wrong, although the tone may be somewhat serious.

Tibetan Astrology

Lunar Day 26: Bliss

A very auspicious day for travel, with good results. A day that produces fame and honor from society, but not good for undertaking new projects or construction. The direction North is favorable.

Favorable for Hair Cutting
Not Favorable for Building

For those born on this lunar day, wealth is very good. Marriages and children are favored. Intelligent and pure of mind. Very good for religious practice.

Tibetan Astrology

Lunar Day 27: Splendid

A good lunar day to undertake new projects and for construction, in general. Not a good day for traveling, and doing so may result in the loss of wealth. Very favorable for study and learning.

Favorable for Hair Cutting

Persons born on this lunar day are somewhat restless, and the mind may wander.

Lunar Day 28: Victory

Travel on this lunar day is said to be favorable for making friends and creating alliances. A good day for undertaking new projects and beginning construction, as well as education. Good for making friends, pleasures, and enjoyment of all kinds.

A person born on this lunar day has kindness, charity, and hospitality.

Tibetan Astrology

Lunar Day 29: Fierce

No travel is to be undertaken on this day. The direction East is favorable. Starting new projects and construction in general is not favored

Not Favorable for Journeys
Not Favorable for Agriculture

A person born on this day is somewhat aggressive, even bold and daring. Honor from society may come. Wealth is favored and religious activities. Hot temper.

Lunar Day 30: Ancestral

Travel is forbidden on this lunar day. Good for invoking the ancestors, religious practice, and ceremonies. New projects and construction should not be undertaken. The direction to the South-West is favored.

Not Favorable for Journeys
Not Favorable for Marriage
Not Favorable for Agriculture
Not Favorable for Hair Cutting

Persons born on this lunar day may have mental and physical disturbances. There could be a tendency toward cruelty.

The Karanas: Lunar Half-Days

The Karanas are taken from the Kar-Tsi, that part of
Tibetan astrology derived from Indian astrology, where
they are much used. A Karana is one half a lunar day
(tithie) or six degrees of solunar angular separation.
Keep in mind that a lunar day is the time it takes the
Moon to travel (in relation to the Sun) 12 degrees of arc.
There are thirty lunar days in a month and thus sixty
Karanas.

There are eleven types of Karana, four of them occur
just once a month and are called the Fixed Karanas:
Kintughna, Chatushpada, Sakuni, and Naga.

The other seven are movable and follow one another in
strict rotation: Bava, Balava, Kaulava, Taitila, Gara,
Vanija, Vishti

Each of the Karanas is said to have a particular
influence and interpretation, with "Vishti" being the most
inauspicious of the group. Nothing of importance is
done during the hald lunar day of Vishti.

In the Tibetan almanacs the Karana is usually listed for
each day as it exists at sunrise, about 5 A.M. of the
current calendar day.

On the next page is a list of the sixty Karanas,
beginning with the moment of the New Moon and
extending to the next New Moon.

30 Lunar Days, Sixty Karanas

First half		Second half
1	Kintughna	Bava
2	Balava	Kaulava
3	Taitila	Gara
4	Vanija	Vishti
5	Bava	Balava
6	Kaulava	Taitila
7	Gara	Vanija
8	Vishti	Bava
9	Balava	Kaulava
10	Taitila	Gara
11	Vanija	Vishti
12	Bava	Balava
13	Kaulava	Taitila
14	Gara	Vanija
15	Vishti	Bava
16	Balava	Kaulava
17	Taitila	Gara
18	Vanija	Vishti
19	Bava	Balava
20	Kaulava	Taitila
21	Gara	Vanija
22	Vishti	Bava
23	Balava	Kaulava
24	Taitila	Gara
25	Vanija	Vishti
26	Bava	Balava
27	Kaulava	Taitila
28	Gara	Vanija
29	Vishti	Sakuni
30	Chatushpada	Naga

The Eleven Karanas

Bava Karana

An auspicious karana, one excellent for all activities that increase one's strength and vitality - health.

Tibetan Astrology

Balava Karana

A karana that is auspicious for undertaking good acts and performing religious practices and ceremonies.

Tibetan Astrology

Kaulava Karana

This is a karana that is favorable for relationships, whether friends or lovers - anything done with love. Also good for choosing a spouse.

Tibetan Astrology

Taitila Karana

A karana that is auspicious for becoming known and more popular. Also good for things having to do with building homes and construction.

Tibetan Astrology

Gara Karana

A karana good for agriculture and anything having to do with the cultivation of the land, planting and sowing seeds, undertaking projects, building, etc.

Tibetan Astrology

Vanija Karana

A karana that is excellent for all business and exchange, relating to other people and building permanent relationships.

Vishti Karana

Said not be a good karana for any activity other than being aggressive and attacking enemies and obstacles. This is the "bad" karana and nothing positive should be undertaken.

Tibetan Astrology

Sakuni Karana

This karana is favorable for healing and health, in general and for taking medicine and herbs.

Tibetan Astrology

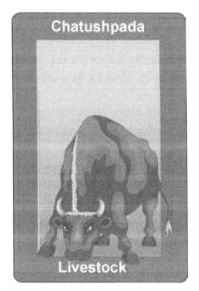

Chatushpada Karana

This is the karana of politics and the affairs of state. Also said to be good for animal husbandry.

Tibetan Astrology

Naga Karana

A more negative karana, one having to do with aggression, forceful activities, and cruelty, in general.

Tibetan Astrology

Kintughna Karana

This is a good karana for marriage and any religious or auspicious ceremony. Also good for virtue, making sacrifices, and good acts, in general.

The Indian Tithies or Lunar Days

The system of "Tithies" or Lunar Days is part of the "Kar-Tsi," the stream of Tibetan astrology that came to Tibet from India, along with the Kalachakra Tantra and, of course, the Dharma itself. Since much of this book is my attempt to collect and pass on for your review what I have found over the years, it won't hurt to list out some of the various details and correspondences connected to this most important topic. Here are the descriptive details:

Lunar Day: The Lunar Day Number

Keyword: Key Concept

Comments: Traditional Comments

Degrees: The range of degrees of this Tithie

Degrees-2: The 2nd half and Karana

Karana: Name of Karana

Nanda: The 1st, 6th and 11 th lunar days are known as Nanda. The the 2nd, 7th and 12th lunar days are known as Bhadra.The 3rd, 8th and 13th lunar days are known as Jaya. The 4th, 9th and 14th lunar days are known as Riktha. The 5th, 10th and 15th lunar days are known as Poorna.

Nanda +/-: Nanda rating, "0" is lowest, "00" is next best, and "000" is best Nanda.

Planet: Planet connected with the Lunar Day.

Nature: Planet's nature or temperament.

Nakshatra: Lunar Mansion connected with Tithie.

Deity: Assiciated deity.

Lunar Day: 01
Lunar Day: Pratami
Keyword: Seed Is Sown
Comments: Favorable day, offerings, vows, practice
Degrees: 000-006
Degrees-2 000-012
Karana: Kintughna
Nanda: Nanda - Gaining Happiness
Nanda +/-: O
Planet: Venus
Nature: Increasing
Nakshatra: Rohini, Krittika
Deity: Brahma, Agni

Lunar Day: 01
Lunar Day: Pratami
Keyword: Seed Is Sown
Comments:
Degrees: 006-012
Degrees-2
Karana: Bava
Nanda: Nanda
Nanda +/-:
Planet: Venus
Nature: Increasing
Nakshatra: Rohini, Krittika
Deity: Brahma, Agni

Lunar Day: 02
Lunar Day: Bava
Keyword: Germination
Comments: Favorable day, but unproductive
Degrees: 012-018
Degrees-2 012-024
Karana: Balava
Nanda: Bhadra - Starting Things
Nanda +/-: O
Planet: Mercury
Nature: Auspicious
Nakshatra: Rohini
Deity: Vidhaatri, Brahma

Lunar Day: 02
Lunar Day: Bava
Keyword: Germination
Comments:
Degrees: 018-024
Degrees-2
Karana: kaulava
Nanda: Bhadra
Nanda +/-:
Planet: Mercury
Nature: Auspicious
Nakshatra: Rohini
Deity: Vidhaatri, Brahma

Lunar Day: 03
Lunar Day: Tritiya
Keyword: Spread The Word
Comments: Minor Healing. Start things good
Degrees: 024-030
Degrees-2 024-036
Karana: Taitila
Nanda: Jaya - Overcome Obstacles
Nanda +/-: O
Planet: Mars
Nature: Strong
Nakshatra: Sravana
Deity: Vishnu, Gauri

Lunar Day: 03
Lunar Day: Tritiya
Keyword: Spread The Word
Comments:
Degrees: 030-036
Degrees-2
Karana: Gara
Nanda: Jaya
Nanda +/-:
Planet: Mars
Nature: Strong
Nakshatra: Sravana
Deity: Vishnu, Gauri

Lunar Day: 04
Lunar Day: Chaturthi
Keyword: Step Forward
Comments: unfruitful day.
Degrees: 036-042
Degrees-2 036-048
Karana: Vanija
Nanda: Rikta - Destroying
Nanda +/-: O
Planet: Saturn
Nature: Cruel
Nakshatra: Bharani
Deity: Yama, Ganesha

Lunar Day: 04
Lunar Day: Chaturthi
Keyword: Step Forward
Comments:
Degrees: 042-048
Degrees-2
Karana: Vishti
Nanda: Rikta
Nanda +/-:
Planet: Saturn
Nature: Cruel
Nakshatra: Bharani
Deity: Yama, Ganesha

Lunar Day: 05
Lunar Day: Panchami
Keyword: Plan It Out
Comments: Bad reaction day, moral failure
Degrees: 048-054
Degrees-2 048-060
Karana: Bava
Nanda: Purna - Harvesting
Nanda +/-: O
Planet: Jupiter
Nature: Prosperous
Nakshatra: Mrigasira, Aslesha
Deity: Chandra, Sarpa

Lunar Day: 05
Lunar Day: Panchami
Keyword: Plan It Out
Comments:
Degrees: 054-060
Degrees-2
Karana: Balava
Nanda: Purna
Nanda +/-:
Planet: Jupiter
Nature: Prosperous
Nakshatra: Mrigasira, Aslesha
Deity: Chandra, Sarpa

Lunar Day: 06
Lunar Day: Shashthi
Keyword: Handle On It
Comments: Not Favorable to Travel
Degrees: 060-066
Degrees-2 060-072
Karana: Kaulava
Nanda: Nanda - Gaining Happiness
Nanda +/-: OO
Planet: Venus
Nature: Glorious
Nakshatra:
Deity: Kartikeya

Lunar Day: 06
Lunar Day: Shashthi
Keyword: Handle On It
Comments:
Degrees: 066-072
Degrees-2
Karana: Taitila
Nanda: Nanda
Nanda +/-:
Planet: Venus
Nature: Glorious
Nakshatra:
Deity: Kartikeya

Lunar Day: 07
Lunar Day: Saptami
Keyword: Warts And All
Comments: Favorable to Travel
Degrees: 072-078
Degrees-2 072-084
Karana: Gara
Nanda: Bhadra - Starting Things
Nanda +/-: OO
Planet: Mercury
Nature: Friendly
Nakshatra: Jyesthra
Deity: Indra, Ravi

Lunar Day: 07
Lunar Day: Saptami
Keyword: Warts And All
Comments:
Degrees: 078-084
Degrees-2
Karana: Vanija
Nanda: Bhadra
Nanda +/-:
Planet: Mercury
Nature: Friendly
Nakshatra: Jyesthra
Deity: Indra, Ravi

Lunar Day: 08
Lunar Day: Ashami
Keyword: Acceptance
Comments: Emotional upset, bad morals
Degrees: 084-090
Degrees-2 084-096
Karana: Vishti
Nanda: Jaya - Overcome Obstacles
Nanda +/-: OO
Planet: Mars
Nature: Conflictual
Nakshatra: Dhanishta, Ardra
Deity: Vasus, Siva

Lunar Day: 08
Lunar Day: Ashami
Keyword: Come Across
Comments:
Degrees: 090-096
Degrees-2
Karana: Bava
Nanda: Jaya
Nanda +/-:
Planet: Mars
Nature: Conflictual
Nakshatra: Dhanishta, Ardra
Deity: Vasus, Siva

Lunar Day: 09
Lunar Day: Navami
Keyword: Make The Point
Comments: Good. long journeys, marriage, teachings
Degrees: 096-102
Degrees-2 096-108
Karana: Balava
Nanda: Rikta - Destroying
Nanda +/-: OO
Planet: Saturn
Nature: Pierce
Nakshatra: Aslesha
Deity: Sarpa, Durga

Lunar Day: 09
Lunar Day: Navami
Keyword: Make The Point
Comments:
Degrees: 102-108
Degrees-2
Karana: Kaulava
Nanda: Rikta
Nanda +/-:
Planet: Saturn
Nature: Pierce
Nakshatra: Aslesha
Deity: Sarpa, Durga

Lunar Day: 10
Lunar Day: Dasami
Keyword: Lock It In
Comments: Daka Day. Good travel, everything
Degrees: 108-114
Degrees-2 108-120
Karana: Taitila
Nanda: Purna - Harvesting
Nanda +/-: OO
Planet: Jupiter
Nature: Gentle
Nakshatra: Bharani
Deity: Dharmaraja

Lunar Day: 10
Lunar Day: Dasami
Keyword: Lock It In
Comments:
Degrees: 114-120
Degrees-2
Karana: Gara
Nanda: Purna
Nanda +/-:
Planet: Jupiter
Nature: Gentle
Nakshatra: Bharani
Deity: Dharmaraja

Tibetan Astrology

Lunar Day: 11
Lunar Day: Ekadasi
Keyword: Field Response
Comments: Good firm action, starting, spiritual
Degrees: 120-126
Degrees-2 120-132
Karana: Vanija
Nanda: Nanda - Gaining Happiness
Nanda +/-: OOO
Planet: Venus
Nature: Blissful
Nakshatra: Ardra, Uttarashadra
Deity: Rudra, Visvadevas

Lunar Day: 11
Lunar Day: Ekadasi
Keyword: Field Response
Comments:
Degrees: 126-132
Degrees-2
Karana: Vishti
Nanda: Nanda
Nanda +/-:
Planet: Venus
Nature: Blissful
Nakshatra: Ardra, Uttarashadra
Deity: Rudra, Visvadevas

Lunar Day: 12
Lunar Day: Dvadasi
Keyword: Embody It
Comments: Day of Wisdom
Degrees: 132-138
Degrees-2 132-144
Karana: Bava
Nanda: Bhadra - Starting Things
Nanda +/-: OOO
Planet: Mercury
Nature: Glorious
Nakshatra: Hasta, Sravana
Deity: Savitri, Vishnu

Lunar Day: 12
Lunar Day: Dvadasi
Keyword: Embody It
Comments:
Degrees: 138-144
Degrees-2
Karana: Balava
Nanda: Bhadra
Nanda +/-:
Planet: Mercury
Nature: Glorious
Nakshatra: Hasta, Sravana
Deity: Savitri, Vishnu

232

Lunar Day: 13
Lunar Day: Trayodasi
Keyword: Extension
Comments: Good clarity, speed, Skillful
Degrees: 144-150
Degrees-2 144-156
Karana: Kaulava
Nanda: Jaya - Overcome Obstacles
Nanda +/-: OOO
Planet: Mars
Nature: Victorious
Nakshatra:
Deity: Kamadeva

Lunar Day: 13
Lunar Day: Trayodasi
Keyword: Extension
Comments:
Degrees: 150-156
Degrees-2
Karana: Taitila
Nanda: Jaya
Nanda +/-:
Planet: Mars
Nature: Victorious
Nakshatra:
Deity: Kamadeva

Lunar Day: 14
Lunar Day: Chaturdasi
Keyword: Infrastructure
Comments: Not Favorable to Travel
Degrees: 156-162
Degrees-2 156-168
Karana: Gara
Nanda: Rikta - Destroying
Nanda +/-: OOO
Planet: Saturn
Nature: Fierce
Nakshatra: Ardra
Deity: Kali, Siva

Lunar Day: 14
Lunar Day: Chaturdasi
Keyword: Infrastructure
Comments:
Degrees: 163-168
Degrees-2
Karana: Vanija
Nanda: Rikta
Nanda +/-:
Planet: Saturn
Nature: Fierce
Nakshatra: Ardra
Deity: Kali, Siva

Lunar Day: 15
Lunar Day: Purnima
Keyword: Completion
Comments: Assembly. Bad travel. Unproductive
Degrees: 168-174
Degrees-2 168-180
Karana: Vishti
Nanda: Purna - Harvesting
Nanda +/-: OOO
Planet: Jupiter
Nature: Gentle
Nakshatra: Uttarashdra, Mrigasira
Deity: Visvadevas, Chandra

Lunar Day: 15
Lunar Day: Purnima
Keyword: Completion
Comments:
Degrees: 174-180
Degrees-2
Karana: Bava
Nanda: Purna
Nanda +/-:
Planet: Jupiter
Nature: Gentle
Nakshatra: Uttarashdra, Mrigasira
Deity: Visvadevas, Chandra

Lunar Day: 16
Lunar Day: Pratami
Keyword: Fullness
Comments: Competition, speed, clarity. Good day.
Degrees: 180-186
Degrees-2 180-192
Karana: Balava
Nanda: Nanda - Gaining Happiness
Nanda +/-: OOO
Planet: Venus
Nature: Increasing
Nakshatra: Rohini, Krittika
Deity: Brahma, Agni

Lunar Day: 16
Lunar Day: Pratami
Keyword: Fullness
Comments:
Degrees: 186-192
Degrees-2
Karana: Kaulava
Nanda: Nanda
Nanda +/-:
Planet: Venus
Nature: Increasing
Nakshatra: Rohini, Krittika
Deity: Brahma, Agni

Lunar Day: 17
Lunar Day: Bava
Keyword: FullBodied
Comments: Dangerous Day. Bad reactions
Degrees: 192-198
Degrees-2 192-210
Karana: Taitila
Nanda: Bhadra - Starting Things
Nanda +/-: OOO
Planet: Mercury
Nature: Auspicious
Nakshatra: Rohini
Deity: Vidhaatri, Brahma

Lunar Day: 17
Lunar Day: Bava
Keyword: FullBodied
Comments:
Degrees: 198-204
Degrees-2
Karana: Gara
Nanda: Bhadra
Nanda +/-:
Planet: Mercury
Nature: Auspicious
Nakshatra: Rohini
Deity: Vidhaatri, Brahma

Lunar Day: 18
Lunar Day: Tirtiya
Keyword: Blink
Comments: Dangerous Day, bad for marality
Degrees: 204-210
Degrees-2 204-222
Karana: Vanija
Nanda: Jaya - Overcome Obstacles
Nanda +/-: OOO
Planet: Mars
Nature: Strong
Nakshatra: Sravana
Deity: Vishnu, Gauri

Lunar Day: 18
Lunar Day: Tirtiya
Keyword: Blink
Comments:
Degrees: 210-216
Degrees-2
Karana: Vishti
Nanda: Jaya
Nanda +/-:
Planet: Mars
Nature: Strong
Nakshatra: Sravana
Deity: Vishnu, Gauri

Lunar Day: 19
Lunar Day: Chaturthi
Keyword: The Dawn
Comments: Good Day to Begin Things
Degrees: 216-222
Degrees-2 216-234
Karana: Bava
Nanda: Rikta - Destroying
Nanda +/-: OOO
Planet: Saturn
Nature: Cruel
Nakshatra: Bharani
Deity: Yama, Ganesha

Lunar Day: 19
Lunar Day: Chaturthi
Keyword: The Dawn
Comments:
Degrees: 222-228
Degrees-2
Karana: Balava
Nanda: Rikta
Nanda +/-:
Planet: Saturn
Nature: Cruel
Nakshatra: Bharani
Deity: Yama, Ganesha

Tibetan Astrology

Lunar Day: 20
Lunar Day: Panchami
Keyword: Me and Mine
Comments: Good Day for action
Degrees: 228-234
Degrees-2 228-246
Karana: Kaulava
Nanda: Purna - Harvesting
Nanda +/-: OOO
Planet: Jupiter
Nature: Prosperous
Nakshatra: Mrigasira, Aslesha
Deity: Chandra, Sarpa

Lunar Day: 20
Lunar Day: Panchami
Keyword: Me and Mine
Comments:
Degrees: 234-240
Degrees-2
Karana: Taitila
Nanda: Purna
Nanda +/-:
Planet: Jupiter
Nature: Prosperous
Nakshatra: Mrigasira, Aslesha
Deity: Chandra, Sarpa

Tibetan Astrology

Lunar Day: 21
Lunar Day: Shashthi
Keyword: Party Is Over
Comments: Bad Day for Travel
Degrees: 240-246
Degrees-2 240-258
Karana: Gara
Nanda: Nanda - Gaining Happiness
Nanda +/-: OO
Planet: Venus
Nature: Glorious
Nakshatra:
Deity: Kartikeya

Lunar Day: 21
Lunar Day: Shashthi
Keyword: Party Is Over
Comments:
Degrees: 246-252
Degrees-2
Karana: Vanija
Nanda: Nanda
Nanda +/-:
Planet: Venus
Nature: Glorious
Nakshatra:
Deity: Kartikeya

Tibetan Astrology

Lunar Day: Saptami
Keyword: Salvage
Comments: Good Travel Day
Degrees: 252-258
Degrees-2 252-270
Karana: Vishti
Nanda: Bhadra - Starting Things
Nanda +/-: OO
Planet: Mercury
Nature: Friendly
Nakshatra: Jyesthra
Deity: Indra, Ravi

Lunar Day: 22
Lunar Day: Saptami
Keyword: Salvage
Comments:
Degrees: 258-264
Degrees-2
Karana: Bava
Nanda: Bhadra
Nanda +/-:
Planet: Mercury
Nature: Friendly
Nakshatra: Jyesthra
Deity: Indra, Ravi

Lunar Day: 23
Lunar Day: Ashami
Keyword: Conservation
Comments: Good action day, begin construction
Degrees: 264-270
Degrees-2 264-282
Karana: Balava
Nanda: Jaya - Overcome Obstacles
Nanda +/-: OO
Planet: Mars
Nature: Conflictual
Nakshatra: Dhanishta, Ardra
Deity: Vasus, Siva

Lunar Day: 23
Lunar Day: Ashami
Keyword: Conservation
Comments:
Degrees: 270-276
Degrees-2
Karana: Kaulava
Nanda: Jaya
Nanda +/-:
Planet: Mars
Nature: Conflictual
Nakshatra: Dhanishta, Ardra
Deity: Vasus, Siva

Lunar Day: 24
Lunar Day: Navami
Keyword: Detachment
Comments: Good travel day. Fruitful activities
Degrees: 276-282
Degrees-2 276-294
Karana: Taitila
Nanda: Rikta - Destroying
Nanda +/-: OO
Planet: Saturn
Nature: Pierce
Nakshatra: Aslesha
Deity: Sarpa, Durga

Lunar Day: 24
Lunar Day: Navami
Keyword: Detachment
Comments:
Degrees: 282-288
Degrees-2
Karana: Gara
Nanda: Rikta
Nanda +/-:
Planet: Saturn
Nature: Pierce
Nakshatra: Aslesha
Deity: Sarpa, Durga

Lunar Day: 25
Lunar Day: Dasami
Keyword: Observation
Comments: Dakini Day. Good Travel.
Degrees: 288-294
Degrees-2 288-306
Karana: Vanija
Nanda: Purna - Harvesting
Nanda +/-: OO
Planet: Jupiter
Nature: Gentle
Nakshatra: Bharani
Deity: Dharmaraja

Lunar Day: 25
Lunar Day: Dasami
Keyword: Observation
Comments:
Degrees: 294-300
Degrees-2
Karana: Vishti
Nanda: Purna
Nanda +/-:
Planet: Jupiter
Nature: Gentle
Nakshatra: Bharani
Deity: Dharmaraja

Lunar Day: 26
Lunar Day: Ekadasi
Keyword: The Critic
Comments: Goof for vows, offerings
Degrees: 300-306
Degrees-2 300-318
Karana: Bava
Nanda: Nanda - Gaining Happiness
Nanda +/-: O
Planet: Venus
Nature: Blissful
Nakshatra: Ardra, Uttarashadra
Deity: Rudra, Visvadevas

Lunar Day: 26
Lunar Day: Ekadasi
Keyword: The Critic
Comments:
Degrees: 306-312
Degrees-2
Karana: Balava
Nanda: Nanda
Nanda +/-:
Planet: Venus
Nature: Blissful
Nakshatra: Ardra, Uttarashadra
Deity: Rudra, Visvadevas

Lunar Day: 27
Lunar Day: Dvadasi
Keyword: Trim It
Comments: Day of wisom
Degrees: 312-318
Degrees-2 312-330
Karana: Kaulava
Nanda: Bhadra - Starting Things
Nanda +/-: O
Planet: Mercury
Nature: Glorious
Nakshatra: Hasta, Sravana
Deity: Savitri, Vishnu

Lunar Day: 27
Lunar Day: Dvadasi
Keyword: Trim It
Comments:
Degrees: 218-324
Degrees-2
Karana: Taitila
Nanda: Bhadra
Nanda +/-:
Planet: Mercury
Nature: Glorious
Deity: Savitri, Vishnu

Lunar Day: 28
Lunar Day: Trayodasi
Keyword: SeedTime
Comments: Success to activities.
Degrees: 324-330
Degrees-2 324-342
Karana: Gara
Nanda: Jaya - Overcome Obstacles
Nanda +/-: O
Planet: Mars
Nature: Victorious
Nakshatra:

Lunar Day: 28
Lunar Day: Trayodasi
Keyword: SeedTime
Comments:
M15: 13
Degrees: 330-336
Degrees-2
Karana: Vanija
Nanda: Jaya
Nanda +/-:
Planet: Mars
Nature: Victorious
Nakshatra:
Deity: Kamadeva

Lunar Day: 29
Lunar Day: Chaturdasi
Keyword: Encapsulate
Comments: Bad travel day
Degrees: 336-342
Degrees-2 336-354
Karana: Vishti
Nanda: Rikta - Destroying
Nanda +/-: O
Planet: Saturn
Nature: Fierce
Nakshatra: Ardra
Deity: Kali, Siva

Lunar Day: 29
Lunar Day: Chaturdasi
Keyword: Encapsulate
Comments:
Degrees: 342-348
Degrees-2
Karana: Sakuni
Nanda: Rikta
Nanda +/-:
Planet: Saturn
Nature: Fierce
Nakshatra: Ardra
Deity: Kali, Siva

Lunar Day: 30
Lunar Day: Amavasya
Keyword: Dark Night of the Moon
Comments: Bad travel day
Degrees: 348-354
Degrees-2 348-360
Karana: Chatushpada
Nanda: Purna - Harvesting
Nanda +/-: O
Planet: Jupiter
Nature: Ancestral
Nakshatra: Magha, Mrigasira
Deity: Pitris, Chandra

Lunar Day: 30
Lunar Day: Amavasya
Keyword: Dark Night of the Moon
Comments:
Degrees: 354-360
Degrees-2
Karana: naga
Nanda: Purna
Nanda +/-:
Planet: Jupiter
Nature: Ancestral
Nakshatra: Magha, Mrigasira
Deity: Pitris, Chandra

The 27 Nakshatras: Lunar Mansions

The Moon at the time of birth (or an event) is located in one of 27 lunar mansions or Nakshatras as they are called in Vedic astrology. The Moon moves through the 360 degrees of the zodiac in the course of one month and spends about one day in each of the Nakshatras. A Nakshatra is simply the familiar zodiac divided into 27 parts, each 13-degrees 20-minutes of angular arc.

We all know that the zodiac most familiar to us is divided into 12 sections, one for each month the Sun spends in that sign. With the Nakshatras, the zodiac is divided into 27 sections and it is the Moon that we watch move through these areas of the sky. We could say that the Nakshatra you were born in is another kind of Moon sign.

The Nakshatras are ancient and are used by virtually all Vedic/Hindu astrologers in many different ways. The Nakshatra in which you were born is an important key to your character.

The lunar mansion or nakshatra is typically calculated at daybreak (about 5 A.M.). Whichever Nakshatra the Moon is in a daybreak is considered the one to use for that day. However, it is also important to note when (during that 24-hour day) the Moon moves into the next subsequent Nakshatra. That Nakshatra and the time it is entered are usually listed in most Tibetan calendars.

Each lunar mansion has its own flavor and interpretation, just as the familiar zodiac signs have their meaning. In Tibet, the tropical zodiac is used to measure the lunar mansions or Nakshatras.

Tibetan Astrology

The 27 Nakshatras or Lunar Mansions

Tibetan	Sanskrit	Element
00 Ta-Kar	Asvini	Wind
01 Bhya-Nnye	Bharani	Fire
02 Min-Druk	Kritika	Fire
03 Nar-Ma	Rohini	Earth
04 Go	Mrgasira	Wind
05 Lak	Ardra	Water
06 Nap-So	Punarvasti	Wind
07 Gyal	Pusya	Fire
08 Kak	Aslesa	Water
09 Chu	Magha	Fire
10 Dre	Purva-Phalguni	Fire
11 Wo	Uttar-Phaluni	Wind
12 Me-Shi	Hasta	Wind
13 Nak-Pa	Citra	Wind
14 Sa-Ri	Svata	Wind
15 Sa-Ka	Visakha	Wind
16 La-Tsem	Anuradha	Earth
17 Nron	Jestha	Earth
18 Noop	Mula	Water
19 Chu-Do	Purvasadha	Water
20 Chu-Me	Uttarasadha	Earth
21 Dro-Shin	Uttara-Asadha	Earth
22 Non-Dre	Dhaniastha	Water
23 Non-Dru	Satabhisak	Earth
24 Drum-To	Purvabaad-rapada	Fire
25 Dru-Me	Uttara-bhadrapada	Water
26 Namdru	Revati	Water

Nakshatra 00: Healing

The Healer. The power of this mansion is that of healing, and quickly at that, rushing whatever aid and cures that are required to those most in need, human or animal. Very active in curing whatever needs remedy, and at the same time working to remove disease and excess from the world.

This Day:
Favorable for Building
Favorable for Giving a Name
Favorable for Hair Cutting
Favorable for Medicine (giving remedies)
Journeys: Favorable
Not Favorable: Move New House
Not Favorable: Cultivating Ground

Tibetan Astrology

Nakshatra 01: Removal

This lunar mansion is very disciplined and self-sacrificing, and has to due with helping things to pass, the taking away of that which is near death and, in general, the removal of excess in all forms - removing whatever has reached beyond its point of fruition, taking the soul into the bardo and on toward another life or project.

Tibetan Astrology

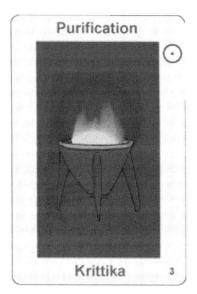

Purification

Krittika   3

Nakshatra 02: Purification

This lunar mansion has to due with purification, the ripening of all things, and, in particular, the burning off of the dross, removing by fire all that which should be removed, and is excess, and leaving all that good. Pure purification.

Nakshatra 03: Growth

This lunar mansion's power is that of growth, growth to abundance, and has to due with matters of fertility, with preparing the ground, and thus growth, and prosperity - always in abundance.

This Day:
Favorable for Building
Favorable for Giving a Name
Favorable for Medicine (giving remedies)
Favorable, Move New House
Favorable for Marriage
Not Favorable for Cultivating Ground

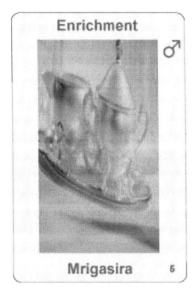

Enrichment ♂

Mrigasira 5

Nakshatra 04: Enrichment

The power of this mansion is that of enhancing and enriching our life beyond or to the limits of our dreams - what we dreamed life could offer. It is ruled by the Moon, Soma, and always acts to fulfill what we already have, showing us the richness and beauty if our lives.

This Day:
Favorable for Building
Favorable for Giving a Name
Favorable for Hair Cutting
Favorable for Medicine (giving remedies)
Favorable: Journeys
Favorable: Marriage

Nakshatra 05: Great Effort

Hitting the target. This mansion is typified by hard, ceaseless effort, a perpetual struggle to overcome life's obstacles, to push past them, and strive forward to reach the goal. Fierce.

This Day:
Favorable for Starting a Fight
Not Favorable for Journeys

Tibetan Astrology

Nakshatra 06: Renewal

This lunar mansion has the power to renew and refresh, like the spring rains, bringing forth new growth and abundance - revitalization. Creativity.

This Day:
Favorable for Hair Cutting
Favorable for Medicine (giving remedies)
Favorable for Journeys
Not Favorable: Move New House
Not Favorable for Cultivating Ground

Nakshatra 07: Spiritual Energy

This lunar mansion has to do with the bringing forth of renewed spiritual energy through prayer, meditation, and any kind of ritual worship. Creating good karma.

This Day:
Favorable for Giving a Name
Favorable for Hair Cutting
Favorable: Journeys, Favorable
Not Favorable: Move New House

Tibetan Astrology

Nakshatra 08: Remove Obstacles

This mansion brings the power of worldly wisdom, and is very practical, especially in how to bring down and paralyze enemies and remove the obstacles in life's path.

This Day:
Not Favorable for Journeys,
Not Favorable for Cultivating Ground

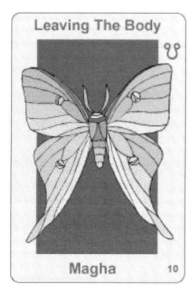

Leaving The Body

Magha   10

Nakshatra 9: Leaving the Body

This mansion's power is that of the end of things, whether that is a cycle or any body of involvement, and the leaving of whatever we happen to find our self in - a kind of death. The leaving of the body.

This Day:
Favorable for Marriage

Tibetan Astrology

Nakshatra 10: Procreation

Procreation is the nature and power of this lunar mansion, based on a coming together, bonding, and marriage - productive alliances. Union.

This Day:
Favorable for Starting a Fight
Not Favorable for Cultivating Ground

Nakshatra 11: Abundance

The power of this mansion is the prosperity and the accumulation of wealth, based on a successful union or marriage - wealth and abundance through partnership. Resources through union.

This Day:
Favorable for Building
Favorable for Giving a Name
Favorable for Medicine (giving remedies)
Favorable for Marriage
Not Favorable for Cultivating Ground

Nakshatra 12: Fulfillment

This mansion puts the power to achieve our goals (whatever it is we are seeking) into our own hands - fulfillment for whatever we search for. And quickly.

This Day:
Favorable for Building
Favorable for Giving a Name
Favorable for Hair Cutting
Favorable for Medicine (giving remedies)
Favorable for Journeys
Favorable for Marriage
Not Favorable: Move New House
Not Favorable: Cultivating Ground

Nakshatra 13: Merit

This mansion has to due with the accumulation of merit and honor, whatever can be achieved through righteousness - very spiritual energy. The power of righteousness.

This Day:
Favorable for Building
Favorable for Hair Cutting
Favorable for Medicine (giving remedies)
Not Favorable for Journeys

Nakshatra 14: Transformation

The power of the wind. Transformation and change is the key to this lunar mansion, altering the stagnant course of things, and taking away and scattering whatever is negative or excessive - stripping it bare. Removing negativity.

This Day:
Favorable for Building
Favorable for Hair Cutting
Favorable for Medicine (giving remedies)
Favorable for Marriage
Not Favorable: Move New House

Tibetan Astrology

Nakshatra 15: Harvesting

The power of heat, producing the fruit of the harvest, attaining aspirations and goals, perhaps not all at once, but gradually, over time, like the fruit ripening in the sun.

This Day:
Favorable for Medicine (giving remedies)

Tibetan Astrology

Nakshatra 16: Middle Way

This lunar mansion brings the power of balance and treading the middle way, in particular with relationships, both bringing honor to others and to us, an even inward-outward flow.

This Day:
Favorable for Building
Favorable for Starting a Fight
Favorable for Giving a Name
Favorable for Journeys
Favorable for Marriage

The Hero

Jeshtha   18

Nakshatra 17: The Hero

The hero, filled with courage and determination to overcome, is the key to the power of this lunar mansion, and through effort and skillful means, vanquishes all obstacles and opposing forces.

This Day:
Favorable for Starting a Fight
Favorable for Hair Cutting
Not Favorable for Journeys

Nakshatra 18: Cutting the Root

Cutting the very root of attachments and afflictions, this lunar mansion destroys and takes away only what must be destroyed and should be removed, making way for liberation and new creation. Negating negativity.

This Day:
Favorable for Building
Favorable for Starting a Fight
Favorable for Journeys
Favorable for Marriage
Not Favorable for Medicine

Nakshatra 19: Cleansing

The power of water, with its purification and sense of regeneration, provides magnetizing energy and results in both inner and outer cleansing.

This Day:
Favorable for Building
Not Favorable for Cultivating Ground

Nakshatra 20: The Champion

The summit. The champion and unchallenged victor, the result of a righteous cause and support of others in that cause. With these alliances, we sit on the top of the mountain, the pinnacle of the career, the head of the army - the winner.

This Day:
Favorable for Giving a Name
Favorable for Medicine (giving remedies)
Favorable, Move New House
Favorable for Marriage
Favorable for Building
Not Favorable for Cultivating Ground

Tibetan Astrology

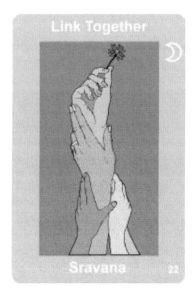

Nakshatra 21: Link Together

Receptivity to others brings the power of linking all things, people, and projects together, each to each, and always appropriately.

This Day:
Favorable for Giving a Name
Favorable for Hair Cutting
Favorable for Medicine (giving remedies)
Favorable for Journeys
Not Favorable: Move New House

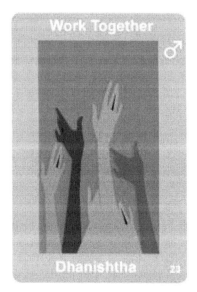

Nakshatra 22: Work Together

The power of this lunar mansion is to bring fame and abundance, and the ability to unite diverse people into a single fabric, held together by natural practicality and mutual benefit.

This Day:
Favorable for Giving a Name
Favorable for Hair Cutting
Favorable for Medicine (giving remedies)
Not Favorable for Journeys
Not Favorable for Cultivating Ground

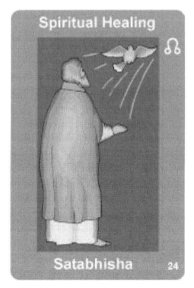

Nakshatra 23: Spiritual Healing

Healing, not just of the body, but of the mind and spirit as well, is the power of this lunar mansion. Resolving obstinate karma over time, humbling us, bringing things to a crisis, and then washing all things clean.

This Day:
Favorable for Hair Cutting
Favorable for Medicine (giving remedies)
Not Favorable for Cultivating Ground

Tibetan Astrology

Spiritual Fire

Purvabhadra-Pada 26

Nakshatra 24: Spiritual Fire

Internal Purification. Burning spiritual fire that cleanses our deepest pain and raises in us a pure aspiration, one that makes it easy to put behind us more personal concerns.

Nakshatra 25: Auspicious Rain

The power of an auspicious rain that brings forth growth and prosperity, enough to create a rising tide that raises all boats. Pure creative power.

This Day:
Favorable for Giving a Name
Favorable, Move New House
Favorable for Marriage
Not Favorable for Cultivating Ground

Tibetan Astrology

Nakshatra 26: Nourishment

Great abundance through rich and proper nourishment, protecting and gathering all together, and urging us on to ever greener pastures is the power of this lunar mansion.

This Day:
Favorable for Giving a Name
Favorable for Hair Cutting
Favorable for Medicine (giving remedies)
Favorable for Trade
Favorable for Marriage

The Nine Mewas of the Lo-Shu

The Nine Mewa Square

Mewa means "mole" or birth mark and the nine Mewa numbers stem from an ancient system of numerology used for centuries by the Chinese. These Mewa numbers are said to indicate a karmic relation from life to life. There are nine Mewas and they are often arranged in the so-called Magic Square that gives totals of 15, whichever way the lines are totaled up.

It is said that the original magic square was engraved on the lower shell (the outside bottom) of the cosmic tortoise, from which (in legend) all Tibetan astrology springs. It has, aside from the numbers themselves, a distinct orientation in space, not to mention colors, elements, and so on:

The nine Mewas or 'moles' are an integral part of Tibetan astrology, just as they are in Chinese astrology. Nine-Star systems abound in oriental astrology and geomancy, and they all are based on the numbers 1

Tibetan Astrology

through 9 arranged in various ways, usually in a matrix of nine squares, as shown above.

The nine Mewa are:

Mewa	Element
1 White	Iron or Metal
2 Black	Water
3 Blue	Water
4 Green	Wood
5 Yellow	Earth
6 White	Iron or Metal
7 Red	Fire
8 White	Iron or Metal
9 Maroon	Fire

There is a Mewa for each year, and the Mewa numbers for years revolve backward in strict rotation. You can find the Mewa for the year you were born by referring to the table on the following pages.

There is a Mewa for each year

Year Mewa Tables for 200 Years

Year	1900	1901	1902	1903	1904	
Mewa	1 White	9 Maroon	8 White	7 Red	6 White	
Year	1905	1906	1907	1908	1909	
Mewa	5 Yellow	4 Green	3 Indigo	2 Black	1 White	
Year	1910	1911	1912	1913	1914	
Mewa	9 Maroon	8 White	7 Red	6 White	5 Yellow	
Year	1915	1916	1917	1918	1919	
Mewa	4 Green	3 Indigo	2 Black	1 White	9 Maroon	
Year	1920	1921	1922	1923	1924	
Mewa	8 White	7 Red	6 White	5 Yellow	4 Green	
Year	1925	1926	1927	1928	1929	
Mewa	3 Indigo	2 Black	1 White	9 Maroon	8 White	
Year	1930	1931	1932	1933	1934	
Mewa	7 Red	6 White	5 Yellow	4 Green	3 Indigo	
Year	1935	1936	1937	1938	1939	
Mewa	2 Black	1 White	9 Maroon	8 White	7 Red	
Year	1940	1941	1942	1943	1944	
Mewa	6 White	5 Yellow	4 Green	3 Indigo	2 Black	
Year	1945	1946	1947	1948	1949	
Mewa	1 White	9 Maroon	8 White	7 Red	6 White	
Year	1950	1951	1952	1953	1954	
Mewa	5 Yellow	4 Green	3 Indigo	2 Black	1 White	
Year	1955	1956	1957	1958	1959	
Mewa	9 Maroon	8 White	7 Red	6 White	5 Yellow	
Year	1960	1961	1962	1963	1964	
Mewa	4 Green	3 Indigo	2 Black	1 White	9 Maroon	
Year	1965	1966	1967	1968	1969	
Mewa	8 White	7 Red	6 White	5 Yellow	4 Green	
Year	1970	1971	1972	1973	1974	
Mewa	3 Indigo	2 Black	1 White	9 Maroon	8 White	
Year	1975	1976	1977	1978	1979	
Mewa	7 Red	6 White	5 Yellow	4 Green	3 Indigo	
Year	1980	1981	1982	1983	1984	
Mewa	2 Black	1 White	9 Maroon	8 White	7 Red	
Year	1985	1986	1987	1988	1989	
Mewa	6 White	5 Yellow	4 Green	3 Indigo	2 Black	
Year	1990	1991	1992	1993	1994	
Mewa	1 White	9 Maroon	8 White	7 Red	6 White	
Year	1995	1996	1997	1998	1999	
Mewa	5 Yellow	4 Green	3 Indigo	2 Black	1 White	
Year	2000	2001	2002	2003	2004	
Mewa	9 Maroon	8 White	7 Red	6 White	5 Yellow	
Year	2005	2006	2007	2008	2009	

Tibetan Astrology

```
Mewa        |4 Green |3 Indigo|2 Black |1 White |9 Maroon|
Year        |2010    |2011    |2012    |2013    |2014    |
Mewa        |8 White |7 Red   |6 White |5 Yellow|4 Green |
Year        |2015    |2016    |2017    |2018    |2019    |
Mewa        |3 Indigo|2 Black |1 White |9 Maroon|8 White |
Year        |2020    |2021    |2022    |2023    |2024    |
Mewa        |7 Red   |6 White |5 Yellow|4 Green |3 Indigo|
Year        |2025    |2026    |2027    |2028    |2029    |
Mewa        |2 Black |1 White |9 Maroon|8 White |7 Red   |
Year        |2030    |2031    |2032    |2033    |2034    |
Mewa        |6 White |5 Yellow|4 Green |3 Indigo|2 Black |
Year        |2035    |2036    |2037    |2038    |2039    |
Mewa        |1 White |9 Maroon|8 White |7 Red   |6 White |
Year        |2040    |2041    |2042    |2043    |2044    |
Mewa        |5 Yellow|4 Green |3 Indigo|2 Black |1 White |
Year        |2045    |2046    |2047    |2048    |2049    |
Mewa        |9 Maroon|8 White |7 Red   |6 White |5 Yellow|
Year        |2050    |2051    |2052    |2053    |2054    |
Mewa        |4 Green |3 Indigo|2 Black |1 White |9 Maroon|
Year        |2055    |2056    |2057    |2058    |2059    |
Mewa        |8 White |7 Red   |6 White |5 Yellow|4 Green |
Year        |2060    |2061    |2062    |2063    |2064    |
Mewa        |3 Indigo|2 Black |1 White |9 Maroon|8 White |
Year        |2065    |2066    |2067    |2068    |2069    |
Mewa        |7 Red   |6 White |5 Yellow|4 Green |3 Indigo|
Year        |2070    |2071    |2072    |2073    |2074    |
Mewa        |2 Black |1 White |9 Maroon|8 White |7 Red   |
Year        |2075    |2076    |2077    |2078    |2079    |
Mewa        |6 White |5 Yellow|4 Green |3 Indigo|2 Black |
Year        |2080    |2081    |2082    |2083    |2084    |
Mewa        |1 White |9 Maroon|8 White |7 Red   |6 White |
Year        |2085    |2086    |2087    |2088    |2089    |
Mewa        |5 Yellow|4 Green |3 Indigo|2 Black |1 White |
Year        |2090    |2091    |2092    |2093    |2094    |
Mewa        |9 Maroon|8 White |7 Red   |6 White |5 Yellow|
Year        |2095    |2096    |2097    |2098    |2099    |
Mewa        |4 Green |3 Indigo|2 Black |1 White |9 Maroon|
```

283

Tibetan Astrology

The Birth Mewa

The Mewa for the year of your birth is the most important Mewa. Everything else is referenced to this number.

Another important Mewa is the Mewa for the current year, which can be determined by looking up that year in the table on the preceding pages.

The element of Natal Mewa is then compared to the element of the current year in terms of the standard element comparisons like, Mother, Child, Enemy, Friend, and so forth. The following diagram illustrates the various element relationships.

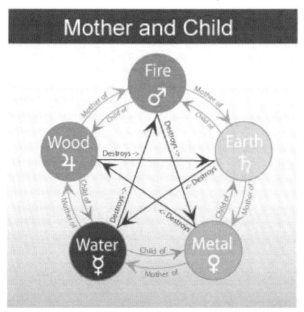

Below are actual translations from the original Tibetan. Pardon the use of only the masculine gender.

The Nine Mewas: Cards and Text

Mewa 01

Mewa: 1 White
Color: White
Element: Iron
Direction: North

Length of life: 71 years. There will be four difficult times during the life.

Birthmark: Has a birth-mark or mole on the right side. Is left-handed.

Practice: The practice involves obtaining a Chenresik statue (loving kindness, compassion) and practicing this sadhana.

Mantra: OM MANI PADME HUM

Either an only child or only one child turns out useful and carries on the generation. He travels a lot. Good in social work, where others are benefited. If a male, then brave. If female then a strong one. Could have three children. Likes to move about here and there. Snakes are their protector. Difficult with children, meaning: not so good for the kids -- things happen to them.

Possessions and jobs are very unstable. He is bad tempered, but has a good mind. A difficult early life, but the longer the life the better it gets. He is a clean person physically and likes white things like milk, butter, etc.

Mewa Day: Keep children close at hand. Good day for purification, making offerings to deities and invoking the nagas - protectors.

Favorable Action (Purification)
Favorable for Feast Days, Offerings
Favorable for Irrigation/water

Tibetan Astrology

Mewa 02

Mewa: 2 Black
Color: Black
Element: Water
Direction: S.W.

Length of life: 61 years. There will be three bad periods.

Birthmark: There is a birthmark on the right-hand or arm, the heartside, or the neck.

Practice: The practice is that of Vajrapani, which is strength and the clearing of obstacles. Become like the vajra -- indestructible. Get a statue of Vajrapani or a stupa.

Mantra: OM VAJRA PANI HUM

If the child is first born, it will be easy to care for him, an easy child. Is often sick when a child. He has nice speech, but a bad mind. He has a dark appearance, mean and horrible. Always sad. He tries to do good things, but no one likes him. If a monk or a member of the Bon religion, then he is a very strong practitioner. He likes meat and alcohol. He has many friends, which he loves, but seldom has an opportunity to be with them -- and thus no result. If sick when an adult, will be hard to cure.

Mewa Day: Not a good day for marriage, making complaints, prayer in general, and traveling at night. Good time for various magical rituals and dispelling negative influences, in particular offerings to the various semi-divine protectors, like Mamo, Düd, and Shin spirits.

Marriage Not-Favorable
Favorable for Banishing Negativity

Tibetan Astrology

Mewa 03

Mewa:	3
Mewa Color:	Blue
Element:	Water
Direction:	East

Length of life: 50 years with three difficult periods.

Birthmark: On the calf of the left leg.

Practice: The suggested practice is that of Vajrasattva (Dorje-Sempa) practice. Vajrasattva purifies and removes the limitations, obstacles and imperfections of the mind.

Mantra: OM VAJRA SATTVA HUM

He likes to sleep. He has a strong mind, but there is much instability in his life. He is a little bit greedy. At work, he is not able to concentrate, and tends to skip around. If male, he will talk less and if female will tend to be sad. He is difficult to change. Blame comes even if he does good things for others. He may have many wives (husbands) but no children. He will go to and die in another country. He may have paralysis.

Mewa Day: Avoid anything to do with lakes, rivers, wells, and irrigation and water, in general. Not a good day for marriage or standard religious prayer. However, a good day for medicine and healing, and making offerings to local deities, such as the earth lords, nagas, and so forth.

Favorable for Local Deities
Favorable for Medicine
Marriage, Not-Favorable
Not Favorable for Felling Trees
Not Favorable for Irrigation/water

Mewa 04

Mewa: 4
Color: Green
Element: Wood
Direction: S.E.

Length of Life: 65 years. There are four difficult periods.

Birthmark: On either thigh is a black circle birthmark.

Practice: The practice is that of Vajrapani, which is strength and the clearing of obstacles. Become like the vajra -- indestructible. Get a statue of Vajrapani or a stupa.

Mantra: OM VAJRA PANI HUM

He should avoid funerals. Cleanliness is very important, else the nagas (snakes) bring a bad disease. He likes to travel. He has a deep mind, but is sometimes bad. Perhaps difficulty having children. If he has property, then it is farmland. The life is unstable, with a lot of ups and downs. There is sadness sometimes. People gossip about him. He does good things, but others get the credit. He does not like to be lower than others, but finds little opportunity to rise. Whatever he has inside, stays with him. The nagas (snakes) are his protector. He is a vegetarian with four children. No wedding.

Mewa Day: Preparing medicine, healing, and medial procedures, in general, are good. Also good are making offerings to the nagas, the various semi-divine protectors. Traditionally, it is a bad day for a widow to wash her hair and an inopportune time to take a young child out of the house.

Favorable for Medicine

Tibetan Astrology

Mewa 05

Mewa: 5
Color: Yellow
Element: Earth
Direction: Center

Length of Life: 50 years. There will be two difficult periods.

Birthmark: His birthmark is a certain nervousness.

Practice: The suggested practice is that of Shakyamuni Buddha called the diamond vehicle (Dorje Chopa) (Prajnaparamita), cutting the vajra.

Mantra: TADYATA OM MUNE MUNE MAHAMUNI SHAKYAMUNAYE SWAHA

This is a dharma person. This is also the astrologer's Mewa. A monk's monk. He was a monk in the last life, reborn into a noble family in this life. Here is a very devoted person, with a stable mind. Very intelligent and religious. Obedient to his parents, he follows their customs or carries on their traditions. He does not travel much, or go far from his birthplace.

He has a protector coming from his ancestors, whom he has ignored, and who is thus a little bit angry.He has strong dreams because his protector is angry. He is hard to please. Before becoming a monk, he was a saint, also a normal dharma teacher. He talks a lot, but often misses the point. He is very smart, a quick thinker. Should be a religious person in this life. He is restless, moving here and there. He has very high expectations of others. He always helps others, but they become his enemies. They gossip about him. He has five children.

He has wealth in the form of property, houses, land. He will live long if he is religious. He is virtuous and educated. His possessions can be somewhat unstable. If female, he gets more gossip from others. If he is angry, it is difficult to please him. He has a good and stable mind. Tends to diseases of the gall-bladder, heart attack.

Mewa Day: This is a bad time for digging, plowing, excavating, and the like. Celebrations and festivals should be avoided, as well as purchasing a dog. It is a good day to making repairs to a church or religious building, ordinations, consecrations, and making petitions to authorities.

Not Favorable Agricultural

Mewa 06

Mewa:	6
Color:	White
Element:	Iron
Direction:	N.W.

Length of life: 70 years. There will be five difficult periods.

Birthmark: Calf of the left leg.

Practice: The practice suggested is that of the long-life (and purification) deity Vijaya Vsnisa (Tsuk Tor Nam Gyal Ma).

Mantra: OM AMRITA A YUR DADE SWAHA

He is intelligent. His mood and appearance are always changing. He travels a lot. If female, then will have nice speech, but the mind is not good. Receives protection from his own local deities. Possibly he could be very poor. He will not be living near his birthplace, but instead, elsewhere. He will be able to build himself up greater than his parents. He is seldom sick, but if sick, he will be hard to cure. He has many relatives, none of whom offer him much help. There will be many enemies. He does good for others, but is still blamed. He will have three to five children. Children possibly handicapped. There is not much power in the family, but wife is powerful. He is quite bad-tempered.

Mewa Day: This is not a day to complain or lament, to get into fights, or to praise others. The day is positive to going outside, making confessions, bathing, purification, marriage, and successful actions.

Favorable Action (Purification)
Favorable for Wealth Jzambhalla
Journeys, Favorable
Marriage, Favorable
Not Favorable for Starting a Fight

Tibetan Astrology

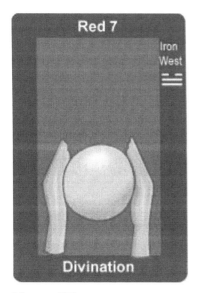

Mewa 07

Mewa: 7
Color: Red
Element: Fire
Direction: West

Length of Life: 80 years and there will be 4 difficult periods.

Birthmark: On the backside or chest.

Practice: The practice is that of tara (green Tara), and thus healing, protection, wealth and a good birth.

Mantra: OM TARE TUTTARE TURE SWAHA

If female, then she likes to sleep. If married, it will not last long. He likes to fight, has a strong body and a ruddy complexion. Possibly may succumb from a sudden disease. Could die from his love of meat and similar things. His generation always shows suicide and murder. Seven children. The life very unstable.

Tibetan Astrology

Mewa Day: This is a day to avoid the slaughter of animals, trading with meat, and, in particular, the cooking of red meat. Also bad for stealing, fire pujas, and aggression - making war on your enemies. It is good day for making offerings to local deities.

Favorable for Local Deities
Not Favorable for Starting a Fight

Tibetan Astrology

Mewa 08

Mewa: 8
Color: White
Element: Metal
Direction: N.E.

Length of Life: 50 years and there are 3 difficult periods.

Birthmark: On right cheek.

Practice: The suggested practice is that of Shakyamuni Buddha called the diamond vehicle (Dorje Chopa) (Prajnaparamita), cutting the vajra.

Mantra: TADYATA OM MUNE MUNE MAHAMUNI SHAKYAMUNAYE SWAHA

He should avoid dirty things, and stay clean. There is protection by local deities. He could go to another place from where born. Pleasant, but proud. Good hands for arts and crafts. Older life will be better than younger life. He is religious and virtuous. Could have four to six children. Elegant people like him. The bad people don't like him. Could have a tendency to gossip, causing bad relations.

Mewa Day: It is a good day for marriages, making confessions, prayer, and making offerings to the protectors. It is important to maintain one's strength and not become weak. A bad day to burn refuse or otherwise scorch the earth.

Favorable for Action (Purification)
Favorable for Irrigation/water
Marriage, Favorable

Tibetan Astrology

Red 9

Fire
South

Success

Mewa 09

Mewa: 9
Color: Red
Element: Fire
Direction: South

Length of Life: 73 years with five difficult periods.

Birthmark: On face, neck or left-leg.

Practice: Suggested practice is that of Manjushri, the development of the mind and intellect.

Mantra: OM ARA PATSA NA DHI

An image of one holding seven glorious flowers in hands. If he keeps flowers well, then will be a very rich man. Could be proud or greedy. His older life will be better than young life. Very brave. He may well live other than where born. Wealth includes cows, animals, livestock in general. Has to keep his wealth with care or obstacles could destroy it. This is a good Mewa for females, but not for monks or Bon.

Tibetan Astrology

Mewa Day: This is a good day for long-life ceremonies, invoking prosperity, and receiving money and goods. Not a good day to send someone on a task for you, and not good to pay out money. If an old man dies today, it is a sign that monetary resources are nearing exhaustion.

Favorable for Wealth (Dzambhala)
Trade: Not Favorable (purchase only)

Other Uses for Mewa

Daily Mewa

Asidr from the annual Mewa, the Mewa for any day can be calculated if you have the lunar month and day. The year is not necessary. Note the Tsurphu and Phugpa traditions use different results, so choose which system you prefer. The Dalai Lama is Phugpa, the Karmapa is Tsurphu.

Lunar Month	Tsurphu	Phugpa
Lunar Month #01	4 Green	[7 Red]
Lunar Month #02	7 Red	[1 White]
Lunar Month #03	1 White	[4 Green]
Lunar Month #04	4 Green	[7 Red]
Lunar Month #05	7 Red	[1 White]
Lunar Month #06	1 White	[4 Green]
Lunar Month #07	4 Green	[7 Red]
Lunar Month #08	7 Red	[1 White]
Lunar Month #09	1 White	[4 Green]
Lunar Month #10	4 Green	[7 Red]
Lunar Month #11	7 Red	[1 White]
Lunar Month #12	1 White	[4 Green]

Mewa-Key is the 1st day of the Month.
Mewa for day = Mewa-Key + Days-in-Month - 1

Worked Example
Lunar Month = 6, Day = 5
Mewa-Key = 1 White

Mewa for day = 1 + 5 – 1 = 5

Mewa for Day = 5 Yellow
(You may have to remove cycles of nine)

Tibetan Astrology

Annual or Birth Mewa Vital Forces

Mewas also have the equivalent of vital force indicators for any given year, either the natal year or any subsequent year. Given the birth (or current) year's Mewa, using the table below, you can determine the Vitality and Power Mewas as follows:

Given Mewa	Vitality Mewa	Power Mewa
Birth Mewa 1|	Vitality Mewa = 7,	Power Mewa = 4
Birth Mewa 2|	Vitality Mewa = 8,	Power Mewa = 5
Birth Mewa 3|	Vitality Mewa = 9,	Power Mewa = 6
Birth Mewa 4|	Vitality Mewa = 1,	Power Mewa = 7
Birth Mewa 5|	Vitality Mewa = 2,	Power Mewa = 8
Birth Mewa 6|	Vitality Mewa = 3,	Power Mewa = 9
Birth Mewa 7|	Vitality Mewa = 4,	Power Mewa = 1
Birth Mewa 8|	Vitality Mewa = 5,	Power Mewa = 2
Birth Mewa 9|	Vitality Mewa = 6,	Power Mewa = 3

```
Body Mewa = Birth Year Mewa
```

Note: The Body Mewa will be the same as the birth (or given) Mewa.

The elements of the birth Mewa Vital Forces are then compared to the elements of the Current Year Vital Forces in the usual way, as follows:

Elemental Comparison

Mother of the birth power: "000" Best
Friend of the birth power: "00" Next Best
Son of the birth power: "0X" Neutral
Enemy of the birth power: "XX" Worst

If it is the same as the birth power then:
If Water or Earth: "0" Good
If Fire, Iron or Wood: "X" Bad

Tibetan Astrology

The Papme Mewa

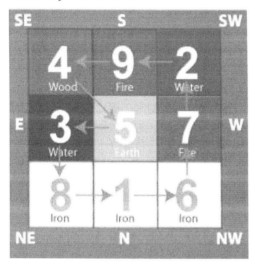

Determining the Papme for Men

Another form of annual Mewa is to start with your natal year and count up to your current age. Remember that in Tibetan counting, the starting point is considered year number one of your age, which is different than how we do it here in the West.

First, pick the Magic Square (following pages) that has your natal Mewa in the center and count counter-clockwise in the direction of the arrows. Note the counting direction for woman is different from men and is shown on the following page.

Men count starting with the first year (#1) in the center and proceeding around the square as shown by the arrows above. When you reach you current age, that particular Mewa is your Papme Mewa and should be compared (using the five-element comparison) with your natal Mewa.

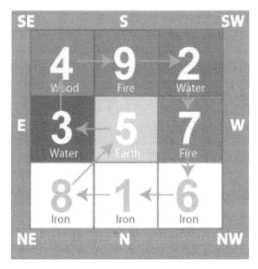

Determining the Papme for Women

First, pick the Magic Square (following pages) that has your natal Mewa in the center and count in the direction of the arrows- clockwise. Note: for woman, we are starting in the same place, moving to the left, but then upward and around – clockwise.

The Nine Papme Magic Squares

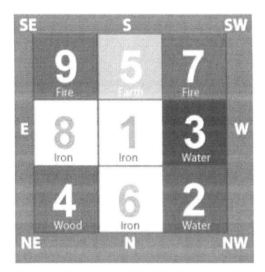

Magic Square with #1 Iron or Metal

Compare Metal with natal Element.

Tibetan Astrology

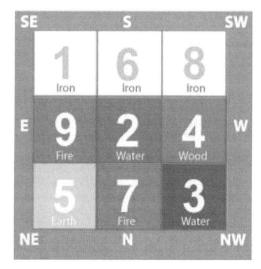

Magic Square with #2 Water

Compare Water with natal Element.

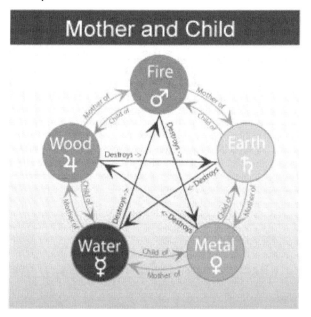

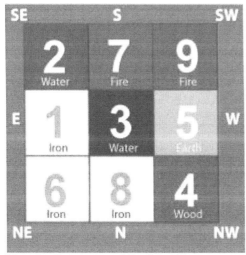

Magic Square with #3 Water

Compare Water with natal Element.

Tibetan Astrology

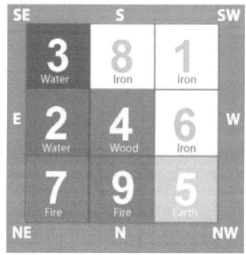

Magic Square with #4 Wood

Compare Wood with natal Element.

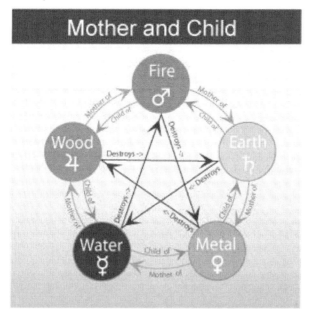

Tibetan Astrology

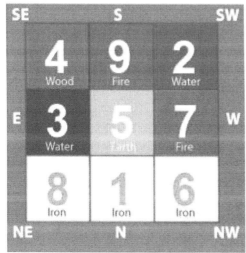

Magic Square with #5 Earth

Compare Earth with natal Element.

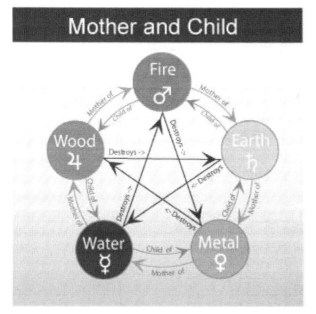

Tibetan Astrology

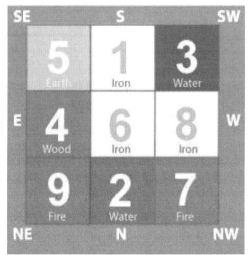

Magic Square with #6 Iron or Metal

Compare Iron with natal Element.

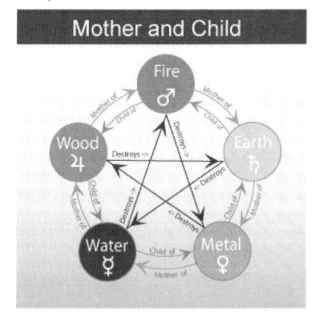

Tibetan Astrology

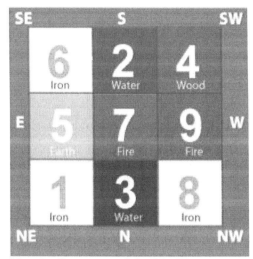

Magic Square with #7 Fire

Compare Fire with natal Element.

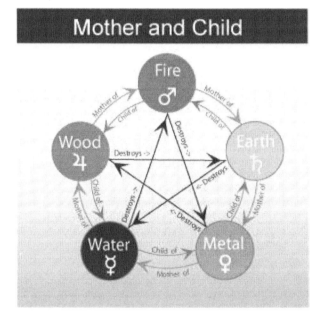

Tibetan Astrology

Magic Square with #8 Iron or Metal

Compare Metal with natal Element.

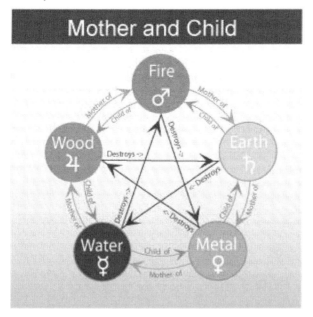

Tibetan Astrology

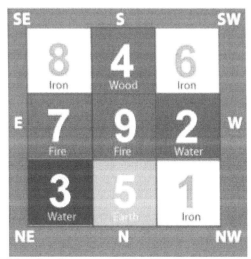

Magic Square with #9 Fire

Compare Fire with natal Element.

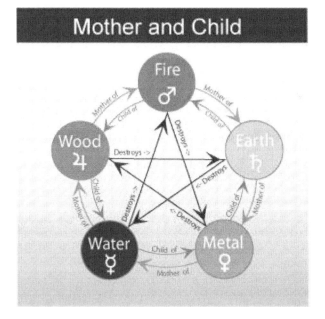

Parkhas: The Eight Trigrams

The eight Parkhas or trigrams are related to the Chinese Pa-Qua, connected to the I-Ching (Book of Changes), one of the oldest and most important writings in the history of the Chinese language. These eight trigrams represent the interdependent relation of the two great opposites, `Yang' and `Yin'.

Yang (translation: "Sunny side of the hill") is the male, positive, and active force, while Yin (translation: "Shaded side of the hill") is female, receptive, and passive. Their interrelationship creates the eight trigrams, any two of which can be used to form the six-lined hexagram, found in the I-Ching.

The active yang force is symbolized by an unbroken line, while the passive yin force is a 2-section broken line. These are then placed, one above the other to form the eight possible combinations or 3-lined trigrams.

In Tibetan astrology, these eight trigrams are placed at the eight directions in space as follows. There are two styles of transliteration for Chinese words:

The Eight Trigrams

Pinyin	Wade-Gilles	Direction
Li	Li	South
Kun	Khon	S.W.
Dui	Dha	West
Qian	Khen	N.W.
Kan	Kham	North
Gen	Kin	N.E.
Zhen	Zin	East
Xun	Zon	S.E.

Tibetan Astrology

The Ba-Gua

The Ba-Gua, a Chinese term that translates to the "eight areas" came from ancient China, along with Taoism, and is associated with the theory of Yin and Yang, and their endless interaction and permutations. For our practical purposes here, the Ba-Gua refers to the set or circle of eight trigram that represent how all things ceaselessly turn into their opposites and back into themselves. These same eight trigrams make up the 64 hexagrams that are the heart of the Yi-Ching, the popular Chinese divinatory oracle and philosophical refuge.

The trigrams each have a particular kind of Qi (pronounced "Chee") associated with them, and it is this Qi that we are concerned about here. Each of us, personally, and every building (and its direction), has a governing trigram of Gua. Personally, we determine our birth Gua by looking up the year of our birth in a simple

317

table. The resulting numbers: 1, 2, 3, 4, 6, 7, 8, or 9 (there is no # '5') becomes our personal Gua number, which is associated with a particular trigram. Numbers for men are different from numbers for women. The personal Gua table looks like this:

Later one, I have included a list, including the meaning as suggested in the now-famous book on the I-Ching by Wilhelm.

Solar Sector Numbers

Annnual 1940-1979

Feb 4 1940 22:50 M6 F9	Feb 4 1960 19:23 M4 F2
Feb 4 1941 04:42 M5 F1	Feb 4 1961 01:15 M3 F3
Feb 4 1942 10:34 M4 F2	Feb 4 1962 07:07 M2 F4
Feb 4 1943 16:26 M3 F3	Feb 4 1963 12:58 M1 F5
Feb 4 1944 22:17 M2 F4	Feb 4 1964 18:48 M9 F6
Feb 4 1945 04:07 M1 F5	Feb 4 1965 00:37 M8 F7
Feb 4 1946 09:57 M9 F6	Feb 4 1966 06:26 M7 F8
Feb 4 1947 15:46 M8 F7	Feb 4 1967 12:14 M6 F9
Feb 4 1948 21:34 M7 F8	Feb 4 1968 18:01 M5 F1
Feb 4 1949 03:22 M6 F9	Feb 3 1969 23:49 M4 F2
Feb 4 1950 09:09 M5 F1	Feb 4 1970 05:36 M3 F3
Feb 4 1951 14:57 M4 F2	Feb 4 1971 11:24 M2 F4
Feb 4 1952 20:44 M3 F3	Feb 4 1972 17:11 M1 F5
Feb 4 1953 02:32 M2 F4	Feb 3 1973 22:60 M9 F6
Feb 4 1954 08:20 M1 F5	Feb 4 1974 04:49 M8 F7
Feb 4 1955 14:09 M9 F6	Feb 4 1975 10:39 M7 F8
Feb 4 1956 19:59 M8 F7	Feb 4 1976 16:30 M6 F9
Feb 4 1957 01:49 M7 F8	Feb 3 1977 22:21 M5 F1
Feb 4 1958 07:40 M6 F9	Feb 4 1978 04:13 M4 F2
Feb 4 1959 13:32 M5 F1	Feb 4 1979 10:05 M3 F3

Annual Number 1900-1939

Each person has an Annual Number, the number for everyone born in that year. It is useful in itself, but you will also need it to determine your Natal Number in the next section. Finding your Annual Number is easy.

In the table above (or the next couple of pages if you are younger), find the year of your birth. In the row

318

(horizontal line) next to your year, you will see a number for men and one for woman, marked as follows:

Feb 4 1900 05:45   M1 F5

In the above example for 1900, "M1" stands for Male and the annual number is "1" for men, and the "F5" stands for Female and the annual number is "5" for women.

Be sure that your birth date and time or equal to or follow that date and time given for each year. Otherwise use the pervious year. Here is an example, using Feb 4 1902.

Feb 4 1901 11:37   M9 F6

Feb 4 1902 17:28   M8 F7

If you were born on February 4th 1902 at 17:28 GMT or later, then use the numbers for 1902. If you were born before 17:28 on February 4th, 1902, then use the numbers for February 4, 1901.

Note: All times are given in military or 24-hour time, thus 17:28 equals 5:28 PM, and so forth. Also all times are given in GMT (Greenwich Mean Time), which is that used in Great Britain and has a time zone of 0 hours. If you were born in the U.S., you would have to deduct the number of hours for your time zone to determine the correct time. For example, using the time of 17:28 given above, here is what that time would be for the four U.S. time zones:

17:28 GMT = 5:28 PM Greenwich Mean Time

12:28 EST = 12:28 PM Eastern Standard Time (-5 hours)

11:28 CST = 11:28 AM Central Standard Time (-6 hours)

10:28 MST = 10:28 AM Mountain Standard Time (-7 hours)

09:28 PST = 09:28 AM Pacific Standard Time (-8 hours)

And last, but also important, if you are on Daylight Savings Time, there would be one hour less or using the same times above, but in summer time (DST), the times would be:

17:28 GMT = 5:28 PM Greenwich Mean Time
13:28 EDT = 01:28 PM Eastern Daylight Time (-4 hours)
12:28 CDT = 12:28 AM Central Daylight Time (-5 hours)
11:28 MDT = 11:28 AM Mountain Daylight Time (-6 hours)
11:28 PDT = 10:28 AM Pacific Daylight Time (-7 hours)

Don't get mad at me if the above is tricky. I didn't invent the time zones.

Annnual 1940-1979

Feb 4 1940 22:50	M6 F9		Feb 4 1960 19:23	M4 F2
Feb 4 1941 04:42	M5 F1		Feb 4 1961 01:15	M3 F3
Feb 4 1942 10:34	M4 F2		Feb 4 1962 07:07	M2 F4
Feb 4 1943 16:26	M3 F3		Feb 4 1963 12:58	M1 F5
Feb 4 1944 22:17	M2 F4		Feb 4 1964 18:48	M9 F6
Feb 4 1945 04:07	M1 F5		Feb 4 1965 00:37	M8 F7
Feb 4 1946 09:57	M9 F6		Feb 4 1966 06:26	M7 F8
Feb 4 1947 15:46	M8 F7		Feb 4 1967 12:14	M6 F9
Feb 4 1948 21:34	M7 F8		Feb 4 1968 18:01	M5 F1
Feb 4 1949 03:22	M6 F9		Feb 3 1969 23:49	M4 F2
Feb 4 1950 09:09	M5 F1		Feb 4 1970 05:36	M3 F3
Feb 4 1951 14:57	M4 F2		Feb 4 1971 11:24	M2 F4
Feb 4 1952 20:44	M3 F3		Feb 4 1972 17:11	M1 F5
Feb 4 1953 02:32	M2 F4		Feb 3 1973 22:60	M9 F6
Feb 4 1954 08:20	M1 F5		Feb 4 1974 04:49	M8 F7
Feb 4 1955 14:09	M9 F6		Feb 4 1975 10:39	M7 F8
Feb 4 1956 19:59	M8 F7		Feb 4 1976 16:30	M6 F9
Feb 4 1957 01:49	M7 F8		Feb 3 1977 22:21	M5 F1
Feb 4 1958 07:40	M6 F9		Feb 4 1978 04:13	M4 F2
Feb 4 1959 13:32	M5 F1		Feb 4 1979 10:05	M3 F3

Annual Number 1940-1979

Here are the annual numbers for 1940 to 1979.

Annnual 1980-2019

Feb 4 1980 15:56	M2 F4	Feb 4 2000 12:28	M9 F6
Feb 3 1981 21:48	M1 F5	Feb 3 2001 18:19	M8 F7
Feb 4 1982 03:38	M9 F6	Feb 4 2002 00:08	M7 F8
Feb 4 1983 09:28	M8 F7	Feb 4 2003 05:57	M6 F9
Feb 4 1984 15:17	M7 F8	Feb 4 2004 11:45	M5 F1
Feb 3 1985 21:06	M6 F9	Feb 3 2005 17:33	M4 F2
Feb 4 1986 02:53	M5 F1	Feb 3 2006 23:20	M3 F3
Feb 4 1987 08:41	M4 F2	Feb 4 2007 05:07	M2 F4
Feb 4 1988 14:28	M3 F3	Feb 4 2008 10:55	M1 F5
Feb 3 1989 20:15	M2 F4	Feb 3 2009 16:43	M9 F6
Feb 4 1990 02:03	M1 F5	Feb 3 2010 22:31	M8 F7
Feb 4 1991 07:51	M9 F6	Feb 4 2011 04:20	M7 F8
Feb 4 1992 13:40	M8 F7	Feb 4 2012 10:10	M6 F9
Feb 3 1993 19:29	M7 F8	Feb 3 2013 16:00	M5 F1
Feb 4 1994 01:20	M6 F9	Feb 3 2014 21:52	M4 F2
Feb 4 1995 07:11	M5 F1	Feb 4 2015 03:43	M3 F3
Feb 4 1996 13:02	M4 F2	Feb 4 2016 09:35	M2 F4
Feb 3 1997 18:54	M3 F3	Feb 3 2017 15:27	M1 F5
Feb 4 1998 00:46	M2 F4	Feb 3 2018 21:18	M9 F6
Feb 4 1999 06:37	M1 F5	Feb 4 2019 03:09	M8 F7

Annual Number 1980-2019

Here are the annual numbers for 1980 to 2019.

The Natal Number

Annual Number ->		1-4-7	2-5-8	3-6-9
Jan 5-7	15° ♑ to ♒ 15°	M6 F9	M9 F6	M3 F3
Feb 4-5	15° ♒ to ♓ 15°	M8 F7	M2 F4	M5 F1
Mar 5-7	15° ♓ to ♈ 15°	M7 F8	M1 F5	M4 F2
Apr 4-6	15° ♈ to ♉ 15°	M6 F9	M9 F6	M3 F3
May 5-7	15° ♉ to ♊ 15°	M5 F1	M8 F7	M2 F4
Jun 5-7	15° ♊ to ♋ 15°	M4 F2	M7 F8	M1 F5
Jul 7-8	15° ♋ to ♌ 15°	M3 F3	M6 F9	M9 F6
Aug 7-9	15° ♌ to ♍ 15°	M2 F4	M5 F1	M8 F7
Sep 7-9	15° ♍ to ♎ 15°	M1 F5	M4 F2	M7 F8
Oct 8-9	15° ♎ to ♏ 15°	M9 F6	M3 F3	M6 F9
Nov 7-8	15° ♏ to ♐ 15°	M8 F7	M2 F4	M5 F1
Dec 7-8	15° ♐ to ♑ 15°	M7 F8	M1 F5	M4 F2

The Natal Number

For this calculation you will need your Annual Number, which is explained in the preceding lesson, so be sure to have that with you.

The Natal Number is derived from the solar month during which you were born. Solar months are measured in the Tropical Zodiac, as measured from the 15th degree of each zodiac sign until the 15th degree of the next zodiac sign.

If you look at the accompanying table, you can see the twelve solar months as measured from January through December of any year. Just look for the interval during which you were born.

For example, I was born on July 18th, so I see from the table that the nearest solar month begins around July 7th and 8th and extends until August 7th to the 9th. July

Tibetan Astrology

18th is safely within that range, so I don't have to look any farther.

I will be looking for my Natal Number in the horizontal row to the right of the dates July 7-8. My Annual Number is "2," so I must use the column with the number "2" in it, shown in red at the top of the diagram. There is a column that covers the numbers 2, 5, and 8, so that is my column.

Now, looking across (horizontally) the row from July 7-8, and under the second column I see "M6 F9," where the "M" stands for male and the "F" for female. Since I am a male, my Natal Number is "6." If I were female, my number would be "9." That's it.

However, if I were born on July 7th or 8th, things are not so simple, but still workable. These starting dates change very slightly from year to year, and there is one simple way of establishing whether I use the July row or have to use the row before it, which would be June. For this you will need your astrology chart.

There are all kinds of free services online that will calculate your natal chart and give you an on-screen list of your planet positions. The only position you need is that of the Sun, showing you which degree of the zodiac the Sun is in.

In order for me to use the Jul 7-8 row, the position of my Sun would have to be greater or equal to 15-degrees of the zodiac sign Cancer and less than 15-degrees of the zodiac sign Leo. This is fairly easy to establish. Using this method you can be sure which Natal Number is your number.

Origins: The Cosmic Tortoise

The concept of a tortoise upon which is inscribed the Lo-Shu diagram (mentioned earlier) and the eight trigrams, and so forth, is found in both Tibet and China (but not India), and this image of a tortoise shell on which are inscribed key divinatory elements essential to astrology is considered the source of much of the astrological tradition, although the appearance of the tortoise is apparently a symbolic event, and by most scholars is considered more-or-less pre-historical.

Xiantian "Prior To Heaven"

At the heart of the history of both feng-shui and the Yi-Ching is the legend of the Ho-Tu, the proverbial river map that is said to have appeared ages ago. As one story goes, the Ho-Tu diagram was carried on the back of a dragon-horse that arose out of the Huan-Ho (the Yellow River). On the flank or side of this creature was a plate with an inscription indicating the order of the eight trigrams and directions, one trigram for each of the basic compass directions. This arrangement of trigrams has come to be known as the Former Heaven sequence or arrangement of the trigrams, sometimes called the Early Heaven sequence or the Ho-Tu diagram.

As mentioned, the Former Heaven sequence assigns a single trigram (and number) to each of the eight primary directions. The number "5" is assigned to the center, which represents where one resides. This in itself is fascinating, but even more interesting is the fact that the arrangement of the eight trigrams is such as to indicate how these trigrams change, producing and endless cycle of Yin and Yang.

The trigram Qian (three solid or Yang) lines represents the father and the direction south. The trigram Kun (three broken lines) represents the mother and the direction north. The six other trigrams fill in the sequence, each changing one line to become the next phase in the cycle. The arrangement is remarkable and offers an endless cycle of phases - changes. In fact, it is said of this Former Heaven sequence that it is perfect in itself, a template of what life should and could be on earth, but not as it is today.

The Lo-Shu Diagram or Houtian

For life as you and I live it, there is a second diagram that has evolved, historically somewhat later that the Former Heaven se quence, It is called, appropriately enough, the Later Heaven sequence, or more popularly the "Lo-Shu" diagram. It was also derived from a natural event, just like the original River Map, but this time the map (so the story goes) was inscribed on the breast plate (some say the back) of a large tortoise that emerged from the Lo River during a flood. On the bottom of the tortoise was inscribed a series of nine numbers in a particular order. This diagram is called the Lo-Shu diagram and the inscription on the shell is that of the Magic Square, a square containing nine numbers in rows of three, all three numbers in any row adding up to 15.

The arrangement of the eight trigrams in the Later Heaven sequence comes directly from the numbers in the classic lo-shu diagram, what is called the Magic Square.

The Magic Square

The Later Heaven sequence is a direct pull of these numbers (as they represent the trigrams), placing the trigram that corresponds with the number in the direction the number appears in the Magic Square or lo-shu. This assumes that the Magic Square is positioned with the "9" (trigram Li) pointing South, the "1" (trigram

Kan) pointing North, "3" (trigram Zhen) pointing East, and on around.

In other words, the placement of the nine numbers in the traditional lo-shu diagram indicates which trigram governs each of the eight directions. If we superimpose the nine numbers of the magic square on the traditional arrangement of the Parkhas or Trigrams, we get one number paired with each trigram, leaving the number "5" for the center, as is traditional.

Below is a description of each of the eight trigrams.

Details on The Eight Trigrams

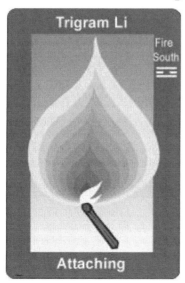

Trigram #1: Li

Direction: South
Element: Fire
Meaning: Clinging
Animal: Bird

The trigram Li (Clinging) represents the element fire, and thus burning passion and attachment. It brings light and brilliance and has been associated with the eye and perception, and glory, fame, light, in general. Also aggression and war.

Li Day: A good day for fire offerings, painting, melting iron in an earthen crucible, and playing chess are good. It is a bad day for marriages, theft, and preparing a corpse for burial.

Favorable for Fire rituals
Marriage, Not-Favorable
Not Favorable for Funeral

Tibetan Astrology

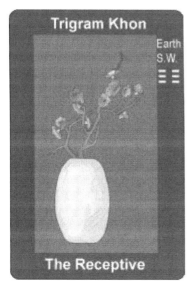

Trigram #2: Kun (Khon)

Direction: S.W.
Element: Earth
Meaning: The Receptive
Animal: Ox

The trigram Khon (The Receptive) is linked to the element Earth and to the female principle and receptivity, in general. It is the matrix, vase, earth, and receptacle, ready to receive and be fertilized. Sexuality. Pure yin. The mother.

Kun Day: It is a bad day for funerals, bathing, laying foundations, or arguments and fighting. It is a good day for cutting word, and performing the various rituals for exorcism and suppression.

Favorable for Banishing Negativity

Favorable for Felling Trees
Not Favorable for Building
Not Favorable for Funeral
Not Favorable for Starting a Fight

Trigram #3: Dui (Dha)

Direction: West
Element: Iron
Meaning: Joyous
Animal: Sheep

The trigram Dha (Joyous Lake) is associated with the element Iron, and also wives, children, and pleasure, in general - reproduction. It also symbolizes decline, autumn, and death.

Dui Day: Travel toward the East or working in that sector on this day is good, as is hunting, cutting wood, making friends, and theft. This is a bad day to make war or aggressions or make business investments.

Favorable for Felling Trees
Journey for Favorable to East
Not Favorable for Trade

Tibetan Astrology

Trigram #4: Qian

Direction:	N.W.
Element:	Sky
Meaning:	The Creative
Animal:	Horse

The trigram Khen (Creative) is called the "Creative," and is the most masculine and forceful of the Parkhas - the ruler. Pure yang. The father.

Qian Day: This is a good day to meet important people and to perform good deeds. This is not a good day to begin new projects or to lay foundations. Also bad are celebrations and parties. If you are ill, it is best to stay on the ground floor of the house, and one should not sleep in a shrine that day.

Favorable for Banishing Negativity
Favorable for Building, Favorable for Local Deities
Not Favorable for Building, Favorable for Trade

Trigram #5: Kham

Direction: North
Element: Water
Meaning: The Abysmal
Animal: Pig

The trigram Kham (Abysmal Water) is the Parkha of the element Water, and suggest a pause in activity - cessation. Also the water brings needed moisture. It's danger is that of stagnation and smothering - rotting.

Kham Day: This is not a good day for crossing water, fishing, and anything to do with waterways. It is a good day to perform rituals to protectors to ward off harm, and working with iron.

Favorable for Banishing Negativity
Favorable for Local Deities
Not Favorable for Irrigation/water

Tibetan Astrology

Trigram #6: Zhen

Direction:	N.E.
Element:	Mountain
Meaning:	Keeping Still
Animal:	Dog

The trigram Gin (Keeping Still) is Parkha of the Mountain, providing stability and protection, a force against whatever would seek to invade and conquer us. "Keeping Still" also refers to the process of meditation. This is the trigram of the dharmapalas or protector of the truth.

Zhen Day: This is not a good day for important meetings or to have any kind of inauguration ceremony. Buying and selling should be avoided, as should reading dharma texts. It is a good day to enter into dharma practice, perform protector rituals, and start new projects, like laying foundation stones. Favorable for planting but not cutting trees, Favorable for Building, Favorable for Local Deities,

Trigram #7: Zin

Direction: East
Element: Wood
Meaning: Arousing
Animal: Dragon

The trigram Tsin (Arousing) is the Parkha of Wood, and represents movement and steady growth, whatever arouses us to action. It also calls or awakens us to action, helping to get us moving.

Zin Day: This is a good day to start new projects, lay foundations, dress up, and make offerings to local deities. It is a bad day to cut trees or make any promises of friendship or loyalty.

Favorable for Agricultural
Favorable for Building
Favorable for Local Deities
Favorable for Planting Trees
Not Favorable for Felling Trees

Tibetan Astrology

Trigram #8: Zon

Direction: S.E.
Element: Wind
Meaning: The Gentle
Animal: Sheep

The trigram Zon (Gentle) is the Parkha of Wind, and suggests dispersion, penetrating everywhere, and working around anything in its way.

Zon Day: This is a bad day to have a party, for entertainment, and for making overtures of friendship. This is a good day for reciting mantras, and for performing rituals to the protectors, to ward off harm.

Favorable for Banishing Negativity

Birth Year Parkha

In general, Tibetans use a progressed Parkha called the "Bap-Par" or descending Parkha. While a natal Parkha does exist, it is not often used.

Natal Parkha: Method One

When a natal Parkha is used, it is based on the Bap-Par or descending Parkha of the mother. Use the formula for the descending Parkha, which stars with the trigram "Li" for men, and the trigram "Kham" for women and count until your birth year. The mother;s birth year must be used. That is your natal or birth Parkha. Remember that "Li" (or "Kham," for women) will count as number one, and so on.

Natal Parkha: Method Two

Some authorities just say that the natal Parkha for all men is "Li," and the natal Parkha for all women is "Kham," and leave it go at that.

The Current Year Parkha

To determine an individual's personal Parkha for the current year, start with your current age. Tibetans count age differently than Westerners, in that they say you are one-year old the moment you are born. That birth moment marks year "one." Also, for this calculation, men count clockwise and women, counterclockwise. Here is how:

Men: Star with the Trigram Li (top of chart). This is number one. Then continue counting in a clockwise direction around the wheel of eight trigrams until you come to your current age. The trigram you stop at is your trigram for this current year.

Women: Star with the Trigram Kan (Kham) (bottom of chart). This is number one. Then continue counting in a counter-clockwise direction around the wheel of eight trigrams until you come to your current age. The trigram you stop at is your trigram for this current year.

One you have the name of the Parkha for the current year, find that Parkha (Trigram) in the next eight pages of the same name. It will have the name of the Parkha in the center of the wheel.

Now look at the eight directions (North, South, East, West, N.E., S.E., S.W, and N.W.) and notice that each direction has a colored square in it. There are four shades of green and four shades of red. The green squares are auspicious directions for the year, and the red squares are inauspicious directions for the current year.

The brighter the color the more intense the experience, so that bright green is the best direction of all and bright red is the worst direction of all.

On the pages following the Trigram wheels are Astro*Image cards and interpretations for each of the red and green cards, to help you learn more about each direction.

This geomantic directional technique is widely used in Tibetan astrology.

Parkha for the Current Day

The Parkha for the current day may be calculated, given only the current lunar month and lunar day number. Remember, these are not western calendar months and days but lunar months (Measured from Tibetan New Year) and lunar days (measured from New Moon).

Tibetan Months	Key Trigram
Tiger, Horse, Dog	First Day = Li
Pig, Hare, Sheep	First Day = Tsin
Mouse, Dragon, Monkey	First Day = Kham
Ox, Snake, Bird	First Day = Dha

Parkha for Day = Key Trigram + Days-in-Month - 1

Worked Example
Lunar Month = 4, Day = 22
Key Trigram = 7

Parkha for day = 7 + 22 − 1 = 28/8 = remainder= 4
Parkha for Day = Trigram 4, Khen

Trigrams Numbered
1 Li
2 Khon
3 Dha
4 Khen
5 Kham
6 Gin
7 Tzin
8 Zon

The Eight Directions

Four Good Directions:

1) NAM-MEN (sky healer) -- The best one. Good for doctors.

2) SOG-TSO (healthy life) -- Next best. Good for sleeping, point the head in this direction.

3) PAL-KEY (generating, glorious) -- 3rd best, but a lower good. It is good to buy or obtain things from this direction.

4) CHA-LON (bringing auspiciousness, prosperity) -- 4th good, least. Good for traveling.

Four Bad Directions:

5) Na-PA (evil spirit) -- Least bad.

6) DRE-GNA (five ghosts) -- More bad.

7) Dš-CH™ (devil-cutting) -- Even worse, strong negativity, cuts us.

8) LU-CHEY (body destroying) -- Worst one (avoid this direction)

The four good directions are the good side or Zan-shi, while the bad side or four bad ones are Gnen-shi.

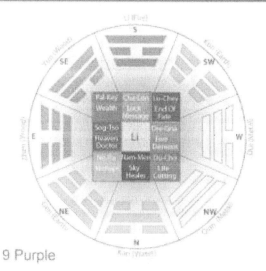

Geomantic Houses for the Trigram Li

The house faces North and sits South. The element is Fire. The trigram is Li. The number is "9." Color is Purple. Your auspicious directions in order of auspiciousness (most to least) are

(1) Name-Men – Sky Healer direction is North.
(2) Sog-Tso - Heavenly Doctor direction is East.
(3) Pal-Key - Wealth direction is S.E..
(4) Pal-Key – Luck Messenger peace direction is South.

Your inauspicious directions are:

(5) Nö-Pa- Injury direction is N.E.
(6) Dre-Gna – Five Demons direction is West.
(7) Dü-Chö– Life Cutting direction is N.W.
(8) Lu-Chey – End-of-Fate direction is S.W.

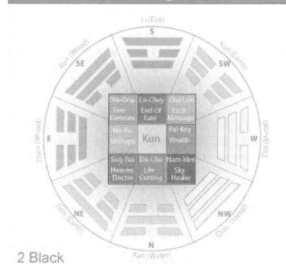

Geomantic Houses for the Trigram Kun

The house faces N.E. and sits S.W. The element is Earth. The trigram is Kun. The number is "2." Color is Black.

(1) Name-Men – Sky Healer direction is N.W.
(2) Sog-Tso - Heavenly Doctor direction is N.E.
(3) Pal-Key - Wealth direction is West.
(4) Pal-Key – Luck Messenger peace direction is S.W.

Your inauspicious directions are:

(5) Nö-Pa- Injury direction is East.
(6) Dre-Gna – Five Demons direction is S.E.
(7) Dü-Chö– Life Cutting direction is North.
(8) Lu-Chey – End-of-Fate direction is South.

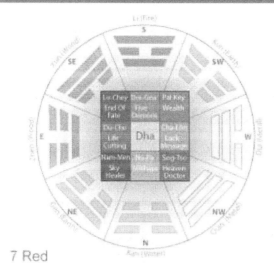

7 Metal Trigram Dui

7 Red

Geomantic Houses for the Trigram Dui

The house faces East and sits West. The element is Metal. The trigram is Dui. The number is "7." Color is Red.

(1) Name-Men – Sky Healer direction is N.E.
(2) Sog-Tso - Heavenly Doctor direction is N.W.
(3) Pal-Key - Wealth direction is S.W.
(4) Pal-Key – Luck Messenger peace direction is West.

Your inauspicious directions are:

(5) Nö-Pa- Injury direction is North.
(6) Dre-Gna – Five Demons direction is South.
(7) Dü-Chö– Life Cutting direction is East.
(8) Lu-Chey – End-of-Fate direction is S.E.

345

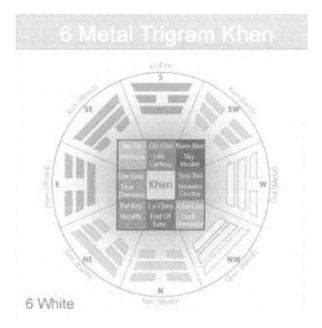

6 White

Geomantic Houses for the Trigram Khen

The house faces S.E. and sits N.W. The element is Metal. The trigram is Qian. The number is "6." Color is White.

(1) Name-Men – Sky Healer direction is S.W.
(2) Sog-Tso - Heavenly Doctor direction is West.
(3) Pal-Key - Wealth direction is N.E.
(4) Pal-Key – Luck Messenger peace direction is N.W.

Your inauspicious directions are:

(5) Nö-Pa- Injury direction is S.E.
(6) Dre-Gna – Five Demons direction is East.
(7) Dü-Chö– Life Cutting direction is South.
(8) Lu-Chey – End-of-Fate direction is North.

Tibetan Astrology

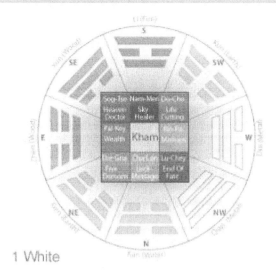

Geomantic Houses for the Trigram Kham

The house faces South and sits North. The element is Water. The trigram is Kan. The number is "1." Color is White.

(1) Name-Men – Sky Healer direction is South.
(2) Sog-Tso - Heavenly Doctor direction is S.E.
(3) Pal-Key - Wealth direction is East.
(4) Pal-Key – Luck Messenger peace direction is North.

Your inauspicious directions are:

(5) Nö-Pa- Injury direction is West.
(6) Dre-Gna – Five Demons direction is N.E.
(7) Dü-Chö– Life Cutting direction is S.W.
(8) Lu-Chey – End-of-Fate direction is N.W.

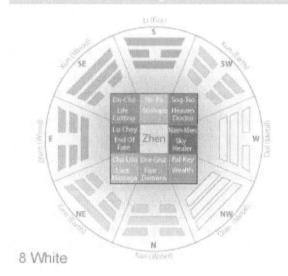

Geomantic Houses for the Trigram Zhen

The house faces S.W. and sits N.E. The element is Earth. The trigram is Gen. The number is "8." Color is white.

(1) Name-Men – Sky Healer direction is West.
(2) Sog-Tso - Heavenly Doctor direction is S.W.
(3) Pal-Key - Wealth direction is N.W.
(4) Pal-Key – Luck Messenger peace direction is N.E.

Your inauspicious directions are:

(5) Nö-Pa- Injury direction is South.
(6) Dre-Gna – Five Demons direction is North.
(7) Dü-Chö– Life Cutting direction is S.E.
(8) Lu-Chey – End-of-Fate direction is East.

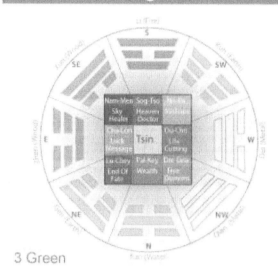

3 Green

Geomantic Houses for the Trigram Tsin

The house faces West and sits East. The element is Wood. The trigram is Zhen. The number is "3." Color is Green.

(1) Name-Men – Sky Healer direction is S.E.
(2) Sog-Tso - Heavenly Doctor direction is South.
(3) Pal-Key - Wealth direction is North.
(4) Pal-Key – Luck Messenger peace direction is East.

Your inauspicious directions are:

(5) Nö-Pa- Injury direction is S.W.
(6) Dre-Gna – Five Demons direction is N.W.
(7) Dü-Chö– Life Cutting direction is West.
(8) Lu-Chey – End-of-Fate direction is N.E.

4 Green

Geomantic Houses for the Trigram Li

The house faces N.W. and sits S.E. The element is Wood. The trigram is Xun. The number is "4." Color is Green.

(1) Name-Men – Sky Healer direction is East.
(2) Sog-Tso - Heavenly Doctor direction is North.
(3) Pal-Key - Wealth direction is South.
(4) Pal-Key – Luck Messenger peace direction is S.E.

Your inauspicious directions are:

(5) Nö-Pa- Injury direction is N.W.
(6) Dre-Gna – Five Demons direction is S.W.
(7) Dü-Chö– Life Cutting direction is N.E.
(8) Lu-Chey – End-of-Fat

The Eight Directions

Four Good Directions:

#1 Nam-Men (Sky Healer)

This is the best one. Good for doctors. The direction where the Sky Healer can be found is the most favorable for healing and medicine. Its image is that of the Sun.

This is the best direction and kind of Qi for a house to face, and represents the life-generating force. Often this direction is recommended for the location of the front door, when a new building is being constructed. This very energizing direction indicates prosperity, excellent business opportunities, plus nobility, statesmanship, and respect, in general. It belongs to the element Wood.

#2 Sog-Tso (Healthy Life)

This is the next best direction. The direction of Vitality and Health is the second-best, and it is traditional to sleep with one's head pointed in this direction. It is good for healing and generating vitality. Its image is the thunderbolt (Dor-Je) or vajra.

This, second-best direction for Qi relates to health and safety matters. It bodes well for finding the best teachers and doctors, and all noble and helpful people. It belongs to the element Earth.

#3 Pal-Key (Generating, Glorious)

The direction of Generating Wealth is the third best direction, and it is best to buy or obtain things from this direction, if possible. Its image is the Knot of Eternity.

Still good, but a lower good. It is auspicious to buy or obtain things from this direction.

This is the third-best direction for Qi and is favorable for longevity, good health, and all kinds of relationships, romantic and otherwise - friends, lovers, co-workers. It also bring public and communication skills. It belongs to the Metal element.

#4 Cha-Lön (Luck Messenger)

The direction of the Auspicious Messenger is the fourth best direction (least beneficial of the "good" directions), and it is considered favorable to travel in this direction. Its image is the swastika.

This is the fourth and lowest of the best directions for Qi, and brings stability and calm, as well as a certain amount of luck. It is recommended for areas where studies or meditation take place, and enhances organizational and management skills.

Tibetan Astrology

Four Bad Directions:

#5 Nö-Pa (Evil Spirit)

The direction of the Evil Spirit is the least bad of the four bad directions. However, this direction should be avoided, under threat of injury and accidents. Its image is the triangle.

This is the weakest or least problematical of the four inauspicious forms of Qi, and refers to loss of money, quarreling, lawsuits, and, in general, obstacles to achieving one's goals.

#6 Dre-Gna (Five Ghosts)

The direction of the Five Demons or Five Ghosts is the second worst of the four bad directions, and should be avoided, lest it expose one to various demonic influences. Its image is five points, like on a die.

This is the second worst of the four inauspicious forms of Qi, and refers to loss, the loss of friends, relatives, and also to fire, accidents, and negative influences, in general. This includes back-stabbing, betrayal, arguments, minor accidents.

#7 Dü-Chö (Devil-Cutting)

The direction of the Devil Cutting is the 3rd worst direction, meaning next to the worst one. It must be avoided under threat of life and limb, and one has to protect one's life force. Its image is the dagger, called in Tibetan "Phurbu."

This, the next to the worst of the four inauspicious forms of Qi refers loss in relationships, bad sexual experiences, and treachery, in general. Also: lawsuits, physical injury, surgery, arguments, and legal problems. The element is Water.

#8 Lu-Chey (Body Destroying)

The direction of the Body Destroying is the very worst direction and should be avoided at all costs. It is said to threaten a particular part of the body depending upon the particular Parkha involved. Its image is a body part of some kind.

This is the worst of the four inauspicious forms of Qi, and is considered to be life threatening, promoting illness, incurable diseases, misfortune, bankruptcy, robbery, and unproductive career, and other fateful occurrences. The element is Metal.

The four good directions are the good side or Zan-shi, while the bad side or four bad ones are Gnen-shi.

The Eight Direction Portents

Eleven Directions

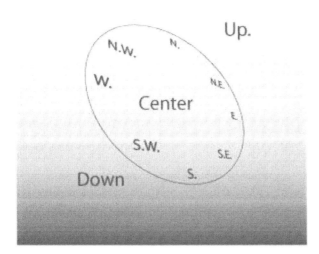

Elements and Directions

From very early on in Tibetan and Chinese history the five elements were associated with the four directions and the stable center. In Tibet there is constant reference to the Three Times (past, present, and future) and the Ten Directions. The ten Directions were, of course, East, South, West, North, and the four intermediate directions S.E., S.W., N.W., and N.E. To these were added the directions above and below. Perhaps the center or non-direction should be added to this, to give 11 directions!

In ancient China, and it is also true today, the future is said to always come to us from one of these directions, so the pairing of the five elements with the four compass directions (and center) took place very early on in history. We either get up and go in a particular direction, or something appears from a direction, coming our way.

Certain directions were favored, like the southern direction, since (at least in the Northern Hemisphere) that was the direction from which the most light and warmth came - the direction of the Sun each day.

South - Fire Element

The South - Element Fire

The direction of the Sun appears always to make a large arc through the sky each day toward the South. The Sun's rays come from the South and cast shadows toward the North.

Since the Sun is where all warmth, light, and life comes from, that direction has always had a special importance. It is obvious that the Sun reaches its maximum heat and strength in the summer, so summertime became associated with heat, brightness, and the color Red, and, of course, Fire. The Fire Element is associated with the direction south.

North - Water Element

The North - Element Water

If south represents summer, heat, and dryness, then north (its opposite) represents winter, cold, and wetness. The north corresponds to the element Water and its traditional color is black (darkness) or a deep blue (indigo). If the front door and windows of houses in the Northern Hemisphere all tend to point to the south, then the north side of homes tend to be closed and windowless. Literally, the north side of a house never sees the rays of the sun, but is always shrouded in shadow. If the south is welcomed, then the north is to be avoided. If the south brings the harvest and plenty, then the north points to mean times and dearth.

The East - Element Wood

The direction east is where the Sun rises, where morning comes, and where things revive and start moving for the day. In most cultures the direction East is considered a very auspicious direction. For one, East is associated with spring and the return of life and green to the world once again. Everything is revitalized and grows, takes fresh form, and has new renewed life, after the harshness of winter. Spring is associated with the Wood Element and, naturally enough, with the color green.

Tibetan Astrology

The West - Element Metal

The West is where the Sun sets, where day ends, and night comes forth. If East is associated with springtime, then West is associated with autumn, with the gathering of the harvest and the preparing for winter - husbanding things inside. In the Eastern culture, the direction West is associated with death and dying, and burial. Amitabha, the Buddha of the West direction, oversees the setting sun, death and burial - preparing us to transition to the bardo or intermediate states.

Unlike here in the West, where the color of death is always black and we dress in black for funerals, in China the traditional color of death is white, and white cloth indicates the dead and funerals. The Metal Element is the element of the direction West and its color is white or silver-gray.

The Center - Element Earth

In the study of the five elements, four of the elements (Wood, Fire, Metal, and Water) indicate a particular kind of movement and change. The so-called fifth element's (Earth) phase is that of no movement - non-movement.

It is positioned at the center, and the other four elements rotate and move around it. The element Earth is stationary, solid, and unmoving. The color of the Element Earth is, of course, earth colored, some shade of yellow or ochre. The Earth element refers to land and all that is most stable and unmoving.

The 27 Yogas of Combination

The 27 "Yogas of Combination" are an integral part of Vedic (Indian) astrology that has carried over into the Tibetan astrology, although the calculation is slightly different from the Hindu methods. The Combination Yogas are usually numbered from "0" to "26," although they are sometimes referenced from"1" to "27."

The Tibetan combination or yoga is arrived at by the simple addition of the Sun and Moon (Tropical zodiac), with no additional sum added to that result. Using a modulus of 27, the combined sum of the Sun and Moon is reduced to a number from 0 to 26, which amounts to dividing the zodiac into equal 27 13-degree 20' segments.

Modern astrologers may want to use the exact positions of the Sun and Moon at birth, but Tibetans tend to be more concerned with determining the Yoga for a particular day, having group practice in mind. Usually the longitude of the Moon is calculated for daybreak, but the longitude of the Sun is frequently used for the time during the previous lunar day (tithie) ended. In other words, there can be at times a considerable discrepancy between the time that the longitudes for the Sun and Moon were calculated.

Modern students of Tibetan astrology are trying to sort things out. I prefer to know the instantaneous postion of the Suna and Moon – which yoga is right now.

Each of the 27 yogas is given a unique interpretation as shown below.

Tibetan Astrology

01 Victorious (Vishkambha)

Victorious over enemies. Vanquishes. Secures wealth and property. More spiritual minded than materialistic, naturally interested in all divine and occult information, and probably have natural predictive talents.

The Day: This yoga brings the power of attraction, and the ability to have victory over your enemies. Not good for making friends or visiting with relatives.

02 Contented (Priti)

Enjoys contented life. Very well-liked by others, including the opposite sex, and the favor is more than returned. May come under the control of the will of the wives of others. Natural workaholics, sincere and generally altruistic.

The Day: This is a very auspicious yoga and virtually every kind of activity is enhanced. Also: perfect for loving all beings, even the not-so-friendlies.

Tibetan Astrology

03 Long Lived

Good health, energy, and longevity. Natural leadership qualities, and a drive for success. Quite happy. Their judgments are accepted by society, without objection.

The Day: This yoga promotes longevity and health, good for almost any activity - everything in abundance. Very favorable.

04 Good Fortune

Happy, comfortable life, filled with good fortune and many opportunities. Could travel and live in distant places. Food, its preparation and quality, is a life-long interest and perhaps a good career move.

The Day: This yoga is favorable for all things, health, longevity, spirituality, wealth - the works. All is well.

05 Voluptuous

Voluptuous. Very sexually oriented, sensual, and taken with lovely bodies, their own or others. Interested in the visual arts, and artistic by temperament. They like good food and possessions. Generally happy, they tend to have good luck.

The Day: A very agreeable yoga, one favoring the accomplishment of most anything, in particular taking action. Strong sexuality.

06 Many Obstacles

Could be numerous obstacles and difficulties, so beware of anger and developing resentment. They love all the arts - visual, music, and film. They are hard to influence and have a natural sense of their own integrity. Quarrelsome.

The Day: One of the so-called "empty" yogas, during which even good deeds may lead to bad results, and the exhaustion of resources. Depletion.

07 Magnanimous

Virtuous and noble in their outlook. Magnanimous, always charitable, and up to noble deeds. Could accumulate wealth. Others are impressed by their actions.

The Day: This yoga is good, in general, and in particular good for clearing away ignorance (what we ignore), and performing good and noble deeds.

08 Enjoyment

Enjoys the hospitality, wealth (and sometimes the spouses) of others. They love and are skilled at communication, and generally like research and scientific knowledge. Strong minded. Like science fiction.

The Day: This yoga is good for the increase in wealth and family - possessions in general. Receiving goods or wealth.

09 Confrontational

Confrontational and perhaps quarrelsome. Anger. A contrarian. Naturally flexible and athletic bodies. Very active and sharp minds. Proud of their skills.

The Day: This is not a favorable yoga, but rather one where enemies, divisiveness, thieves, illness, gossip, and bad people have rule. Real harm can result from any activities.

10 Troublesome

Could have troublesome personality, fueled by flawed morals or loose ethics. Bad habits, or forced to deal with the rough elements in society. They have strong will power and are hard workers.

The Day: A difficult yoga, and one during which illness may arise. If not illness, then a lost of place or a decline in position.

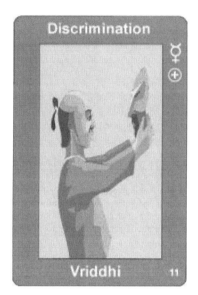

11 Discrimination

Smart, with a natural sense of discrimination, and strong powers of elocution. Tends to opportunism. Get better with age. They love their children and family, and this is worth more than gold to them. Very analytical and intelligent.

The Day: This is a very favorable yoga, during which prosperity of all kinds, wealth, health, longevity, etc. will increase and problems and enemies will decrease.

12 Immovable

Very steady, persistent, with strong powers of concentration. May accumulate wealth. They are physically robust and show great patience. Reliable.

The Day: This is a favorable yoga, one during which intellectual powers, wealth, and all that is good is on the increase, and it is easy to fulfill what you wish. Obstacles and enemies vanish.

13 Fierce

Fierce, prone to anger, and short tempered. Can have a tendency to be harsh or cruel, with a penchant for causing harm to self and others. The world sees them as eccentric, and tends to stay away. They have unusual eyes.

The Day: In general, a bad yoga for most everything. In particular for the health and the physical body. Best to stay away from those who are not well during this time.

14 Thrilled With Joy

A natural leader, they love a good time, jokes, and all kinds of humor. Very intelligent. Loves a party. Could be wise and famous. They are truthful and demand that others be as well.

The Day: A very positive yoga, an indicator of good luck, spiritual growth, and, in general, an increase in all endeavors.

15 Thunderbolt

Strong, even forceful, but also can be unpredictable, and even lecherous. May be wealthy. They have very analytical minds and excel as critics and inspectors. Others may view them as troublemakers.

The Day: A yoga that indicates the fulfillment of wishes and dreams. Also favorable for working through conflicts and resentment.

16 Accomplishment

Accomplished and very skillful, perhaps in more than one career. Tends to support and protect others, in particular, the unfortunate. They are very intelligent, with strong minds. May have many children.

The Day: A very favorable yoga, in particular for spiritual growth, but one in which all projects are encouraged. Plans are fulfilled.

17 Adversity

More than their share of surprises, even mishaps, and possibly reversals of fortune. They are determined in the face of adversity, and usually win out. Can become hard and cruel due to the hardships of their life. May be picky and unreliable at times.

The Day: In general, a yoga during which gossip and loose talk prevail, one in which it is difficult to succeed, and plans go astray. Is said to be bad for travel, in particular, abroad.

18 Lap of Luxury

They loves their ease and a life of comfort, living in the lap of luxury. Could be lascivious. They like religion and philosophy, and are naturally courageous and self-confident.

The Day: A yoga during which to receive dharma initiations and direction, and one in which you can rise above and conquer your enemies.

19 Obstruction

Natural born fighters, they may have to control this tendency. May encounter many obstacles and obstructions in the course of life, perhaps a cause of a natural irritability. May be wealthy. Often small in stature.

The Day: Not a favorable yoga, but one in which you will have to face problems and adversaries, head on, or find your wealth and position taken from you. Fear and injury may be at hand.

20 Benevolent

Learned, very religious, probably wealthy, but very much honored by authority and the public. Cool, calm, and collected. People naturally look up to and respect them.

The Day: A very favorable yoga, one during which almost anything may be accomplished, wealth is received, and the life span extended.

21 Accomplished

Virtuous. Very commanding personality, controlled, pleasant, and interested in spiritual matters. They have a pure heart and natural sincerity, and are usually very successful. Like to acquire knowledge of all kinds.

The Day: A good yoga in which to push forward and accomplish projects and desires, and one during which wealth and lifespan are extended.

22 Amendable

Righteous. Fine etiquette, always well behaved, and very accomplished manners. They are devoted to duty and usually get what they set out for, which may irritate others. They love music and the arts.

The Day: A perfect yoga for doing business, exchanging goods, and generally enjoying good health and happiness.

23 Auspicious

Naturally beautiful. Very fine body and personality, and probably quite wealthy and content, but perhaps some health problems. Could be irritable. Others may envy them. They naturally command the respect of others.

The Day: A favorable yoga, in general, in particular for ritual and religious activities.

24 Brilliance

Impatient, perhaps even impulsive, always changing their mind, with resulting unsteadiness. Could be flighty and quarrelsome. Could be quite a scholar.

The Day: A good yoga for travel or remaining put, during which all things are enhanced or hold steady.

25 The Priest

A natural sense of discernment and good judgment, well liked and trusted by others. Ambitious. They love philosophy and religion and are not afraid to sacrifice for what they believe in. Others love and respect them.

The Day: A yoga of joy and happiness, long life, increased wealth, and reputation. In particular, religious activities are enhanced.

26 The Chief

Naturally brilliant. Very educated or interested in education and knowledge in general. Perhaps will be well off. Helpful to others. Normally gentle, unless provoked. May have to monitor their health.

The Day: A good yoga for being a student, in particular, as relates to a teacher or a spiritual master. All things are accomplished.

27 The Divider

Naturally somewhat of a schemer, with strong critical faculties. May be both physically and mentally overbearing. They may be naturally graceful and beautiful and love the fashion of the day. They may be wealthy. They march to the beat of a different drummer.

The Day: Not a good yoga, in particular when it comes to relations between men and women. Can be deceit, resentment, blame.

The Days of the Week

Practically all nations use the day of the week coupled with one of the traditional planets. In Tibetan astrology, the planets are related to the days of the week in the same way that we do here in the West. Thus Sunday is the day of the Sun, Monday of the Moon, Tuesday of Mars, Wednesday of Mercury, Thursday of Jupiter, Friday of Venus, and Saturday of Saturn.

DAY	Tibetan	Planet	Element
Sunday	Nyi-Ma	Sun	Fire
Monday	Da-Ba	Moon	Water
Tuesday	Mik-Mar	Mars	Fire
Wednesday	Lhak-Pa	Mercury	Water
Thursday	Phur-Bu	Jupiter	Wind
Friday	Pa-Sang	Venus	Earth
Saturday	Pen-Pa	Saturn	Earth

The days of the week are either auspicious or inauspicious, as described on the following pages.

Tibetan Astrology

Sunday

Sunday, the day of the sun, is what Tibetans call an "angry" day, not an auspicious day, and one during which most work does not progress toward completion. It is said to favor official ceremonies, war, fire, religious ceremonies, and preparing medicines.

Favorable Action, (Astrology calc, not reading)
Favorable for Giving a Name
Favorable for Irrigation/water
Favorable, Move New House
Favorable for Planting Trees
Not Favorable Journeys (particularly to East, South OK)
Favorable: Marriage
Not Favorable for Starting a Fight
Not Favorable for Medicine (giving remedies)
Not Favorable for planting (cultivating OK)
Not Favorable for Taking on Responsibility
Not Favorable for Trade (selling)

Tibetan Astrology

Monday

Monday, the day of the Moon, which has been called the body that represents the soul of women, is considered favorable for most things, including agriculture, preparing medicines, trade, divination, astrology, and various religious rites. It is considered a bad day for war, making judgments, funerals, taking journeys, and violence in general.

Favorable for Fire rituals
Favorable for Building
Favorable for Starting a Fight
Favorable for Medicine (making remedies)
Favorable for Taking on Responsibility
Favorable Journeys to North
Not Favorable Journeys to West
Not-Favorable Marriage
Not Favorable for planting trees or Agricultural
Not Favorable for Funeral
Not Favorable for Irrigation/water
Not Favorable, Move New House
Not Favorable for Trade (selling)

Tibetan Astrology

Tuesday

Tuesday is the day of Mars, and one of the "angry" days. It has been called the planet of the soul of men. It is favorable for sports, war, and military action, and conquest, in general. Also good for many rituals, in particular of a wrathful nature. It is not good for marriage, purification, and travel.

Favorable Action (Astrology)
Favorable Action (Purification)
Favorable for Agricultural
Favorable for Building
Favorable for Irrigation/water
Favorable for Wealth (Djzambhala)
Favorable for Medicine (making remedies)
Favorable, Move New House
Favorable for Planting Trees
Favorable for Taking on Responsibility
Favorable for Trade
Not Favorable Journeys (except South)
Favorable Marriage,
Not Favorable for Banishing Negativity, Fire Rituals
Not Favorable for Funeral

Tibetan Astrology

Wednesday

Wednesday is the day of Mercury, is good for travel, commerce, marriage, and most activities. It is said to be good for receiving things, but not for giving them. It is not favorable for funerals, war, and preparing medicines.

Favorable for Banishing Negativity
Favorable for Fire rituals
Favorable for Starting a Fight
Favorable for Giving a Name
Favorable: Moving to New House
Favorable: Taking on Responsibility
Not Favorable Journeys (except Northand East)
Not-Favorable for Marriage
Favorable for Building and for Trade (selling)
Not Favorable Action (Purification)
Not Favorable for Agricultural
Not Favorable for Funeral
Not Favorable for Giving a Name
Not Favorable for Irrigation/water
Not Favorable for Medicine (giving remedies)
Not Favorable for Planting Trees

Tibetan Astrology

Thursday

Thursday is the day of Jupiter, often called the planet of the Bodhisattva, and is good for spirituality of all kinds, ordination, rituals, mantras, and the like. Also good for study, marriage, trade, and most things. It is not good for war, funerals, and the practice of magic.

Favorable Action (Astrology)
Favorable Action, Petitions
Favorable for Agricultural
Favorable for Building
Favorable for Funeral
Favorable for Giving a Name
Favorable for Irrigation/water
Favorable for Planting Trees
Favorable for Trade
Favorable for Journeys (except to North)
Favorable for Marriage
Not Favorable for Fire rituals
Not Favorable for Starting a Fight
Not Favorable for Medicine (making remedies)

Tibetan Astrology

Friday

Friday

Friday is the day of Venus, and is best for learning, overcoming obstacles, magical rituals, trade, agriculture, surgery, astrology, and travel. It is not good for arguments, negotiations, funerals, and the slaughter of animals.

Favorable Action (Astrology)
Favorable Action, Petitions
Favorable for Agricultural
Favorable for Building
Favorable for Giving a Name
Favorable for Medicine (making remedies)
Favorable, Move New House
Favorable for Taking on Responsibility
Favorable for Trade
Favorable for Journey West (Not Favorable to South)
Favorable for Marriage
Not Favorable for Funeral
Not Favorable for Starting a Fight

Tibetan Astrology

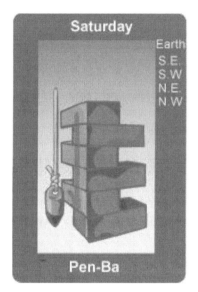

Saturday

Earth
S.E.
S.W
N.E.
N.W

Pen-Ba

Saturday

Saturday, the day of Saturn, is best for receiving goods, but not giving things away. It is good for building, new homes, magical rituals, agriculture, and astrology. It is not good for war, working with fire, surgery, preparing medicines, and giving gifts.

Favorable for Action (Astrology)
Favorable for Agricultural
Favorable for Banishing Negativity
Favorable for Building
Favorable for Funeral
Favorable for Giving a Name
Favorable for Local Deities
Favorable for Medicine (surgery)
Favorable for Move to New House
Favorable for Planting Trees
Favorable for Trade
Favorable for Journeys (except to West)

Good and Bad Days

Animal	Basis	Power	Success	Obstacle	Upheaval	Enemy
Mouse	20th Day	6th Day	3rd Day	26th Day	19th Day	23rd Day
Ox	17th Day	14th Day	12th Day	12th Day	18th Day	5th Day
Tiger	5th Day	27th Day	9th Day	14th Day	12th Day	3rd Day
Hare	11th Day	27th Day	12th Day	25th Day	25th Day	18th Day
Dragon	3rd Day	12th Day	17th Day	8th Day	9th Day	11th Day
Snake	13th Day	12th Day	6th Day	8th Day	9th Day	6th Day
Horse	17th Day	12th Day	6th Day	20th Day	5th Day	27th Day
Sheep	8th Day	1st Day	2nd Day	20th Day	5th Day	27th Day
Monkey	8th Day	1st Day	2nd Day	9th Day	10th Day	17th Day
Bird	14th Day	7th Day	25th Day	3rd Day	11th Day	24th Day
Dog	9th Day	27th Day	5th Day	11th Day	3rd Day	12th Day
Pig	2nd Day	8th Day	11th Day	28th Day	3rd Day	12th Day

These tables relate the animal years to the lunar days of the month. Remember, these are not calendar days, but the "Tithie" or Lunar Day. Each yearly animal sign (birth or current) combines with certain lunar days of the month to create special qualities for that day. The qualities are "Basis" or foundation, "Power" or strength, "Success or achievement, "Obstacles" or blockage, "Upheaval" or stress, and "Enemy" or adversaries.

The qualities are pretty much self explanatory. Look up your natal animal and note which lunar days possess particular qualities for you.

Tibetan Astrology

```
Animal|Best|Good|Bad  |
Mouse |WED |TUE |SAT  |
Ox    |SAT |WED |THU  |
Tiger |THU |SAT |FRI  |
Hare  |THU |SAT |FRI  |
Dragon|SUN |WED |THU  |
Snake |TUE |FRI |WED  |
Horse |TUE |FRI |WED  |
Sheep |FRI |MON |THU  |
Monkey|FRI |THU |TUE  |
Bird  |FRI |THU |TUE  |
Dog   |MON |WED |THU  |
Pig   |WED |TUE |SAT  |
```

Good and Bad Weekdays

The animal sign for your birth (or the current year) also has good and bad weekdays that go along with it. Keep in mind that each weekday stands for a particular planet, as well. For each animal sign, there are best, good, and bad days of the week. The above table lists these for each animal sign.

Good and Bad Days for Travel

Irrespective of animal sign or any other indicators, in Tibet there are good and bad lunar days for travel. Remember these are not calendar days, but the thirty lunar days that make up a lunar month. Here is a list of the good and bad days for travel.

Waxing	Waning
01 Good	16 Good
02 Good	17 Good
03 Good	18 Good
04 Bad	19 Bad
05 Good	20 Good
06 Bad	21 Bad
07 Good	22 Bad
08 Bad	23 Bad
09 Good	24 Good
10 Good	25 Good
11 Good	26 Good
12 Good	27 Good
13 Good	28 Good
14 Bad	29 Bad
15 Bad	30 Bad

Planet	Weekdays	Ele.	Directions
Sun	Sunday	Fire	South
Moon	Monday	Water	North
Mars	Tuesday	Fire	South
Mercury	Wednesday	Water	North
Jupiter	Thursday	Wood	East
Venus	Friday	Iron	West
Saturn	Saturday	Earth,	S.E.,N.W.,S.W., N.E.)
Rahu	All Days	All Elements, all directions	

The day after the New Moon is the 1st day of the month and whatever day of the week it is colors the whole month with the tone or quality of the planet of that day (Sun for Sunday, etc.). Also, the son of the 1st day's element is equally powerful for that whole month. The mother of that element is medium powerful, and the friend or enemy is bad for that entire month.

Example: if Sunday is the first day of the month (as above) then every Sunday in that month is very powerful, but if Sunday is friend or enemy (or otherwise not very good), then it dampens the best day of the month.

Further, if the first day of the month falls on a Sunday, then the planet is Sun, and the element Fire. Therefore, the son of Fire is Earth. Earth is powerful for the month. The Mother of Fire is Wood, so Wood is medium powerful that month. The friend of Fire is Iron, and the enemy of Fire is Water. Fire and Water are bad for that month.

The Portent Techniques
Bad Years

Tibetans have a wide variety of methods to disclose the inauspicious years in your life. I must admit that it was somewhat disheartening when I sat down one day and did all the calculations and then integrated them into a single list of "bad" years. There were very, very few good years left. But that is the way it is.

Below are a number of the most well-known of the so called "portents." Chief among them is Lo-Khak, the most important of the critical year warnings, Dun-Zur is second and so on, in order of difficulty.

Lo-Khak

Every 12th year, whenever the animal sign for the current year is the same as your birth year, is considered Lo-Khak - anauspiciuos. This is the most feared of the inauspicious-years techniques.

You might expect that a year which has the same sign as your birth year would be lucky or auspicious. Not in the Tibetan system. If your birth sign and the current year sign are the same (every 12 years) then this, as mentioned, is an example of LO-KHAK, which is very inauspicious. For men, the year before a LO-KHAK (termed NANG-KHAK) is a little more difficult than the LO-KHAK itself, for women, it is the year after LO-KHAK (termed CHI-KHAK) that is difficult.

Tibetan Astrology

Lo-Khak Years

12 to 13 years age
24 to 25 years of age
36 to 37 years of age
48 to 49 years of age
60 to 61 years of age
72 to 73 years of age
84 to 85 years of age
96 to 97 years of age

During a Lo-khak year, there are reputedly six months of particular danger when you are most vulnerable :

Bird Month	2nd half very bad
Dog Month	1st half very bad
Pig Month	Passable
Mouse Month	2nd half very bad
Ox Month	1st half very bad
Tiger Month	Passable
Hare Month	2nd half very bad
Dragon Month	Entire month very bad
Snake month	1st half very bad
Horse month	Passable
Sheep Month	2nd half very bad
Monkey Month	Entire month very bad
Bird Month	1st half very bad

If the current year sign is the 7th or opposite of the birth sign, this is called Dun-zur and is also bad. If the current year is the 5th sign (i.e. Dragon-Monkey), then this is also not good. If the current year is same element as the birth element, then this too is not-so-good.

Tibetan Astrology

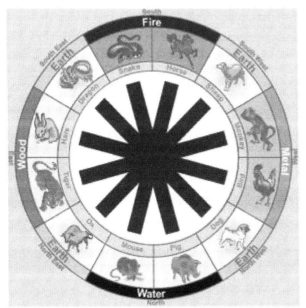

Dun-Zur

The `Dun-Zur' refers to the 6th animal sign, the animal sign exactly opposite your birth animal sign. Any year that matches that opposite sign will be a year to be careful in.

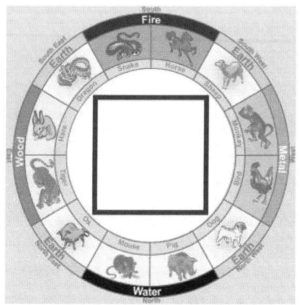

Shi-Shey

This refers to the 4th animal sign (either way) from the birth sign. When either of those signs are the current sign for the year, it is `Shi-Shey'.

Gu-Mik

The Gu-Mik or 9th-Eye Spot. When the animal sign for the year is the ninth animal sign from the birth animal sign, this is Gu-Mik – an inauspicious year. For example, I am born in the year of the Snake. The 9th animal sign from the snake (counting the Snake as #1) is the Ox. That would be tough year.

Mewa Gu-Mik

When the Mewa for the current year is the same as the Mewa for your birth year, this is Mewa Gu-Mik, an inauspicious year.

Tibetan Astrology

Death Spot: Dur-Mik

This is a little more complicated and is based on the current animal sign and particular Parkhas. When they line up, we have the `Death Spot' year, although it is not as horrible as the name suggests. Here is the table:

Tiger and Hare	Khon
Horse and Snake	Khen
Bird and Monkey	Gin
Remainder of Signs	Zon

When the descending Parkha is in any of the above signs, that is Dur-Mik, the Death Spot. For example, if the current year is the Hare and your descending Parkha for that year is Khon, you have Dur-Mik.

Black Year

If the current year animal is Tiger, Monkey, Pig, or Snake and the current yer Mewa is 2 BLACK, then the year is a "Balck Year," inauspicious.

Same Element

When the element for the year is the same element as the birth element, the year is considered inauspicious.

Tibetan Astrology

Log-Men: The Reverse-Year

Log-Men is a form of progression and the word means "not turning back" or "Not returning." It is s method of counting using the following steps:

(1) Determine the Son of the birth Power element, using the standard element cycle as described elsewhere in this book.

(2) Then combine that element with the animal sign Tiger (for men) or Monkey (for women) to form one of the sexagenary pairs, and element and animal combination.

(3) Using the sixty year cycle of element-animal pairs, start counting from the pair (derived above) and count to your current age. Remember that first pair counts as number one, and so on.

Count through the sexagenary pairs until you reach the current age and stop.

(4) The animal of the pair where you stopped is your current Log-Men.

If the current Log-Men is the animal sign Dog, this is called Nam-Go, the `Sky Door.' If it is the animal sign of the `Pig', it is Sa-Go, the `Earth Door'.

On `Sky Door' years, one must be careful of high places, while on `Earth Door' years, one must be careful of underground places.

For females, Nam-Go is the year of the Dragon and Sa-Go is the year of the Snake.

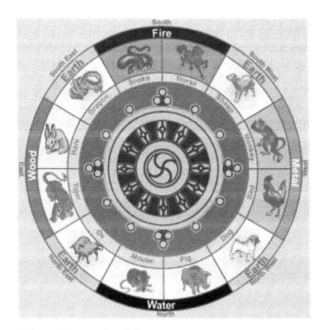

The Tomb Signs

I first learned of the concept of Tomb Signs from Sange Wangchuck, who introduced me to Tibetan astrology. The subject is also covered in considerable detail in Gurme Dorje's Ttibetan Elemental Divination Paintings" and Edward Henning's book "Kalachakra and the Tibetan Calendar." I refer you to those works for more complete details. The concept of Tomb Signs is something almost unique to Asian astrology, but it does have a distant cousin in Western astrology. First, let's understand it.

To understand it, we need to know that the twelve Asian animal signs (like the Western zodiac signs, in this respect) have a traditional order in which they are displayed, based on the compass directions and the five elements. They form a cycle or circle.

Tibetan Astrology

The element "Wood" (or air) is always shown on the left (toward the East), the element "Iron" on the right (toward the West), the element "Fire" at the top (to the South), and the element "Water" at the bottom (to the North). That takes care of four of the elements, leaving only the element "Earth" to place.

The element "Earth" is placed not in a single spot. It is considered to be placed in the center (we all stand on earth), but also on all four corners of the wheel, what are called on the compass, the intermediate directions: S.E., S.W., N.E., and N.W.

In Western astrology, these would be the 45-degree angles or "Semisquares," if we were considering aspects. On the Tibetan wheel of the animal signs, these are called the "Four Tomb Signs," and are considered inauspicious.

They are called Tomb Signs because they are of the "Earth" element and because our bodies are eventually buried in the earth. The similarity with Western astrology, as pointed out, is that the tomb signs and the semisquares are both 45-degree angles, which to many astrologers (including this one) are more "Square" than the 90-degree squares, when it comes to interpretation.

Tibetan Astrology

Each of the 12 animal signs has an associated element and direction. This is traditional:

Animal	Element	Direction	Tomb Sign
Mouse	Water	North	Dragon
Cow	Earth	N.E.	Dragon
Tiger	Wood	East	Sheep
Hare	Wood	East	Sheep
Dragon	Earth	S.E.	Dragon
Snake	Fire	South	Dog
Horse	Fire	South	Dog
Sheep	Earth	S.W.	Dragon
Monkey	Iron	West	Ox
Bird	Iron	West	Ox
Dog	Earth	N.W.	Dragon
Pig	Water	North	Dragon

Each of the animal signs and elements has a Tomb Sign based on the animal element. It is shown above in the fourth column.

There are different methods of examining the tomb signs and the years in an individual's life which they affect. I will list some of them, but I refer you to Edward Henning's book "Kalachakra and the Tibetan Calendar" for complete details. I also have programmed them in my software for the PC, "Tibetan Astrology."

The Eight Trigrams

This is a method of progressing the trigrams, and there is a different method for men and women. The technique is based on determining the trigram that is associated with the corresponding tomb sign.

(1) Starting with the birth year, use the trigram Li for men, and the trigram Kham for women.

(2) Determine the Life Element for the year of birth. The table for this is located elsewhere in this book.

413

Tibetan Astrology

(3) Given the Life Element for the birth year, use this table:

Life Element	KEY	Tomb Sign
Iron	KEY Trigram Gin	Tomb Sign of Ox
Water	KEY Trigram Zon	Tomb Sign of Dragon
Wood	KEY Trigram Khon	Tomb Sign of Sheep
Fire	KEY Trigram Khen	Tomb Sign of Dog
Earth	KEY Trigram Zon	Tomb Sign of Dragon

(4) Count from the birth year as "Li" for men and "Kham" for women. Count to the KEY Trigram in the order of the trigrams for Men; count to the KEY Trigram in the REVERSE order for men. When you reach the KEY Trigram, that year is considered a Tomb Sign and inauspicious.

Example for 1941 Female-Iron-Snake Year

1944 Wood-Monkey4 Khen
1952 Water-Dragon 4 Khen
1960 Iron Mouse   4 Khen

Mewa Progression

This is a method of progressing the nine Moles or Mewa in relation to the tomb signs, but the details are too complex to go into here. The net result is that these years marked are considered inauspicious. Method:

(1) Note your natal Mewa, the Mewa for the year you were born.

(2) Look up the years after the birth when the same Mewa number occurs that was present at birth. These are considered inauspisious.

Example for 1941 Female-Iron-Snake Year

1950 Iron-Tiger   5 Yellow
1959 Earth-Pig   5 Yellow
1968 Earth Monkey 5 Yellow

414

Tibetan Astrology

Combined Method

One counts through the 60-year Animal-Element cycle, but backward. The starting point depends on the animal sign for the year of birth, and then counting continues until the tomb sign for the natal power element is reached, which amounts to the age of nine for each of us.

To do this calculation, you will need a list of the sexagenary Element-Animal cycle, the 60 combinations, which can be found elsewhere in this book.

(1) First note the Animal for the year you were born. In my case, 1941 (Iron-Snake), my animal is the Snake.

(2) Next, locate your birth Animal in the following table:

Animal: Mouse, Pig, Ox, Dragon, Sheep, Dog:
KEY: Start with the Wood-Mouse year.

Animal: Tiger, Hare:
KEY: Start with the Fire-Hare year.

Animal: Horse, Snake:
KEY: Start with the Iron-Horse year.

Animal: Bird, Monkey
KEY: Start with the Water-Bird year.

(3) In the sexagenary list of element-animal combinations (60-year cycle), go to the KEY Element-Animal combination as derived in step #2, and begin to count BACKWARD, making sure to count the Key Element-Animal combination as #1.

(4) Count BACKWARD to the ninth pair, which will be the tomb sign for the natal Power Element. As mentioned, count the Key Element-Animal combination as #1.

(5) This Ninth combination is one of the four Tomb Signs. This will be the ninth year from the birth year, counting the birth year as #1.

(6) Now, using the result of step #5 as your first, count forward through the element-animal combinations in years in multiples of 12. In this case, the first of the twelve numbers will be the element-animal pair following the result of step #5.

(7) Summary: the ninth pair back (Step #4) and all multiples of 12 (going forward) are considered inauspicious years.

Example: 1941 Iron-Snake. Animal "Snake' starts with the combination "Iron-Horse," and the following:

1949 Water-Dog
1961 Iron Dog
1973 Earth-Dog
1985 Fire-Dog
1997 Wood-Dog
2009 Water-Dog

Note: the 5th year following the year the count begins is called an "accursed year," and if it happens to coincide with one of the four tomb-sign years (9th, 21, 33, 45, 57, 69, 81.. year), it is much worse, called a "crucial multiple of nine."

Major/Minor Tomb Signs

This technique produces four results in a 60-year period, what is called:

Major Personal Tomb Year
Minor Personal Tomb Year
Major Enemy Tomb Year
Minor Enemy Tomb Year

Tibetan Astrology

Any of these four are considered inauspicious, with the Major Tomb being worse than the Minor, and the Enemy being worse than the Personal. Here is the method:

(1) Find Starting Animal:

Natal Animal Hare or Tiger: Start with Hare.
Natal Animal Horse or Snake: Start with Horse.
Natal Bird or Monkey: Start with Bird.
Natal Animal Mouse, Pig, Sheep, Ox, Dragon, or Dog: Start with Mouse.

(2) Determine Power Element for natal year. The Power Element is the same as the element in the element-animal combination for that sexagenary year.

(3) Determine the Enemy of the Power Element (you will need it later on) following the standard Destruction Cycle as follows:

Natal Element	Enemy Element
Wood	Metal
Fire	Water
Earth	Wood
Metal	Fire
Water	Earth

(3) Combine the Power Element and the starting Animal (step #1) to form one of the sexagenary combinations and start with that combination as your #1.

(4) Now count BACKWARD using the following table of Animal signs:

Natal Tiger or Hare:

Natal Power Element plus Sheep year = Major Tomb
Natal Power Element plus Ox year = Major Tomb
Enemy Power Element plus Sheep year = Major Enemy-Tomb

417

Enemy Power Element plus Ox year = Major Enemy-Tomb

Natal Horse or Snake:

Natal Power Element plus Dog year = Major Tomb
Natal Power Element plus Dragon year = Minor Tomb
Enemy Power Element plus Dog year = Major Enemy-Tomb
Enemy Power Element plus Dragon year = Minor Enemy Tomb

Natal Bird or Monkey:

Natal Power Element plus Ox year = Major Tomb
Natal Power Element plus Sheep year = Major Tomb
Enemy Power Element plus Ox year = Major Enemy-Tomb
Enemy Power Element plus Sheep year = Major Enemy-Tomb

Natal Mouse, Pig, Dragon, Sheep, Dog, or OX:

Natal Power Element plus Dragon year = Major Tomb
Natal Power Element plus Dog year = Major Tomb
Enemy Power Element plus Dragon year = Major Enemy-Tomb
Enemy Power Element plus Dog year = Major Enemy-Tomb

(5) As mentioned above, count backward until you reach (using the two Animal signs indicated for your natal animal above) either of the two signs for your sign indicated in Step #4, AND that have either the same Power Element OR its Enemy Element (Step #3).

(6) Keep going until all four of the major and minor tomb signs are found in the sixty year cycle.

(7) These years are inauspicious, with the major being more inauspicious than the minor.

Tibetan Astrology

Major Personal Tomb
Minor Personal Tomb
Major Enemy Tomb
Minor Enemy Tomb

Any of these four are considered inauspicious, with the major being worse than the minor.

For my Birth in 1941, the following results are:

1955 Wood-Sheep Major Enemy
1961 Iron-Ox   Minor Tomb
1985 Wood-Ox   Minor Enemy
1991 Iron-sheep Major Tomb

Solitary Tomb Sign

Based on the Power or Destiny Element conjoined with a particular animal sign for men and another for women, and counting backward through the subject's Tibetan age (one year more than Western age) until one of the four tomb signs is reached. Method:

For males, start with animal MOUSE and the Power Element for the year of birth. For example, 1941 has a Power Element of Iron, so would start with the Iron-Mouse.

For females, start with animal BIRD and the Power Element for the year of birth. For example, 1941 has a Power Element of Iron, so would start with the Iron-Bird.

COUNTING is backward by nine, according to the age of the subject, remembering that Tibetans count one from the first point.

So… year 9, 18, 27, 36, 45, 54, 63, 72, 81, 90. etc.

At certain times, particularly at the beginning and the end of some years, the ninth year will occur with a tomb sign, making this particular year more difficult. These are:

For those born in the Tiger or Hare year, the 18th year will be inauspicious for men, and the 36th year will be inauspicious for women.

For those born in the Horse or Snake year, the 36th year will be inauspicious for men, and the 18th year will be inauspicious for women.

For those born in the Bird or Monkey year, the 54th year will be inauspicious for men, and the 72nd year will be inauspicious for women.

For those born in the Pig, Ox, Sheep, Dog, or Dragonyear, the 72nd year will be inauspicious for men, and the 54th year will be inauspicious for women.

Example: 1941

1949 Earth-Ox	Water-Dragon
1958 Earth-Dog	Water-Sheep
1967 Fire-Sheep	Wood-Dog
1976 Fire-Dragon	Wood-Ox

12-Year Animal

This is the reoccurrence of the natal animal sign, every twelve years and is considered inauspicious. In fact, in my experience this 12th year is taken so seriously that some lamas and rinpoches will go into strict retreat for the entire year. Most at least give some observance. This is called Lo-Khak and was described earlier.

Tomb Sign: Ox

This is one of the animals that comprise what are know as the Four Tomb Signs, being the Ox Dragon, Sheep, and Dog. These four animals are situated at the four corners of the directional wheel, the 45-degree angles, at what are called the four intermediate directions. These four signs are said to be not favorable and to be avoided, and when they occur as the animal for the year, month, day, or hour they portend obstacles.

Tibetan Astrology

Tomb Sign: Dragon

This is one of the animals that comprise what are know as the Four Tomb Signs, being the Ox Dragon, Sheep, and Dog. These four animals are situated at the four corners of the directional wheel, the 45-degree angles, at what are called the four intermediate directions. These four signs are said to be not favorable and to be avoided, and when they occur as the animal for the year, month, day, or hour they portend obstacles.

Tibetan Astrology

Tomb Sign

Khon
S.W.
Wood

Sheep

Tomb Sign: Sheep

This is one of the animals that comprise what are know as the Four Tomb Signs, being the Ox Dragon, Sheep, and Dog. These four animals are situated at the four corners of the directional wheel, the 45-degree angles, at what are called the four intermediate directions. These four signs are said to be not favorable and to be avoided, and when they occur as the animal for the year, month, day, or hour they portend obstacles.

Tomb Sign: Dog

This is one of the animals that comprise what are know as the Four Tomb Signs, being the Ox Dragon, Sheep, and Dog. These four animals are situated at the four corners of the directional wheel, the 45-degree angles, at what are called the four intermediate directions. These four signs are said to be not favorable and to be avoided, and when they occur as the animal for the year, month, day, or hour they portend obstacles.

Shi-Shey

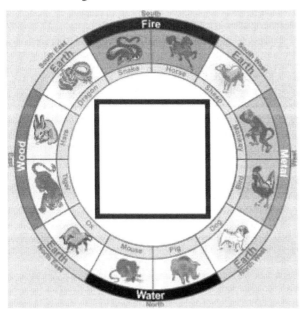

She-Shey: Dragon, Sheep, Dog, Ox

SHI-SHEY refers to the signs that are four up and back from the birth-year sign. For example, my birth in 1941 in the year of the snake makes the Tiger and the Monkey signs fit this description (always counting from the birth sign as one). If the current year is either of these signs, then it is called SHI-SHEY -- which is not so good.

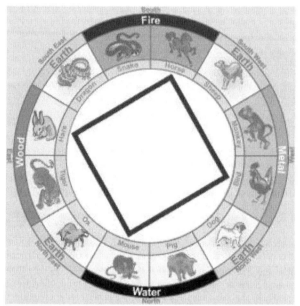

She-Shey: Mouse, Hare, Horse, Bird

Also, for the current year sign ... count four up and four back and the months of that year with the same sign are called "black months." If these months are Tiger, Monkey, Pig or Snake then the whole month is black, but the first ten days are the worst, the 2nd ten days a little better, and the last ten days better still.

Tibetan Astrology

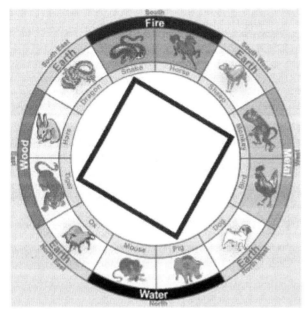

She-Shey: Tiger, Snake, Monkey, Pig

If the month signs are the Mouse, Horse, Bird and Hare, then the days of the month from 10th-20th are the bad ones. If the month signs are Ox, Sheep, Dog or Dragon, then the last 10 days of the month are bad. All days being calculated from the New Moon.

Thun-Sun (3 Friends)

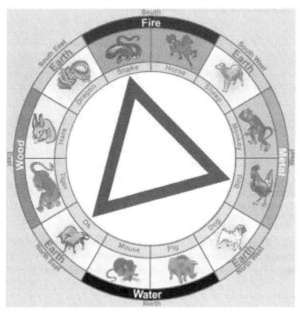

3 Friends = Bird, Ox, Snake

The Chinese call them the three friends, but the Tibetans call them the three destroyers. Here the Bird, Ox, and Snake are marked.

Tibetan Astrology

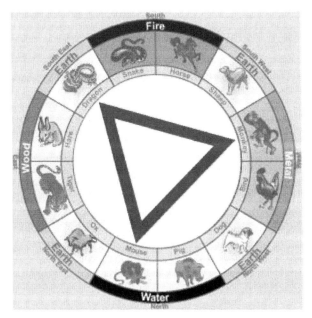

3 Friends = Mouse, Dragon, Monkey

The Chinese call them the three friends, but the Tibetans call them the three destroyers. Here the Mouse, Dragon, and Monkey are marked.

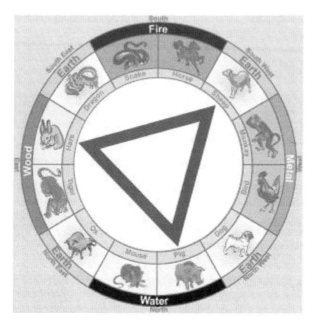

3 Friends = Pig, Sheep, Hare

The Chinese call them the three friends, but the Tibetans call them the three destroyers. Here the Pig, Sheep, and Hare are marked.

Tibetan Astrology

3 Friends = Tiger, Horse, Dog

The Chinese call them the three friends, but the Tibetans call them the three destroyers. Here the Tiger, Horse, and Dog are marked.

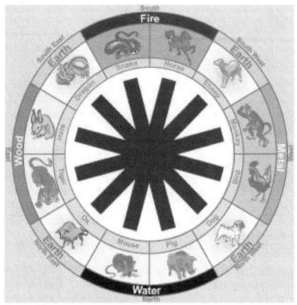

Dun-Zur

The worst or opposites (Dun-zur: which means 7th corner or opposite) are:

Sign, DUN-ZUR (Opposite Sign)

Horse	Mouse
Ox	Sheep
Tiger	Monkey
Hare	Bird
Dog	Dragon
Snake	Pig

Tibetan Astrology

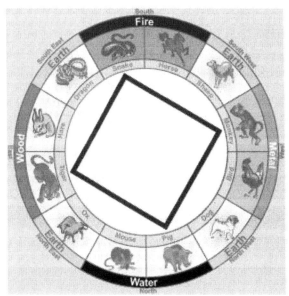

Animal Sign Power: Best

The signs have different power or importance as shown in the table below. By far, the most important are the first four, which are similar to what are called cardinal signs in Western astrology. These signs rule the four major directions as follows: Tiger (East), Pig (North), Monkey (West), and Snake (South).

Signs	Power
Tiger, Monkey, Pig, Snake	Best

Tibetan Astrology

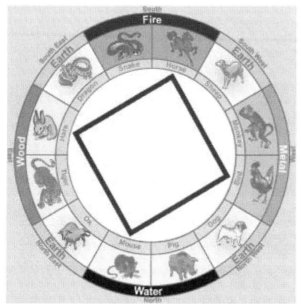

Animal Sign Power: Moderate

The signs have different power or importance as shown in the table below. The next most important are the four which are similar to what are called mutable signs in Western astrology. These are the next best set of four animal signs.

Signs	Power
Mouse, Horse, Bird, Hare	Next-Best

Tibetan Astrology

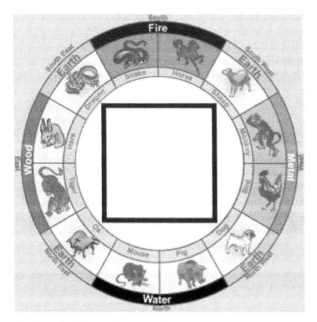

Animal Sign Power: Least

The signs have different power or importance as shown in the table below. The least important are the four which are similar to what are called fixed signs in Western astrology. These are the least powerful set of four animal signs.

Signs	Power
Ox, Dragon, Sheep, Dog	Least

The 24 Solar or Seasonal Sectors

Inherited from Chinese Astrology are the 24 solar terms or seasonal indicators, starting with the moment that the Sun reaches 15-degrees of the tropical sign Aquarius, which is usually somewhere around February 4th or 5th. These solar terms mark the beginning (zero degrees) and the middle (15-degrees) of each zodiac sign, using the tropical zodiac.

Zodiac Point	Season
15° Aquarius	Coming of Spring
00° Pisces	Rain Water
15° Pisces	Insects Awaken
00° Aries	Spring Equinox
15° Aries	Clear and Bright
00° Taurus	Grain Rain
15° Taurus	Summer Starts
00°Gemini	Grain Full
15° Gemini	Last Planting
00° Cancer	Summer Solstice
15° Cancer	Small Heat
00° Leo	Great Heat
15° Leo	Autumn Starts
00° Virgo	Cooling
15° Virgo	White Dew
00° Libra	Fall Equinox
15° Libra	Black Dew
00° Scorpio	Deep Frost
15° Scorpio	Winter Begins
00° Sagittarius	Small Snow
15° Sagittarius	Great Snow
00° Capricorn	Winter Solstice
15° Capricorn	Slight Cold
00° Aquarius	Great Cold

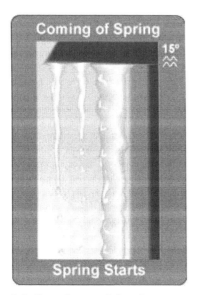

01 Coming of Spring

The Coming of Spring occurs when the Sun enters the 15th degree of the tropical sign Aquarius, and marks the first impulse of spring.

02 Rain Water

Rain Water occurs when the Sun enters the tropical sign Pisces, and marks when the snow begins to show some rain.

Tibetan Astrology

Insects Awaken

15°
♓

Spring Winds

03 Insects Awaken

Insects Awaken occurs when the Sun enters the 15th degree of the tropical sign Pisces, and marks the first stirring of life, and the advent of the great wind of spring.

Tibetan Astrology

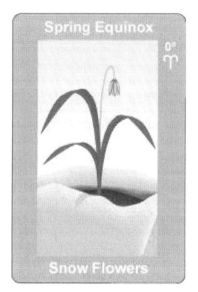

04 Spring Equinox

The Spring Equinox occurs when the Sun enters the tropical sign Aries, and marks the point of equal day and night.

Tibetan Astrology

05 Clear and Bright

Clear & Bright occurs when the Sun enters the 15th degree of the tropical sign Aries, and marks the time when the first seedlings may be planted. The sap is rising.

Tibetan Astrology

06 Grain Rain

Grain Rain occurs when the Sun enters the tropical sign Taurus, and marks the point when the rains are plentiful, and most crops can be planted.

Tibetan Astrology

07 Summer Starts

Summer Starts occurs when the Sun enters the 15th degree of the tropical sign Taurus, and marks the time when the songbirds return.

08 Grain Full

Grain Full occurs when the Sun enters the tropical sign Gemini, and marks the point when the flowers are blooming and everything is growing.

Tibetan Astrology

09 Last Planting

Last Planting occurs when the Sun enters the 15th degree of the tropical sign Gemini, and marks the time when all crops must be planted. This is the time when the first spring crops are picked.

Tibetan Astrology

10 Summer Solstice

The Summer Solstice occurs when the Sun enters the tropical sign Cancer, and marks the point of the longest day of the year.

Tibetan Astrology

11 Small Heat

Slight Heat occurs when the Sun enters the 15th degree of the tropical sign Cancer, and marks the time when the heat comes on in earnest.

12 Great Heat

The Great Heat occurs when the Sun enters the tropical sign Leo, and marks the point of the greatest heat, also when the summer rains come, and rivers swell.

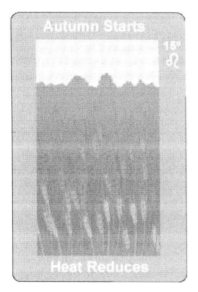

13 Autumn Starts

Autumn Starts occurs when the Sun enters the 15th degree of the tropical sign Leo, and this marks the first reduction in heat..

14 Cooling

Cooling occurs when the Sun enters the tropical sign Virgo, and marks the point when the rivers recede and it begins to cool.

Tibetan Astrology

15 White Dew

White Dew occurs when the Sun enters the 15th degree of the tropical sign Virgo, and this marks when it starts to get cold.

16 Fall Equinox

The Fall Equinox occurs when the Sun enters the tropical sign Libra, and marks the point when day and night are of equal length.

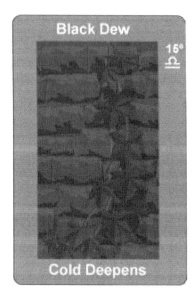

17 Black Dew

Black Dew occurs when the Sun enters the 15th degree of the tropical sign Libra, and this marks when it starts to get colder, and frost is coming.

18 Deep Frost

Frost Starts occurs when the Sun enters the tropical sign Scorpio, and marks the point when the frosts begin, and the birds head south.

Tibetan Astrology

19 Winter Begins

Winter Begins occurs when the Sun enters the 15th degree of the tropical sign Scorpio, and this marks when the cold grows stronger and ice forms.

Tibetan Astrology

20 Small Snow

Small Snow when the Sun enters the tropical sign Sagittarius, and marks the point when the winter cold begins to take a grip.

Tibetan Astrology

21 Great Snow

Great Snow occurs when the Sun enters the 15th degree of the tropical sign Sagittarius, and this marks when the cold is pretty much permanent.

22 Winter Solstice

The Winter Solstice is when the Sun enters the tropical sign Capricorn, and marks the point of the longest night of the year.

Tibetan Astrology

23 Slight Cold

Lesser Cold occurs when the Sun enters the 15th degree of the tropical sign Capricorn, and this marks when the cold is deepening.

24 Great Cold

The Great Cold is when the Sun enters the tropical sign Aquarius, and marks the point of greatest cold.

The 28 Great Conjunctions

The 28 Great Conjunctions are an integral part of Tibetan astrology and represent the meeting of the daily planet (planet of the weekday) and the current lunar mansion. The Nakshatras or Lunar Mansions are 27 divisions of the zodiac (tropical for Tibetan astrology) through which the Moon travels. Each Nakshatra is 13°20' of the zodiac, so the moon enters a new Nakshatra about once a day. When we know what Nakshatra the Moon is in AND what day of the week it is, we come up with the 28 Great Conjunctions. These 28 yogas or conjunctions combine the day-of-the-week and the Nakshatra.

The resulting combination is a traditional keyword and image that is important on that particular day.

28-Conjunctions: 01 Joy

Favorable. Good for just about everything, in particular receiving wealth and gifts.

29-Conjuctions: 02 The Staff of Time

Very unfavorable. Brings fear of destruction and loss.

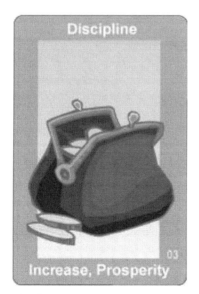

28-Conjunctions: 03 Discipline

Favorable, bringing great increase in wealth and possestions. Prosperity.

28-Conjunctions: 04 Multitude

Happiness in Love

Favorable. Brings happiness, good luck, and the love of a woman. Good for mothers and children.

28-Conjunctions: 05 Youth

Favorable. All dreams and wishes will be attained.

Tibetan Astrology

28-Conjunctions: 06 Raven

Unfavorable. Brings arguments, wars, destruction, and loss. Marriage should not be undertaken.

Tibetan Astrology

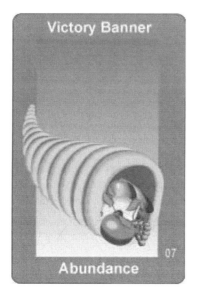

28-Conjunctions: 07 Victory Banner

Favorable. Brings great prosperity, and an abundance of wealth and possessions.

Tibetan Astrology

28-Conjunctions: 08 Knot of Eternity

Favorable. Brings the accumulation of precious gems.

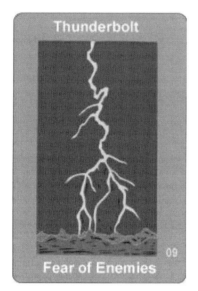

28-Conjunctions: 09 Thunderbolt

Unfavorable. Said to bring fear of natural phenomena, such as lightning.

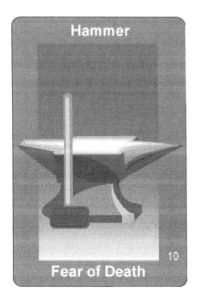

28-Conjunctions: 10 Hammer

Unfavorable. Said to bring the fear of death in the near future.

28-Conjunctions: 11 Parasol

Favorable. Indicates strong action, the removal of obstacles, and the conquering of enemies.

28-Conjunctions: 12 Friends

Favorable. Indicates that one will find and meet with friends.

28-Conjunctions: 13 Attainment

Favorable. An indication that one will obtain wealth, in abundance.

Tibetan Astrology

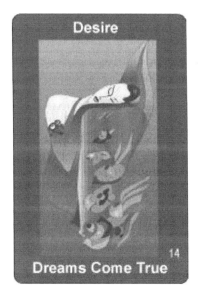

28-Conjunctions: 14 Desire

Favorable. Indicates the realization ideas and wishes. Dreams come true.

28-Conjunctions: 15 Firebrand

Unfavorable. An indication that arguments and conflict will ensue.

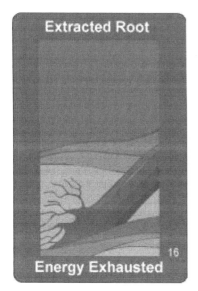

28-Conjunctions: 16 Extracted Root

Unfavorable. An indication that one's lifespan may be diminished.

28-Conjunctions: 17 Death Lord

Unfavorable. An indication that death may occur.

28-Conjunctions: 18 Arrow

Unfavorable. An indication that the mind will be in turmoil, with disruptive thoughts holding sway.

Tibetan Astrology

28-Conjunctions: 19 Success

Favorable. Whatever you begin will be completed.

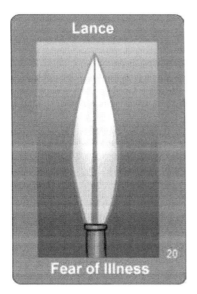

28-Conjunctions: 20 Lance

Unfavorable. An indication that the fear of illness or illness itself will arise.

28-Conjunctions: 21 nectar

Favorable. An indication that enemies and obstacles will be destroyed.

Tibetan Astrology

28-Conjunctions: 22 Pestle

Favorable. An indication that understanding will arise.

28-Conjunctions: 23 Elephant

Favorable. All undertakings will be successful.

Tibetan Astrology

28-Conjunctions: 24 The Tigress

Favorable. Good for travel. The proper vehicle will be found.

Tibetan Astrology

28-Conjunctions: 25 Exhaustion

Unfavorable. An indication that friends and possessions will diminish.

28-Conjunctions: 26 Movement

Favorable. All action, if undertaken promptly, will succeed.

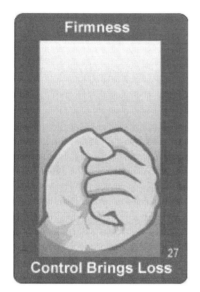

28-Conjunctions: 27 Firmness

Unfavorable. Seizing control or moving too fast will bring losses.

Tibetan Astrology

28-Conjunctions: 28 Increase

Favorable. An indication that wealth and prosperity will increase.

The Ten Yogas: Element Combinations

Perhaps the single most-used technique in Tibetan astrology are the day-of-the-week element and the Lunar Mansion element combinations, often called the Ten Yogas. Layman and clergy alike use the Ten Yogas. They are always included in any almanac, large or small.

Each weekday has a particular element permanently attached to it, so these 28 yogas or conjunctions combine the day-of-the-week element and the Nakshatra.

Combination	Meaning
Earth + Earth	Accomplishment
Water + Water	Nectar
Earth + Water	Youth
Fire + Fire	Advancement
Wind +Wind	Excellence
Fire + Wind	Powerful
Earth + Wind	Deficiency
Water + Wind	Disharmony
Earth + Fire	Burning
Fire + Water	Death

Tibetan Astrology

Table of Weekday Element and Lunar Mansion

Tibetan	Sanskrit	Element
00 Ta-Kar	Asvini	Wind
01 Bhya-Nnye	Bharani	Fire
02 Min-Druk	Kritika	Fire
03 Nar-Ma	Rohini	Earth
04 Go	Mrgasira	Wind
05 Lak	Ardra	Water
06 Nap-So	Punarvasti	Wind
07 Gyal	Pusya	Fire
08 Kak	Aslesa	Water
09 Chu	Magha	Fire
10 Dre	Purva-Phalguni	Fire
11 Wo	Uttar-Phaluni	Wind
12 Me-Shi	Hasta	Wind
13 Nak-Pa	Citra	Wind
14 Sa-Ri	Svata	Wind
15 Sa-Ka	Visakha	Wind
16 La-Tsem	Anuradha	Earth
17 Nron	Jestha	Earth
18 Noop	Mula	Water
19 Chu-Do	Purvasadha	Water
20 Chu-Me	Uttarasadha	Earth
21 Dro-Shin	Uttara-Asadha	Earth
22 Non-Dre	Dhaniastha	Water
23 Non-Dru	Satabhisak	Earth
24 Drum-To	Purvabaad-rapada	Fire
25 Dru-Me	Uttara-bhadrapada	Water
26 Namdru	Revati	Water

Tibetan Astrology

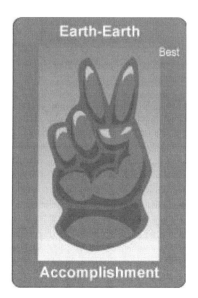

Element: Earth-Earth

This is considered the single most auspicious element combination and is an indication that whatever one desires will be fulfilled.

Tibetan Astrology

Element Water-Water

This is the second most auspicious of the combinations, and is an indication of an increase in strength and greater longevity.

Tibetan Astrology

Element: Earth-Water

This, the third most auspicious combination, is an indication of great happiness.

Tibetan Astrology

Element: Fire-Fire

This is the most auspicious of the "Favorable" combinations, and is an indication that what is needed will be obtained.

Tibetan Astrology

Element: Wind-Wind

This is the second most auspicious of the "Favorable" combinations, and is an indication of success in all that is undertaken.

Tibetan Astrology

Element: Fire-Wind

This is the third most auspicious of the "Favorable" combinations, and is an indication of good fortune and luck.

Tibetan Astrology

Element: Wind-Earth

This is the first of the third of the "Unfavorable" combinations, and is an indication that wealth and possessions will decrease.

Tibetan Astrology

Element: Wind-Water

This is the second of the "Unfavorable" combinations, and is an indication of a separation of friends and relatives.

Tibetan Astrology

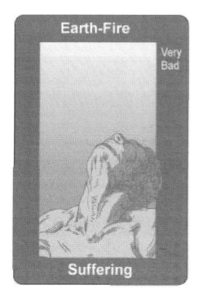

Earth and Fire

This is the third and worst of the unfavorable combinations and is an indication of suffering. Nothing good will work out on an earth-fire day.

Tibetan Astrology

Element: Fire-Water

This is the most "Unfavorable" combinations, and this is an indication that life is threatened and great care should be taken.

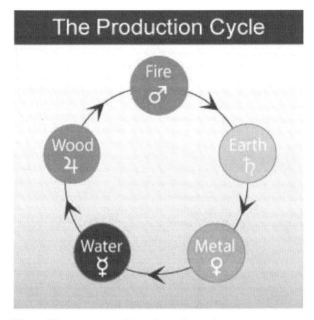

Five Elements: Production Sequence

The Five Elements in Chinese philosophy can be traced back to around 300 B.C. and the work of the philosopher Chou Yen. From the very beginning these five elements were not seen as static states, but were considered phases or stages in the ongoing cyclic process of life. They were said to produce one another, to exhaust one phase and turn into the next. This is what is called the Production Sequence of the five elements, and it takes the order of Wood, Fire, Earth, Metal, and Water, each changing into the next as follows:

Wood burning produces...
Fire, which in the end leaves ...
Earth, as ashes, from which we derive...
Metal, which can be melted down to flow like ...
Water, which nourishes ...
Wood, and so on.

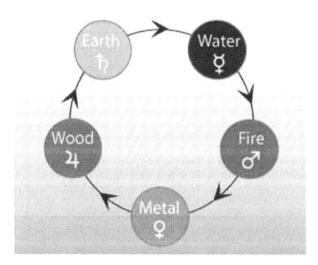

The Destruction Sequence

At the other extreme is what is called the Destruction Cycle. For each element, there is one other element which is particularly adversarial, and "enemy," so to speak. The Destruction Cycle or sequence is: Wood, Earth, Water, Fire, and Metal, and is often explained:

Wood absorbs or eats...
Earth, which drinks up and removes...
Water, which puts out ...
Fire, which melts ...
Metal, which cuts up...
Wood, etc.

In fact, in terms of explanation, the destruction sequence makes more immediate sense than does the production sequence. In comparison to the production sequence, the destruction cycle is simply every other element, in strict rotational order.

503

Tibetan Astrology

In the production cycle, the element that produces the second element is said to be the "mother" of that element, and the element that is produced is said to be the "child" of the mother element. Therefore, the mother element in every combination is considered very important to the health and welfare of the child element. The child element looks to the mother for nourishment and support, just as a human child depends on its mother.

It should not surprise us to learn that when any element is attacked or threatened by the destruction or adversarial element, increasing the strength of the mother element of that element under attack will strengthen and protect it. In fact, as you will soon learn, each of the five elements has a direct and identifiable relationship with each of the other four. From this stems much of the familiar feng-shui remedies, which consist of strengthening or weakening the various elements in order to arrive at a functioning harmony of the elements.

When all is said and done, many of the techniques used for elements has to do with examining the elements relating to the various compass directions, determining their strength or weakness, and adjusting or weakening the strength of one element or another.

Tibetan Astrology

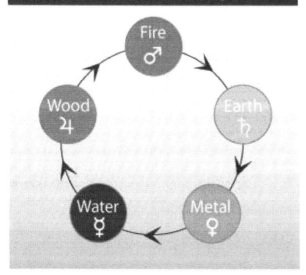

The Production Cycle

Sometimes there is a need to enhance or make an element stronger, to somehow make or produce more of that element, and this is called the Production Cycle. The Production Cycle reveals which element is the mother (or producer) of any given element, and this is what is called the Production Cycle, one element is the mother of or produces another. Here is that cycle:

Wood produces Fire
Fire produces Earth
Earth produces Metal
Metal produces Water
Water produces Wood

There are a number of explanations why a particular element is the mother on another, and some seem more logical than others. One of the more popular ones goes like this:

Tibetan Astrology

Burning Wood produces Fire
Fire produces ash or Earth
Earth contains ore and therefore produces Metal
Metal, when cold, produces Water on its surface
Water produces Wood or plants

There are several variations on how the production cycle of the Five Elements may be derived. While these might be helpful aids to memorize the sequence, they (or parts of them) require stretches of credulity that I find hard to make.

Easier to handle is declaring that these five elements are linked together in a cycle. Once that is known, then the phases of any cycle have to be similar, like the cycle of the breath or the heartbeat - expansion and contraction, and on around.

This cyclic sequence places Wood at the direction East, Fire toward the South, Metal toward the West, and Water to the North. The element Earth is placed in the center of the diagram.

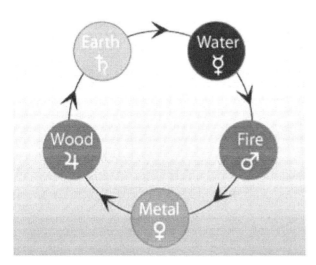

The Destruction Cycle

On the other hand, sometimes an element is just too strong, overbearing, or too dominant. It needs to be removed, and thus the Destruction Cycle. For each element there is a nemesis or anti-element that will destroy it and cause it to go into decline. Here is the list.

Water destroys Fire
Fire destroys Metal
Metal destroys Wood
Wood destroys Earth
Earth destroys Water

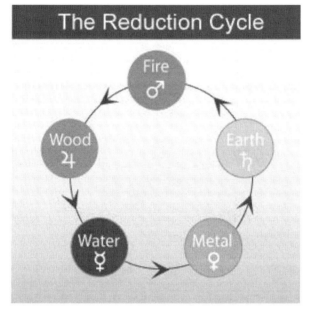

The Reduction Cycle

Sometimes you don't want to out-and-out destroy an element, but just weaken or deemphasize that element. Each element has another element that reduces or weakens that element. This is called the Reduction Cycle, and it is the exact opposite of the Production Cycle. This cycle is also called the Control Cycle, because any element can be controlled (reduced) through invoking a second element.

For example, in the production cycle we know that Water produces (is the mother of) Wood. In the reduction cycle, therefore, Wood weakens Water, by the fact that it drains it in order to make the Wood grow stronger.

For every element there is another element that drains or reduces it. Here is the list:

Earth reduces Fire

Tibetan Astrology

Fire reduces Wood
Wood reduces Water
Water reduces Metal
Metal reduces Earth

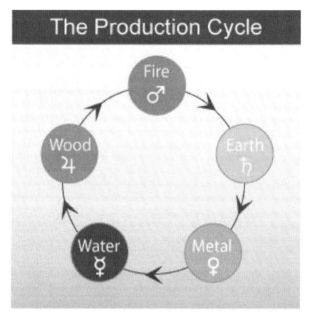

The Production Cycle

The Masking Cycle

The Masking Cycle, which is the same as the Production Cycle, is not as frequently mentioned as the other cycles, and has to do with supporting or propping up an element that, for one reason or another, is being destroyed or harmed.

Using the Masking Cycle, we apply an element to shore up or support the element being destroyed or harmed. The Masking Cycle is:

Wood produces Fire
Fire produces Earth
Earth produces Metal
Metal produces Water
Water produces Wood

Tibetan Astrology

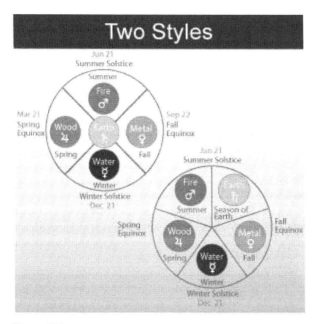

Two Diagrams

So there are two major diagrams that are used to illustrate the sequence of the five elements and, unfortunately, each has flaws. In the one on the left, we see the production sequence clearly, but there is no convenient way to line up five elements with the four seasons, the four directions, and so forth.

With the diagram at the top left, we see how four of the elements line up with the four directions and four seasons, but the Earth element is out of sequence. It is in the center.

The diagram at the lower right shows how the Chinese tradition integrates the Earth element into a five-seasonal approach. Both methods and diagrams are used, but when all is said and done, the four-seasonal diagram (upper left) seems to be the default.

The Five Elements Interpreted

Element: Earth

Element: Earth -- Stable, strength, ground.

The element Earth corresponds to stability and solidity, and among the planets, to Saturn. It typically is placed in the center of the compass, rather than having an outward direction. Earth is the least active element and indicates stasis and duration, often connected with building construction and land. Earth is patient and stubborn.

Tibetan Name: Sa
Color: Yellow
Physical: Flesh
Nature: Stabilize

Tibetan Astrology

Element: Fire

Fire -- Strong, instant, hot, warmth.

The element Fire corresponds to summer among the seasons, the direction South on the compass, and the planet Mars among the planets. Fire brings drive and excitement to a situation - sheer energy. Like its season, Summer, Fire likes things hot and dynamic.

Physically, Fire is related to the heart. Fire's mother is Wood, so Fire always needs something to feed upon, something to stimulate it.

Tibetan: Me
Color: Fire (me), Red, Warmth, Heat, To Burn
Physical: Warmth, Heat
Nature: To Burn

Tibetan Astrology

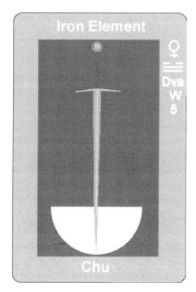

Element: Iron (Metal)

Iron -- Strong, cutting, direct, weapon, changing. (similar to earth)

The element Metal corresponds to autumn among the seasons, the direction West on the compass, and the planet Venus among the planets. Metal is related to business, and to gathering in or accumulation - harvesting. Metal sorts the wheat out from the chaff.

Physically Metal governs the lungs. Metal's mother is Earth, so it needs plenty of stability and support.

Tibetan Name: Chak
Color: White
Physical: Bones
Nature: Hardening

Tibetan Astrology

Element: Water

Water -- Soft, fluid, clear-seeing, flowing, smooth. Often connected to the blood and emotional concerns

The element Water corresponds to winter among the seasons, the direction North on the compass, and the planet Mercury among the planets. Water and the planet Mercury indicates fluidity and communication, sparkling intellect and all things relating to the mind - intelligence. Water governs travel.

Physically Water relates to the kidneys.

Tibetan Name:	Chu
Color:	Blue
Physical:	Blood
Nature:	Moistening

Tibetan Astrology

Element: Wood

Wind (wood, air) -- Long-life, beauty, good

Jupiter among the planets. The keyword for Wood is "Creativity." Wood indicates outward growth and development, a phase where things are born and come into existence. As Jupiter rules Wood, this suggests that this element is progressive, leads us onward, a way into the future, the next logical step.

Wood is supple and strong - fresh. The Yang quality here overcomes the Yin quality, so this is the element of springtime and strong new growth. We expand and continue through Wood. Physically, Wood is said to relate to the liver, the gallbladder, and to digestion, in general. Wood's mother is Water, so Wood always needs moisture or feelings to thrive.

Tibetan Name:	Shing
Color:	Green
Physical:	Veins
Nature:	Cause to Grow

Tibetan Astrology

Western Elements

Element Interplay

The Five Elements (Wood, Fire, Earth, Metal, and Water) are not to be confused with the four elements used by the ancient Greeks (Fire, Air, Earth, and Water), the scientist's Periodic Table of Elements, or the four elements (earth, air, water, fire) as used in astrology. There is no direct relationship between these three groupings of elements and the way the Five Elements are used in China. Although they have many similarities, they are not the same.

Natural Elements

And let's not confuse the Chinese/Tibetan Element "Fire" with the fire in a campfire or the element "Earth" with simple soil, although there is obviously some correspondence.

In the chemist's Periodic Table of Elements, elements refer to physical states like iron, nickel, copper, and so on. The Greeks and others refer to elements as static qualities that make up our universe - things or states. The earth is made up of these elements. The astrological elements Fire, Air, Earth, and Water are also states or qualities.

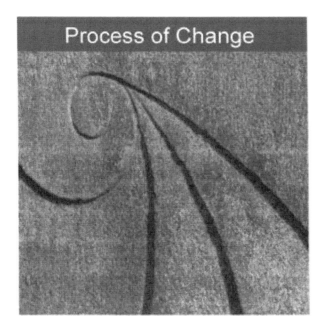

Process and State

The Chinese elements are not so much "things" or states as they are simultaneously both processes and states. In other words, think of the Chinese/Tibetan Five Elements as active and always in motion - pure energy in flux. These five elements mark the kind of changes going on around us all the time, rather than something permanently there and static.

It may be more helpful to think of the Five Elements as reminders or pointers as to the phase or kind of change going on around us rather than something in themselves. When we refer to the element Wood, we are pointing to the act of starting forth and initial growth. Wood is not a place or a state, but a state of change or a way something is changing, in this case developing or growing. That is the general idea.

Process of Change

Process of Change

When all is said and done, these five elements are of critical importance to Tibetan Astrology and feng-shui-stle analysis as they constitute one of the principal forms through which astrology is used by the lay person and through which feng-shui remedies can be applied.

In the cycles of change going on in the life around us, everything is constantly turning into its opposite and back around again - transformation. One thing leads to the next, and then turns into the next, and so on. The Five Elements mark distinct phases or ways of changing in the endless cycles of life.

Element Remedies

Elemental remedies are key to understand, if you want to work with feng-shui. Without grasping the theory of the five elements and how to balance them, them, most of the modern traditional of feng-shui will remain a mystery to you. So, although this type of theory can at first appear to be difficult to understand, you will be much better off if you just bite the bullet and learn it now. Otherwise, you will close the door on most of what feng-shui remedies are all about. I know this from experience, because I tried to ignore or put it off for a long time, and finally have to return to the beginning and just learn it. It really helps.

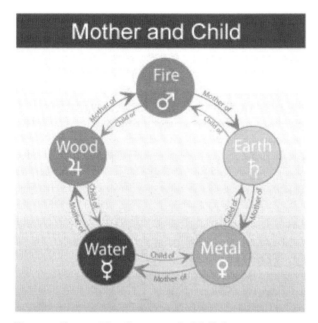

Remedies - Mother and Child

The most important elemental relationship may be that of mother and child. In the standard elemental sequence Wood, Fire, Earth, Metal, and Water, when considered in a clockwise rotation, the element clockwise to any other element is the child. The element counterclockwise to any other element is the mother.

The mother produces the child and is capable of providing or withholding nourishment and strength.

In fact, any particular element is positioned between its mother and its child, each of which are capable of affecting its health and strength. In fact, manipulating the mother and child of an element as a standard way to increase or decrease its strength and power.

If an element is too strong and that increased strength is causing problems in the feng-shui analysis, one remedy is to simply decrease its strength using either its mother, its child, or both.

By removing or decreasing the mother element, you automatically cut of the supply of nourishment to its child, the element that is getting out of hand. On the other hand, by increasing the strength of the child element to the element that is too strong, it automatically demands more nourishment and strength from its mother, and decreases its strength accordingly. So an element can be controlled by increasing or decreasing its mother, its child, or both.

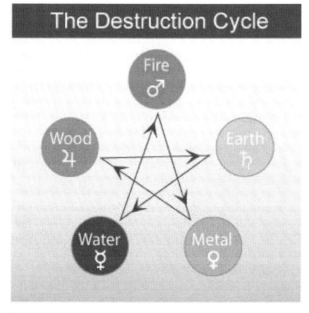

The Destruction Cycle

Destroying Element

An even more aggressive approach to toning down an unruly element is to invoke the element that destroys it. For each element, there is one other element that is its destroyer. Looking at the standard production sequence for any element, its destroyer element is always that element that is two elements back, that is the third element counterclockwise to the element you are considering, given that the element you are seeking to control is the first element.

This destroying element is also called the Grandparent of the element that needs to be controlled, in other words: the parent of the parent of the element you are looking at. This is the destroyer. By increasing the strength of the destroyer element, you automatically decrease the strength of the element you wish to control. This is about as aggressive a measure of control as you can leverage.

Of course, in many or even most cases, you don't need to go to the extreme of invoking the destroyer element. Often just backing off the strength of the parent or increasing the strength of the child is enough to temper and tone down the element that needs some adjustment.

The only other measure that can be undertaken is to increase the strength of the element called the "grandchild," which is the third element forward from the element that needs toning down, counting that element as number one. By increasing the grandchild element, which is automatically under attack from the element you want to tone down, it draws strength away from your element, thus contributing to decreasing its strength.

Helping an Element

The reverse process is also true. Sometimes what is needed is to strengthen an element that is weakened, one that needs a boost. There are several ways to do that, as well.

You can increase the strength of its parent, so that it receives more nourishment and protection. You can decrease the strength of its child, so it does not pull so much strength from its mother, the element you are considering. By the same token, you can decrease the strength of its destroying element, so that it does not impinge on your chosen element, and lastly, you can decrease the strength of the grandchild element, so that it takes less strength to attach. You get the idea.

The Chinese concept of the Five Elements and feng-shui for that matter is all about balance and harmony. To show what I would consider a perfect example of the difference between Eastern and Western philosophy:

Tibetan Astrology

Looking at the elemental balance from a Western perspective, if you are missing an element, you are said to lack that quality. However, in the Easter view of the five elements, when you are missing an element, this element is termed your "Luck Element," because only when you add it or come across it can you ever be balanced. In other words, it is through what you want or lack that you will become whole, so that missing element is lucky.

The difference between the two views may be subtle, but very revealing in how the Chinese approach works.

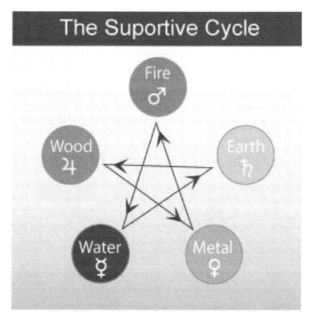

The Suportive Cycle

The Enemy of the Enemy Is My Friend

Another valuable feng-shui tool, when it comes to elemental balance, is to invoke the "enemy of my enemy, which is my friend." Let's take an example:

Supposing that we are looking at the element Earth, which happens to be weakened for some reason, and is under intense attach from a very strong Wood element. Remember that Wood is the natural enemy of Earth. A common remedy is to increase the strength of Wood's enemy, which as it turns out is the child of Earth, Metal. In fact, the enemy of your enemy will always by your child. In this sense, the child comes to the aid of the parent.

By increasing the strength of the child element, it automatically puts your enemy under direct attack, which means they have less strength to waste on destroying the element you are trying to protect.

Element-Animal Combinations

Year Elemental Animal Combination

This is the Element-Animal combination the current year, one of the cycle of sixty years, sometimes called the great cycle of Jupiter. The Twelve Animals each rule the year, in succession (Mouse, Ox, Tiger, Hare, Dragon, Snake, Horse, Sheep, Monkey, Bird, Dog, and Pig) and coupled with the Five Elements (Iron, Water, Wood, Fire, and Earth). The elements only change every two years, and in the order just given above. The total cycle takes sixty years to complete. They animal-element combination is a key factor in Tibetan astrology and the current pair are given great importance.

Current Month Animal-Element Combination

This is the Element-Animal combination the current month, one sixty animal-element pairs. The animal for the first month of the year is always the Tiger, and the rest of the months follow in the standard order of the Tibetan animal cycle. The element that goes with the first month is always the son of the element of the year. Each element holds for two months, and the order of the element is in the standard order: iron, water, wood, fire, and earth.

Current Day Animal-Element Combination

This is the Element-Animal combination the current day is determined as follows: the male or odd-numbered months (1, 3, 5, etc.) always start with the day of the Tiger. The six female or even-numbered months start with the day of the Monkey. Successive days follow the traditional order of the animals.

As for the elements, the element for the first day of the month is always the son of the element of that month. The elements change each day and are not doubled as they are for the year and the month.

Element Relationships

Best Friend

This is the best possible combination. Very auspicious.

Tibetan Astrology

Friend

This is a very good combination, and is considered auspicious.

Neutral

This is a neutral combination, and is not considered wither good nor bad.

Tibetan Astrology

Enemy

This is a bad combination, and is considered to be inauspicious.

Tibetan Astrology

Worst Enemy

This is the worst possible combination, and is considered very inauspicious.

Tibetan Astrology

The Vital Forces

There are five major factors that are taken into consideration when examining the nature and qualities of a given calendar year. They are listed here in order of their importance:

Major Life Factors	Tibetan Name
Life Force (holder of the life)	(SOK)
Power	(WANG)
Bodily Health	(Lü)
Luck	(LUNG TA)
Soul	(LA)

As regards these major elements, the life force is the most important of them, for both sexes. It represents the life strength or elan vital -- how you hold your life.

Then comes the power element, how you overcome obstacles, and achieve goals. This is of special interest for women. The function of power is spontaneous, instantaneous -- you must have it now.

Bodily health, physical health or sickness is important for all.

The luck element, also called Lung-Tha or "Wind Horse," is special for men, while soul, which is somewhat similar to the life force but more concerned with the emotional or psychological state, is not used very much.

The Soul or "La" element is the spirit in the body. It can be dislodged to sickness or shock and become separated from the physical. In this case, there are rituals to recall it back into the body.

Tibetan Astrology

	M/F	Ele. Animal	Vital	Body	Power	Wind	La
4	Female	Fire-Hare	Wood	Fire	Fire	Fire	Water
5	Male	Earth-Dragon	Earth	Water	Earth	Water	Fire
6	Female	Earth-Snake	Fire	Wood	Earth	Water	Wood
7	Male	Iron-Horse	Fire	Earth	Iron	Iron	Wood
8	Female	Iron-Sheep	Earth	Earth	Iron	Fire	Fire
9	Male	Water-Monkey	Iron	Iron	Water	Wood	Earth
10	Female	Water-Bird	Iron	Iron	Water	Water	Earth
11	Male	Wood-Dog	Earth	Fire	Wood	Iron	Fire
12	Female	Wood-Pig	Water	Fire	Wood	Fire	Iron
13	Male	Fire-Mouse	Water	Water	Fire	Wood	Iron
14	Female	Fire-Ox	Earth	Water	Fire	Water	Fire
15	Male	Earth-Tiger	Wood	Wood	Earth	Earth	Iron
16	Female	Earth-Hare	Wood	Earth	Earth	Fire	Water
17	Male	Iron-Dragon	Earth	Iron	Iron	Wood	Fire
18	Female	Iron-Snake	Fire	Iron	Iron	Water	Wood
19	Male	Water-Horse	Fire	Wood	Water	Iron	Wood
20	Female	Water-Sheep	Earth	Wood	Water	Fire	Fire
21	Male	Wood-Monkey	Iron	Water	Wood	Wood	Earth
22	Female	Wood-Bird	Iron	Water	Wood	Water	Earth
23	Male	Fire-Dog	Earth	Earth	Fire	Iron	Fire
24	Female	Fire-Pig	Water	Earth	Fire	Fire	Iron
25	Male	Earth-Mouse	Water	Fire	Earth	Wood	Iron
26	Female	Earth-Ox	Earth	Fire	Earth	Water	Fire
27	Male	Iron-Tiger	Wood	Wood	Iron	Iron	Water
28	Female	Iron-Hare	Wood	Wood	Iron	Fire	Water
29	Male	Water-Dragon	Earth	Water	Water	Wood	Fire
30	Female	Water-Snake	Fire	Water	Water	Water	Wood
31	Male	Wood-Horse	Fire	Iron	Wood	Iron	Wood
32	Female	Wood-Sheep	Earth	Iron	Wood	Fire	Fire
33	Male	Fire-Monkey	Iron	Fire	Fire	Wood	Earth
34	Female	Fire-Bird	Iron	Fire	Fire	Water	Earth
35	Male	Earth-Dog	Earth	Wood	Earth	Iron	Fire
36	Female	Earth-Pig	Water	Wood	Earth	Fire	Iron
37	Male	Iron-Mouse	Water	Earth	Iron	Wood	Iron
38	Female	Iron-Ox	Earth	Earth	Iron	Water	Fire
39	Male	Water-Tiger	Wood	Iron	Water	Iron	Water
40	Female	Water-Hare	Wood	Iron	Water	Fire	Water
41	Male	Wood-Dragon	Earth	Fire	Wood	Wood	Fire
42	Female	Wood-Snake	Fire	Fire	Wood	Water	Wood
43	Male	Fire-Horse	Fire	Water	Fire	Iron	Wood
44	Female	Fire-Sheep	Earth	Water	Fire	Fire	Fire
45	Male	Earth-Monkey	Iron	Earth	Earth	Wood	Earth
46	Female	Earth-Bird	Iron	Earth	Earth	Water	Earth
47	Male	Iron-Dog	Earth	Iron	Iron	Iron	Fire
48	Female	Iron-Pig	Water	Iron	Iron	Fire	Iron
49	Male	Water-Mouse	Water	Wood	Water	Wood	Iron
50	Female	Water-Ox	Earth	Wood	Water	Water	Fire
51	Male	Wood-Tiger	Wood	Water	Wood	Iron	Fire
52	Female	Wood-Hare	Wood	Water	Wood	Fire	Water
53	Male	Fire-Dragon	Earth	Earth	Fire	Wood	Fire
54	Female	Fire-Snake	Fire	Earth	Fire	Water	Wood
55	Male	Earth-Horse	Fire	Fire	Earth	Iron	Wood
56	Female	Earth-Sheep	Earth	Fire	Earth	Fire	Fire
57	Male	Iron-Monkey	Iron	Wood	Iron	Wood	Fire
58	Female	Iron-Bird	Iron	Wood	Iron	Water	Earth
59	Male	Water-Dog	Earth	Water	Water	Iron	Fire
60	Female	Water-Pig	Water	Water	Water	Fire	Iron
01	Male	Wood-Mouse	Water	Iron	Wood	Wood	Iron
02	Female	Wood-Ox	Earth	Iron	Wood	Water	Fire
03	Male	Fire-Tiger	Wood	Fire	Fire	Iron	Water

Tibetan Astrology

Vital Force – Life force or Sok

The Life Force is the vitality, the very heart strength of the person, and as long as it is strong, life lasts. This is our essential vitality or life force. We need it to sustain life. We become sick and even die, if this force becomes too weak.

Determination:

The life force is determined according to the following table. The left-hand column is the animal for the current year, while the right-hand column is the element for that year's life force:

Current Year Animal	Life Force Element
Snake, Horse	Fire
Hare, Tiger	Wood
Mouse, Pig	Water
Monkey, Bird	Iron
Dragon, Sheep	Earth
Ox, Dog	Earth

Tibetan Astrology

Vital Force – Power or Wang-Thang

The Power or Destiny Element (Wang Thang) refers to our personal power and our ability to achieve the goals we set out for ourselves. When it is strong, we are victorious and draw to ourselves: wealth, strength, power, and so on. When it is weak, we experience losses.

This Power Element indicates the ability to overcome obstacles and to achieve success. When the relationship is positive, we overcome obstacles to achieve wealth, well-being, and success. When it is weak, we succumb to the trials of life more than we overcome them

Determination:

The Power element will always be identical to the element determined for the current year. For example, 1991 is the year of the Iron Sheep. Therefore the power element for 1991 will be "iron."

Vital Force – Body or Lü

The Bodily Health is just that, the general state of good or poor health for the body. This is our overall bodily health, warding off illness, when strong, and succumbing to sickness, when weak.

Determination:

With Bodily Health, calculation is a little more complicated. First determine the key element:

Current Year Animal	Health Key Element
Mouse, Ox, Horse, Sheep	Wood as Key
Tiger, Hare, Bird, Monkey	Water as Key
Dog, Pig, Dragon, Snake	Iron as Key

Next, using this key element, take the Power Element (as calculated above, this will always be identical to the ELEMENT determined for the current year) according to the following rules:

Tibetan Astrology

If Power Element is:	Bodily Health
Son of Health Key Element	Water
Mother of Health Key Element	Wood
Enemy of Health Key Element	Earth
Friend of Health Key Element	Fire
Same Element Health Key Element	Iron

Tibetan Astrology

Vital Force – Soul or La

The Spirit or "La" as the Tibetans call it refers to our psychic vitality, a kind of centered-ness, in which mind and body are connected and work as one. Sometimes the La becomes disconnected and wanders from the body and needs to be brought back. This has more to do with our psyche. It is often associated with Sok, the life force. an indicator of our psychic well-being.

The "La" is not considered our Self, but a kind of God or being (other than ourselves) that inhabits persons and is separated from our consciousness (the one that proceeds into the Bardo) at death. The La sticks around our body at and after death, and this is why it is considered important to place the physical remains or the ashes of the deceased in a secure (geomantically-speaking) place. We have a new "La" for each rebirth we take. It is not us.

In fact, if an improper burial is undertaken and the La is seriously affected, the main remedy is to disinter the body and bury it properly. In fact, the body should be buried at a depth of one cubit for each year since the death.

The Tibetans and the Chinese do not considering the scattering of one's ashes auspicious. In fact, it is just the opposite. Both Tibetans and Chinese believe that such a a burial will affect the descendants either auspiciously or inauspiciously.

Tibetans believe that the "La" can be stolen while we are alive and somehow separated from the physical body, stolen usually by mischievous spirits of one kind or another. When this happens, we can become ill and feel out of sorts, literally beside ourselves. There are different rituals that can be performed to make the La return to the body.

It is also said that our La is what senses danger at times and warns us, like when we enter a house that contains ghosts or unhappy spirits. It is our La that senses the unhappy spirits and makes us feel uneasy.

Determination:

The Soul Element is always the Mother of the Life Force Element.

Life Force Element	Soul Element
Fire	Wood
Wood	Water
Water	Metal (Iron)
Iron (Metal)	Earth
Earth	Fire

Tibetan Astrology

Vital Force – Luck or Lung-Ta

The Luck Element or Wind Horse is a general indicator of one's good luck, either at birth or for the coming year. This force is connected with the more subtle and psychic energies. The Lung Ta acts as a coordinator of all of the other forces, uniting them to a coordinated whole when strong, causes the forces to work inharmoniously, when weak. It is said to be our luck, good luck, when strong, bad luck, when weak.

Determination:

Current Year Animal	Luck Element
Tiger, Horse, Dog	Iron
Pig, Sheep, Hare	Fire
Mouse, Dragon, Monkey	Wood
Ox, Snake, Bird	Iron

Planets and Vital Forces

In the 12-year cycle of the animal signs, each sign has particular planets that are powerful or rule for that sign. For example, the Snake has Mars as the planet that controls the `La' force. There are a number of key categories, with planetary rulers. These are:

The Planet of the `La' - Good. Overcoming obstacles.

The Planet of Vitality - Good luck and success.

The Planet of Destruction - Bad. Destructive forces.

In addition, there are a number of special asterisms (stars) that are associated with each sign. They are:

The `La' Star - Good. Success, overcoming.
The Star of Vitality - Good. Success, overcoming.
The Power Star - Good. Success, overcoming.
the `Keh' Star - Bad omen.
The Demon Star - Bad. Obstacles.
The Star of Destruction - Bad. Worst

The Deu Khamar

One of the more popular of the Tibetan astrological techniques is the various Vital Forces for each year, compared to the natal Vital Forces. These are compared and the current relationship is rated using a system of circles and crosses:

Rating	Symbol
The Best	000
Very Good	00
Good	0
Neutral	0X
Bad	X
Worst	XX

The range is from `Best' to `Worst', with several grades in-between. The Vital Forces rated are: the Life Force, Power, Bodily Health, Luck, and Soul.

Method

Compare your birth Major Vital Forces and those of the current year as follows. For example, using the Power Element, if the current year's power element is:

Mother of my birth power than mark 000
Son of my birth power than mark 0X
Friend of my birth power than mark 00
Enemy of my birth power than mark XX

if it is the same as my birth power then:
If Water or Earth, Mark 0
If Fire, Iron or Wood then Mark X

Tibetan Astrology

Deu: Earth-Earth/Water-Water

Good. Third best.

The Deu

Deu: Friend

Very good. Second best.

Tibetan Astrology

Deu: Mother

Most favorable.The best.

Tibetan Astrology

Deu: Son

Neutral.

Tibetan Astrology

Deu: Power

The Power or Destiny Element (Wang Thang) refers to our personal power and our ability to achieve the goals we set out for ourselves. When it is strong, we are victorious and draw to ourselves: wealth, strength, power, and so on. When it is weak, we experience losses.

Tibetan Astrology

Deu: Power

Bad.

Tibetan Astrology

Deu: Enemy

The worst. Very bad.

The Fifteen Conjunctures

These come from the conjunction of the planet of the day with a particular Nakshatra (Lunar Mansion), and are used for daily analysis and not natal astrology.

The Fifteen Great Conjunctions are similar to the "28 Conjunctions," with the exception that here only certain of the 27 Nakshatras are paired with the planet for the day-of-the- week. The result is a traditional keyword and image that is important for that particular day. Of these fifteen conjunctures, by far the most important and well-known is the first one, which is called "Drupjor," which only happens rarely.

Drubjor signifies the obtaining of what you have wished and worked for, some positive results. It marks a periof of up to a week when things will go well.

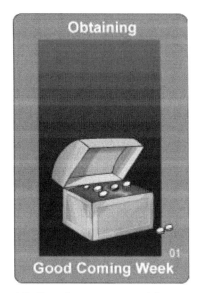

15 Conjunctures: 01

Favorable. For the next seven days, in general, all things are positive and moving forward.

Tibetan Astrology

15 Conjunctures: 02

Generally favorable. For the next seven days, practices and rituals of a gentle kind are suggested having to do with magnetizing, prosperity, and pacification. Fierce practices should be avoided.

15 Conjunctures: 03

This is favorable only for the wrathful practices, those devoted to the various protectors.

Tibetan Astrology

15 Conjunctures: 04

This day is favorable for all major activities.

Tibetan Astrology

15 Conjunctures: 05

A day favorable for performing good and virtuous deeds, as well as consecrations.

Tibetan Astrology

15 Conjunctures: 06

A day is favorable for education, any kind of study and learning. Also for working with land and water, irrigation, digging wells, and the like.

Tibetan Astrology

15 Conjunctures: 07

Generally favorable. For the next seven days, practices and rituals of a gentle kind are suggested, having to do with magnetizing, prosperity, and pacification. Fierce practices should be avoided. Favorable for good and virtuous deeds.

Tibetan Astrology

15 Conjunctures: 08

This time is favorable for getting things done, and all work-related activities. Also a favorable time of being social, making friends and influencing people.

Tibetan Astrology

15 Conjunctures: 09

This day is favorable for astrology and divination, as well as putting on festivals, and, generally, promoting good deeds. The wrathful practices should be avoided.

15 Conjunctures: 10

Unfavorable day, and just about all activity should be avoided. Even good and virtuous deeds and practices will have no beneficial result, and may actually harm. No travel, funerals, marriages, etc. Wrathful practices are favorable.

15 Conjunctures: 11

Unfavorable day, and just about all activity should be avoided. Even good and virtuous deeds and practices will have no beneficial result, and may actually harm. No travel, funerals, marriages, etc. Wrathful practices are favorable.

Tibetan Astrology

15 Conjunctures: 12

Unfavorable day, with even good acts bringing bad results. The prescribing and preparation of medicine should be avoided. Marriage on this day will have bad results.

Tibetan Astrology

15 Conjunctures: 13

Unfavorable day. Nothing good will come of positive actions. Only bad actions and causing problems will succeed. Marriage will have negative results, and should be avoided. Funerals will also have bad results that impact the family. All important business should be postponed.

15 Conjunctures: 14

Unfavorable day. Almost all activities will have negative results, in particular marriages, which should be avoided on this day. No travel or funerals. Bad actions are successful.

15 Conjunctures: 15

Unfavorable day. Almost all activities will have negative results. In particular, anything relating to fire or fire offerings should not be attempted. Surgery should be avoided on this day.

Year Element

Element Relationships

There are preferred relationships between the elements. Mother is the best because then you are the Son. Son is the next best. Friend is less important, but acceptable. Enemy is, as might be expected, not so good.

Element Togetherness:

Certain elements go (or do not go) well together. Earth and Water are good, while Wood, Iron and Fire (in combination) are not as good.

Good Relationship:

Water is the Mother of Wood
Iron is the Mother of Water
Earth is the Mother of Iron
Fire is the Mother of Earth
Wood is the Mother of Fire

Friendly or Beneficial Relationship:

Earth is the Friend of Wood
Wood is the Friend of Iron
Iron is the Friend of Fire
Water is the Friend of Earth
Fire is the Friend of Water

Neutral or Filial Relationship:

Fire is the Son of Wood
Earth is the Son of Fire
Iron is the Son of Earth
Water is the Son of Iron
Wood is the Son of Water

Tibetan Astrology

Antagonistic Relationship:
Iron is an Enemy of Wood
Fire is an Enemy of Iron
Water is an Enemy of Fire
Earth is an Enemy of Water
Wood is an Enemy of Earth

Electional Astrology

Electional issues are of great concern to the Tibetan astrologer and to the Tibetan people. Where here in the West astrologers often speak of predicting events, this is not the approach taken in the Asia. Rather than predict this or that, the Tibetan astrologer consults a variety of traditional indicators to see what they suggest, indictors like the current Nakshatra or Lunar Mansion, which lunar day is in effect, as well as the weekdays, Mewas, Par-khas, and animals for the current day.

Each of these factors already has an established meaning for its various members, and the Tibetans draw on that meaning. In this sense they don't "predict," per se, but since they have established, for example, that a particular lunar day may be good (or bad) for a particular activity, they approach the future with that experience. They elect to enter into certain activities on a given day based on whether that day is considered auspicious or inauspicious based on these factors.

Some well-know activities are listed below, along with which indicators are considered auspicious and inauspicious. Factors considered include:

Legend

Weekdays
LD = Lunar Days
LM Lunar Mansions of Nakshatras
Mewa – The Nine Mewa Numbers
Par-Kha – the Eight Trigrams or Par-Khas
The Twelve Animals

Astrology

Auspicious: Sun, Wed, Thu, Fri, Sat, Mouse

Tibetan Astrology

Building Shrines,

Auspicious: Dog, Dragon, Mon, Wed, Thu, Fri, LD01, LD08, LD10, LD12, LD13, LD15, LD18, LM02, LM03, LM04, LM06, LM07, LM10, LM11, LM13, LM14, LM16, LM18, LM20, LM22, LM23, LM27, Ox, Sheep, Tiger,

Inauspicious: Sat, Sun, Tue, LD19, LD20, LD21, LD22, LD27, LD29, LM01, LM05, LM08, LM12, LM15, LM17

Business Activities

Auspicious: Sun, Wed, Thu, Fri, Bird, Dog, Hare, LM07, LM14, LM20, LM26, Mouse,

Inauspicious: Sat, Dha, Gin, 9-Maroon, Ox, Snake

Cutting Hair

Auspicious: , LD04, LD08, LD11, LM00, LM04, LM06, LM07, LM12, LM13, LM14, LM17, LM21, LM22, LM23, LM26, Pig, Dog, Horse, LD14, LD15, LD16, LD17, Tiger

Destruction of Any Kind

Auspicious: Sun, Tue, Thu, Sat, Dragon, LD04, LD08, LD11, LD15, LD18, LD22, LD25, LD26, LD29, LM01, LM04, LM05, LM08, LM09, LM11, LM12, LM15, LM16, LM17, LM18, LM19, LM25, Tiger,

Inauspicious: Mon, Fri, Dog, Hare, LM00, LM02, LM10, LM23, LM24, LM27, Sheep, Snake, Wed

Divination and Geomancy

Auspicious: Sun, Mon, Wed, Thu, Fri, Sat, Monkey, Snake, Tiger, Dragon, LM02, LM04, LM05, LM06, LM07, LM09, LM10, LM11, LM12, LM18, LM20, LM27,

Inauspicious: Tue, Mouse, LD08, LD09, LD15, LD19, LD29, LD30, LM01, LM08, LM13, LM15, LM17

Tibetan Astrology

Felling Trees

Auspicious: Dha, Khon,

Inauspicious: 3-Blue, Snake

Fire Puja (Purification)

Auspicious: Tue, Bird, Sun, Tiger, Trigram Li,

Inauspicious: Mon, Wed

Funerals

Auspicious: Wed, Thu, Fri, Dog, Monkey, Tiger, LD07, LD15, LD17, LD25, LD27, LM00, LM06, LM07, LM08, LM14, LM18, LM21, LM23, LM25, LM26,

Inauspicious: Sun, Mon, Tue, Sat, Bird, Dragon, Hare, Pig, Snake, LD01, LD05, LD09, LD10, LD19, LD20, LD23, LD28, LD29, LD30, LM01, LM02, LM03, LM04, LM05, LM09, LM10, LM12, LM13, LM15, LM16, LM17, LM19, LM22, LM27

Buying a New Home

Auspicious: Mon, Tue, Wed, Thu, Fri, Sat, LD03, LD07, LD11, LD12, LD14, LD15, LD17, LD19, LD25, LM03, LM04, LM06, LM07, LM09, LM10, LM11, LM12, LM13, LM14, LM15, LM20, LM22, LM23, LM24, LM26, LM27,

Inauspicious: Sun, LD10, LD20, LD22, LD30, LM00, LM08, LM16, LM18, LM25

Increase Activity

Auspicious: Sun, Mon, Wed, Thu, Fri, LD02, LD03, LD06, LD10, LD13, LD17, LD20, LD27, LM00, LM03, LM04, LM06, LM07, LM09, LM12, LM13, LM14, LM15, LM16, LM24, LM26,

Inauspicious: Tue, Sat, LM01, LM05, LM08, LM17, LM18, LM19, LM22, LM25, LM27

Tibetan Astrology

Make Offerings to Local Deities

Auspicious: Fri, Snake, Gin, Tsin, Kham, 3-Blue, 7-Red

Marriage

Auspicious: Mon, Thu, Fri, Monkey, Sheep, Hare, LM04, LM06, LM07, LM11, LM14, LM15, LM20, LM27,

Inauspicious: Sun, Tue, Wed, Sat, Mouse, Ox, Snake, Bird, Dog, Horse, LD01, LD03, LD04, LD05, LD06, LD08, LD12, LD17, LD19, LD21, LD27, LD28, LD30, LM00, LM01, LM02, LM03, LM05, LM08, LM09, LM10, LM12, LM13, LM16, LM17, LM18, LM19, LM22, LM23, LM24, LM25, LM26

Medical Treatment

Auspicious: Sun, Mon, Thu, Fri, Bird, LD04, LD26, LD27, LM00, LM03, LM04, LM06, LM11, LM12, LM13, LM14, LM15, LM20, LM21, LM22, LM23, LM26, 3-Blue, 4-Green,

Inauspicious: Tue, Wed, Sat, Tiger, Dragon, LD30, LM18

Move to New House

Auspicious: Mon, Tue, Thu, Fri, Sat, LM03, LM20, LM25,

Inauspicious: Sun, LM00, LM06, LM07, LM12, LM14, LM21

Naming Children

Auspicious: Sun, Wed, Thu, Fri, LM00, LM03, LM04, LM07, LM11, LM12, LM16, LM20, LM21, LM22, LM25, LM26, Tue, Sat

Make Offerings

Auspicious: , Sun, Mon, Wed, Thu, Fri, Dragon, Horse, Sheep, Snake, Tsin, Kham, Gin, LD15, LM02, LM03,

LM04, LM06, LM07, LM10, LM12, LM14, LM16, LM17, LM18, LM19, LM20, LM21, LM22, LM23, LM26, LM27,

Inauspicious: Tue, Sat, LD01, LM01, LM08, LM09, LM15, LM25, Tiger

Pacification

Auspicious: Mon, Wed, Thu, Fri, LD01, LD05, LD09, LD12, LD16, LD19, LD23, LM00, LM03, LM06, LM07, LM11, LM12, LM14, LM20, LM26,

Inauspicious: Sun, Tue, Sat, LM01, LM05, LM08, LM13, LM15, LM16, LM17, LM18, LM21, LM22, LM24, LM25

Make Petitions

Auspicious: Wed, Thu, Bird, Monkey, Mouse,

Inauspicious: Dog, Horse, Sheep

Planting Trees and Other Plants

Auspicious: Mon, Wed, Fri, Sat, Monkey, Tsin

Inauspicious: Sun, Tue

Prepare Weapons

Auspicious: Sun, Wed, Fri, Sat, Tiger, Dragon, Ox, Kham, LM01, LM04, LM05, LM09, LM12, LM13, LM18, LM19, LM25,

Inauspicious: Mon, Tue, Thu, Bird, Hare, Horse, Mouse, Pig, LM02, LM10, LM20

Good for Prosperity

Auspicious: Sun, Tiger, 6-White, 9-Maroon,

Inauspicious: Hare

Purification

Auspicious: Sun, LD15, 1-White, 6-White, 8-White,

Inauspicious: Tue, Tiger,

Tibetan Astrology

Rain Rituals

Auspicious: Bird, Monkey, Mouse, Pig,

Inauspicious: Dragon, Horse, Ox, Sheep

Removing Obstacles

Auspicious: Tue, Fri, Dragon, Gin, Kham, Khon, 2-Black, Zon,

Inauspicious: Bird, Hare, Mon, Mouse, Ox, Pig, Snake,

Start Building or Project

Auspicious: Mon, Wed, Thu, Fri, Sat, Dragon, Tiger, Ox, Tsin, Gin, LD01, LD03, LD09, LD10, LD11, LD19, LD20, LD23, LD24, LD25, LM00, LM03, LM04, LM11, LM12, LM13, LM14, LM16, LM18, LM19, LM20,

Inauspicious: Tue, Khen, Khon, LD26

Start Fight - Aggression

Auspicious: Sun, Tue, Ox, LM05, LM10, LM17, LM18,

Inauspicious: Wed, Thu, Sat, Dog, Dragon, Hare, Sheep, Tiger, Dha, Kham, Khon, LM16, 6-White, 7-Red

Start on Journey

Auspicious: Bird, Mon, Wed, Thu, Fri, Monkey, LM00, LM06, LM07, LM14, LM16, LM19, LM22, LM25, LM27,

Inauspicious: Sun, Tue, Sat, Dog, Horse, Mouse, Sheep, LM01, LM02, LM03, LM04, LM05, LM08, LM09, LM10, LM11, LM12, LM13, LM15, LM17, LM18, LM20, LM24, LM26

Take Responsibility

Auspicious: Sun, Mon, Tue, Thu, Dragon, Horse,

Inauspicious: Sat, Monkey

Tibetan Astrology

Take Control

Auspicious: Sun, Tue, Thu, Fri, Pig, LD03, LD04, LD07, LD14, LD15, LD21, LD28, LD30, LM00, LM01, LM04, LM06, LM07, LM09, LM11, LM12, LM13, LM14, LM15, LM16, LM18, LM19, LM20, LM22, LM24, LM25, LM26, LM27,

Inauspicious: Mon, Wed, Sat, LM02, LM03, LM05, LM08, LM17

Good for Wealth

Auspicious: Mon, Wed, Thu, Fri, Sat, Bird, Dragon, Monkey, Mouse, Gin, LD01, LD02, LD03, LD04, LD05, LD08, LD10, LD11, LD12, LD13, LD14, LD15, LM03, LM05, LM06, LM07, LM10, LM11, LM13, LM14, LM16, LM17, LM18, LM19, LM24, LM25, LM27,

Inauspicious: Sun, Tue, Sheep, LD06, LD07, LD09, LD16, LD17, LD18, LD19, LD20, LD21, LD22, LD23, LD24, LD25, LD26, LD27, LD28, LD29, LD30, LM00, LM01, LM08,

Work the Land

Auspicious: Sun, Wed, Thu, Fri, Sat, Sheep, LM03, LM04, LM07, LM09, LM11, LM12, LM13, LM20, LM21, LM23, LM25, LM26, Tsin,

Inauspicious: Mon, Tue, Pig, Snake, Dragon, Hare, LD15, LD20, LD23, LD24, LD29, 5-Yellow

The Cosmic Tortoise

Diagrams, like that of the Cosmic Turtle, are common in writings on Tibetan astrology. Often this diagram is shown drawn on the underside of what is called the "Celestial Tortoise." This tortoise represents the universe in both China and Tibet. The upper shell is the dome of Heaven, while on the underside is inscribed the essential elements of the astrological mandala. The above diagram contains the wheel of animal signs, the elements, directions/colors.

This very traditional diagram appears in many forms similar to this throughout the astrological tradition of

579

Tibetan Astrology

Tibet. This is kind of the key diagram or matrix said to have been inscribed on the under-shell of a turtle, thus the name Cosmic Tortoise or Cosmic Turtle. Here is a brief tour of the diagram:

(1) Eight Directions – The entire diagram is in the form of a square, representing the eight cardinal directions, which are inscribed on the outer ring of the diagram. As you can see, we are facing south, with the direction north to our back, and east on left, west on the right.

(2) Twelve Animal Signs – The next ring contains the 12 animal signs in their proper positions, each in alignment with the direction they govern.

(3) Eight Parkhas or Trigrams – Next we find eight trigrams in the Later Heaven sequence, which is the one found in Tibetan astrology. Each trigram is in its proper direction and the good and bad directions for that particular trigram are marked with the letters "A" thorugh "H," with the "good" directions from dark green to light green, and the "bad" directions from dark red to light red. Dark green is the best, dark red the worst.

(4) Magic Square – Next are eight circles, each showing the Magic Square layout for one of the eight numbers that surround the central Magic Square, which itself contains the ninth layout, the traditional Magic Square.

About Mind Practice

In Tibet and the East, the study of astrology is inseparable from the practice of meditation, some form of mind practice. The concept of mind practice is not yet well known here in the West. How many people do you know who consciously practice using their mind for its own sake, anyway? Most of us assume that the mind is quite usable just as we find it, and does not require any special exercise or training.

In many Eastern countries, mind practice is not only acknowledged, it is considered an essential part of an education. This is true for countries like Tibet, Nepal, much of India, and parts of China and Japan, where it is understood that the mind, by nature, is unruly and hard to manage. In these cultures it is assumed that little can be accomplished in life without first learning how to use and work with the mind. In short, mental preparation or mind practice, as it is called, is an important part of life in most parts of Asia.

Why has mind practice as understood in the East never caught on in North America? In part, this may be due to our whole take on the term "meditation," and what we think that is. Meditation here in the West has come to mean something almost like relaxation therapy, a way to relax and get away from the worries of the world, perhaps in the contemplation of some inner landscape.

This approach to meditation, although valid in its own way, shows little resemblance to its Eastern counterpart, which is not primarily concerned with various methods to relax and get rid of tension. The Tibetan or Zen Buddhist concept of meditation or mind practice involves very intense use of the mind. It is unfortunate that here in the West these more active forms of mind practice have been subsumed under the general label of meditation.

Having pointed this out, it may be helpful to clarify and describe what it is that Tibetan Buddhists (and other groups) do when they meditate. In general, if you ask what happens on the cushion, the answer is "practicing", or "sitting". Indeed, that is what takes place. Physically, we sit. The most striking difference between sitting practice (mind practice) and relaxation/meditation as understood in this country is that Tibetan mind practice is anything but relaxing or passive. It is very active.

Tibetan Astrology

Shamata Meditation

This basic form of Buddhist meditation, called shamata, is practiced not only in Tibet, but also by many Eastern countries. Zen Buddhist Zazen meditation is very similar. Shamata is a Sanskrit word meaning peace or calm-abiding, and, although the final result of mind practice is a more peaceful you, the process (at least for beginners) is not exactly what most of us would recognize as peaceful or in any way "fun."

What all forms of shamata share is an emphasis on being present or trying to, just sitting and observing the mind. In this practice, there is no attempt to go anywhere else in the mind other than this present moment. Just sit and observe the mind. Often some object of concentration is selected as the primary focus of attention -- home base so to speak. This can be the simple act of breathing itself. Whenever thoughts or distractions occur, and are recognized (day dreaming, for instance), this is noted and the mind is gently brought back to the breath -- just breathing. Whatever the diversion, the attention is always brought back to the present moment. The distraction is noted, not dwelled on, and the mind returns to the task at hand – sitting. With practice, the mind is trained to be aware of what is happening, without as many excursions or escapes.

It might seem that having nothing to do but sit would be easy enough. However, for most of us, it is anything but that. Confronting restlessness and the endless need for entertainment or escape can be both humbling and frustrating. It is hard for us to sit still for even five minutes much less for the longer sessions usually recommended.

Another common misconception is that the time we spend in mind practice, sitting or meditating, is itself the purpose or goal of practice, that is: one looks forward to the meditation session as an oasis of reverie in the middle of an otherwise hectic day. For the majority of practitioners, mind practice sessions are far from that -- representing some of the more challenging moments in the daily schedule. As mentioned earlier, daily shamata practice seldom results in a more peaceful mind or time out from life, at least in the beginning stages. The results of sitting do not appear at once, sitting there on the cushion, so to speak. Instead, these results show up during the rest of our day in the form of insights and increased awareness as to how to handle whatever comes our way. By learning to calm the mind, it is possible be aware of what happens in the mind.

Tibetan Astrology

In fact, the main result of mind practice is an increased awareness of our own mind and all that goes on in it. With regular sitting practice, we are better able to observe what happens. We begin to catch ourselves being carried away, and can more easily bring our attention back to the task at hand. What we learn on the cushion gradually transfers itself into our daily life.

When we begin to catch our distractions in our day-to-day life, the result is an enhanced concentration and ability to handle situations that present themselves. This kind of result is of far greater practical value than a few peaceful minutes in an otherwise frenzied world. In essence, we learn to train our mind just as we train our body for sports or any learned skill.

In summary, there are two ideas that have been pointed out here regarding meditation or mind practice as used in the East. First, it is anything but a quick escape, and seldom relaxing in the common sense of that word.

Rather than a time for reverie, sitting practice is, at first, very hard work. And second, the purpose or result of mind practice is not some relaxed state to be experienced while sitting on the cushion, although this may be the case for advanced practitioners. I wouldn't know.

Instead, beginning mind practice results in perfecting our eventually being able to grasp real-life situations and, in general, awareness of what is happening to us. The result of sitting meditation or mind practice is an enhanced ability to deal with the world around us with awareness and skillful means. It is this increased ability to respond to whatever presents itself that is the sign of successful shamata meditation. We become peaceful because we are able to handle our lives in a more practical manner.

Once the mind is calmed, a second stage of mediation practice can begin, which is called Vipassana (Lag-Ton), and this involves increasing awareness of what takes place in the mind, and in particular, the actual nature of the mind itself. Yet it all begins with Shamata, the calming of the mind.

Tibetan Astrology

From this very simple practice of observation or mind practice springs much of the long tradition of Tibetan Buddhism -- acknowledged as one of the richest in the world. Shamata meditation is the cornerstone and starting point for many Eastern disciplines. The actual technique is quite simple, taking only a few minutes to learn. It has been described in various books, but it is worth going to the trouble of getting this instruction from someone who is authorized to give it -- who has practiced it. In this way, you are assured of an authentic connection handed down in an unbroken line reaching back at least 1000 years. There are many different forms of Buddhism that teach Shamata and I don't know which to recommend, but you might check Kagyu.org for a center near you. I can vouch for this particular method. Just call them up, and ask for instruction. There should be no fee.

The Twelve Nidanas

The Twelve Nidanas, also called "The Twelve Links of Interdependent Origination," are usually depicted on a wheel, with twelve sections, the Tibetan "Wheel of Life and Death." These twelve phases follow one another like the seasons, each one leading to the next and on around, with no end and no beginning - a circle. In general, the twelve phases are grouped as follows:

"Ignorance" (ignoring the actual truth) has caused us to create...

"Karma," which has resulted in our current state of existence.

The next seven phases describe life as we know it:

Consciousness, Name & Form, The Six Senses, Contact, Craving, Grasping, and Grasping represent the processes we go through in an endless cycle.

The last three are said to be concerned with the life after this one, and they are: Becoming, Rebirth, and Old Age and Death.

This cycle of twelve phases endlessly revolves and we pass through these stages in many different forms, one by one. There is no beginning and no end. Only becoming aware or enlightened allows us to end this perpetual wheel of motion.

The Twelve Nidana

The 12 Nidanas are the various interdependent stages in the development and evolution of consciousness. All twelve are interdependent and follow one after another in an endless cycle. One nidana is assigned to each lunar days in an endless loop. These nidanas traditionally indicate good and bad activities (and directions) for that particular day.

Tibetan Astrology

#1 Consciousness (vijnana)

Nidana 1:   Consciousness
Image: Monky in mango tree
Sanskrit: Vijnana
Time: The Present

The different forms of consciousness.

DAILY: This is a good day for overcoming one's enemies, taking initiations, building, and installing officials. Travel to the North and South are good. Not a good day for bathing or travel to the West and East.

The nidana of Consciousness is favorable for religious initiations, placing statues of deities, conquering, installing officials, and the washing of one's head, and donning new clothes. Also, the directions South and North are favorable. Bathing, in general, is not favorable, nor is travel to the East or West.

#2 Name and Form (nama-rupa)

Two Men in a Boat

Nidana 2:	Identity
Image:	Passenger
Sanskrit:	Nama Rupa
Time:	The Present

The tendency for the discursive mind to name and pigeon-hole things, thus "name and form."

DAILY: This is not a good day to bathe, and travel to the North and West should be avoided. This is a good day for travel to the South and East, and for avoiding what one fears, meeting with religious persons, and praying.

The Name & Form nidana is favorable for meeting with one's guru, doing mantra, cutting hair and finger nails, and travel to the South and east. Travel to the North and west is not favorable, not is bathing.

#3 The Six Senses (shadayatana)

Nidana 3:	The Senses
Image:	House with 6 windows
Sanskrit:	Sadayatana
Time:	The Present

These are the familiar six senses: hearing, seeing, smelling, tasting, touching, and touch, and the sense organs they represent.

DAILY: This is a good day for taking possession of something, staying indoors, hiding a treasure, and travel in any direction. Not a good day for bathing or making obeisance to another.

The nidana of the Sense Fields is favorable for staying indoors, putting on fresh clothes, hiding wealth, conquering a town, and travel in any direction. Bathing and prostrating to another person are not favorable.

Tibetan Astrology

#4 Contact (sparsha)

Nidana 4:   Contact
Image: Couple Making Love
Sanskrit: Sparsha
Time: The Present

The observer and the observed, like the eye and what it sees, the ear and sounds, the nose and incense, and so on.

DAILY: This is a good day for violent actions, such as killing and stealing, black magic, and arguments. Not a good day for to arts and crafts, bathing, and travel to the South. Receiving wealth form the North, changing one's clothes, and wasting time are said to be bad.

The nidana of Contact is favorable for arguing and debating, also: stealing and killing, and any violent actions, and black-magic rituals. Traveling to the south is and craftwork is bad, as is bathing. Also bad are receiving wealth from the North, changing clothes, and delays.

592

#5 Feeling (vedana)

Nidana 5:	Perception
Image:	Arrow in the eye
Sanskrit:	Vedana
Time:	The Present

Feeling or sensation in its dichotomies, such as feeling good or feeling bad, pleasant or unpleasant, and so on.

DAILY: Making love, obtaining wealth, crossing water, and business trade of all kinds, are good, as is travel to the East or North. Travel to the South is bad.

The nidana of Feeling is good for making love, obtaining wealth, and business of all kinds. Also good is changing one's clothes, traveling to the East or North, and crossing over water. It is bad to travel to the North and South, and to bathe.

#6 Craving (trshna)

Nidana 6:   Desire
Image: Sweet drink
             Picnic with Eating and Drinking
Sanskrit: Trishna
Time: The Present

This is the proverbial desire, simple craving for more, and dissatisfaction with never having enough.

This is a good day for quick actions, business of all kinds, and for gathering wealth and materials. Travel to the East, South, or North are good. Travel to the West is to be avoided.

The nidana of Craving is a good one in which to gather wealth, harvest grains, an business in general. Also favored are quick actions, and traveling to the East, provided there is a good reason. It is not a good day to bathe or travel to the West

Tibetan Astrology

#7 Grasping (upadana)

Nidana 7: Attachment
Image: Monkey gathering fruit
Sanskrit: Upadana
Time: The Present

Attachment in all its many forms, clinging to thoughts, ideas, friends, family, and its reverse hatred and dislike.

DAILY: Changing clothes and travel to the West or East should be avoided. This is a good day for preparing medicines, sending messengers, and travel to the North and South.

The nidana of Grasping is good for cutting hair and fingernails, preparing medicine, and bathing. It is also good for any kind of ascetic practice, like fasting, sending messages, and traveling to the South and North. Changing clothes and travel to the West or East should be avoided.

#8 Becoming (bhava)

Nidana 8:	Becoming
Image:	Copulation, Pregnant Woman
Sanskrit:	Bhava
Time:	The Present

This refers to attempts to bring about or create whatever it is that is craved or desired.

DAILY: This is a good day for all activities, bathing, calling for a lover, and travel to the North and South. Changing clothes, arguing, and travel to the East and West are to be avoided.

The nidana of Becoming is good for all activities, calling for your lover, bathing and travel to the South or North. It is not good for changing clothes, travel to the West or East, and arguments of any kind.

Tibetan Astrology

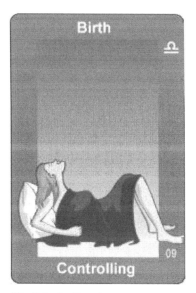

#9 Birth (jati)

Nidana 9:   Rebirth
Image: Woman Giving Birth
Sanskrit: Jati
Time: The Future

Actually bringing into existence that which is craved and desired, causing to happen or exist.

DAILY: Building a house, starting new projects, and activities with important persons are good, as is bathing, and travel to the South, North, or West. Travel to the South should be avoided.

The nidana of Birth is favorable for building a home, bathing, and travel to the South, West, and North. It is also good to engage in the activities of kings, ministers, and householders. It is not good to travel to the South or change one's clothes. Bathing will increase the likelihood of finding a lover.

#10 Old Age and Death (jara-marana)

Nidana 10:   Decline, death
Image: Corpse Carried Away
Sanskrit: Jara marana
Time: The Future

The inevitable playing out of existence to its end, which is death and decay.

DAILY: A good day for consumption, eating, drinking, and washing one's hair. Also good for travel to the North and South, but the West should be avoided. Not a good day for divination, arguments, making offerings, washing the body, and changing clothes.

The nidana of Old Age & Death is good for washing the head, drinking and eating a lot, and taking wealth from someone richer than yourself. Travel is favorable to the East, South, and North. Not favorable is travel to the West, making religious offerings, doing art work, arguing, bathing, changing clothes, and performing divinations.

#11 Ignorance (Avidya)

Nidana 11:   Ignorance
Image: Blind old woman
Sanskrit: Avidya
Time: The Past

Typically, ignorance of the Four Noble Truths that the Buddha taught is what leads to the wheel of suffering and samsara.

DAILY: A good day to bathe, for real estate, making offerings, and travel to the East or North. This is not a good day for important meetings, new clothes, or travel to the West and South.

The nidana of Ignorance is favorable for doing sadhana practice and making offerings. The directions East and North are best, while those of West and South should be avoided. It is not good to hold important meetings or putting on new clothes. It is good to find new land and taking baths.

#12 Karmic Formations (samskaras)

Nidana 12:	Karma
Image:	Potter's wheel
Sanskrit:	Avidya
Time:	The Past

The formation of mental conditions and construct, which results in what we call the Self of the "I," which is from a Buddhist point of view, merely a construct or accumulation that has no true existence, a fiction of our own ignorance or the true nature of the mind.

DAILY: This is a good day for studies, teaching and education, in general. Also good for marriage, overcoming one's enemies, starting new projects, and travel in any direction. This is not a good day for washing one's head and putting on new clothes, as illness will occur.

Tibetan Astrology

The Karma nidana is a good one for travel, in any direction. It is also good to bathe, take action against one's enemies, get married, build homes, and teach or study. Bathing the head and putting on new clothes will bring illness and problems, at once.

Yearly Tables 1900-2099

Year	1900	1901	1902	1903	1904	
Element	Iron	Iron	Water	Water	Wood	
Zodiac	Mouse	Ox	Tiger	Hare	Dragon	
Mewa	1 White	9 Maroon	8 White	7 Red	6 White	
Life Force	Water	Earth	Wood	Wood	Earth	
Health	Iron	Iron	Water	Water	Wood	
Power	Earth	Earth	Iron	Iron	Fire	
Luck	Wood	Water	Iron	Fire	Wood	
Soul	Iron	Fire	Water	Water	Fire	

Year	1905	1906	1907	1908	1909	
Element	Wood	Fire	Fire	Earth	Earth	
Zodiac	Snake	Horse	Sheep	Monkey	Bird	
Mewa	5 Yellow	4 Green	3 Indigo	2 Black	1 White	
Life Force	Fire	Fire	Earth	Iron	Iron	
Health	Wood	Fire	Fire	Earth	Earth	
Power	Fire	Water	Water	Earth	Earth	
Luck	Water	Iron	Fire	Wood	Water	
Soul	Wood	Wood	Fire	Earth	Earth	

Year	1910	1911	1912	1913	1914	
Element	Iron	Iron	Water	Water	Wood	
Zodiac	Dog	Pig	Mouse	Ox	Tiger	
Mewa	9 Maroon	8 White	7 Red	6 White	5 Yellow	
Life Force	Earth	Water	Water	Earth	Wood	
Health	Iron	Iron	Water	Water	Wood	
Power	Iron	Iron	Wood	Wood	Water	
Luck	Iron	Fire	Wood	Water	Iron	
Soul	Fire	Iron	Iron	Fire	Water	

Year	1915	1916	1917	1918	1919	
Element	Wood	Fire	Fire	Earth	Earth	
Zodiac	Hare	Dragon	Snake	Horse	Sheep	
Mewa	4 Green	3 Indigo	2 Black	1 White	9 Maroon	
Life Force	Wood	Earth	Fire	Fire	Earth	
Health	Wood	Fire	Fire	Earth	Earth	
Power	Water	Earth	Earth	Fire	Fire	
Luck	Fire	Wood	Water	Iron	Fire	
Soul	Water	Fire	Wood	Wood	Fire	

Year	1920	1921	1922	1923	1924	
Element	Iron	Iron	Water	Water	Wood	
Zodiac	Monkey	Bird	Dog	Pig	Mouse	
Mewa	8 White	7 Red	6 White	5 Yellow	4 Green	
Life Force	Iron	Iron	Earth	Water	Water	
Health	Iron	Iron	Water	Water	Wood	
Power	Wood	Wood	Water	Water	Iron	
Luck	Wood	Water	Iron	Fire	Wood	
Soul	Earth	Earth	Fire	Iron	Iron	

602

Tibetan Astrology

Year	1925	1926	1927	1928	1929
Element	Wood	Fire	Fire	Earth	Earth
Zodiac	Ox	Tiger	Hare	Dragon	Snake
Mewa	3 Indigo	2 Black	1 White	9 Maroon	8 White
Life Force	Earth	Wood	Wood	Earth	Fire
Health	Wood	Fire	Fire	Earth	Earth
Power	Iron	Fire	Fire	Wood	Wood
Luck	Water	Iron	Fire	Wood	Water
Soul	Fire	Water	Water	Fire	Wood

Year	1930	1931	1932	1933	1934
Element	Iron	Iron	Water	Water	Wood
Zodiac	Horse	Sheep	Monkey	Bird	Dog
Mewa	7 Red	6 White	5 Yellow	4 Green	3 Indigo
Life Force	Fire	Earth	Iron	Iron	Earth
Health	Iron	Iron	Water	Water	Wood
Power	Earth	Earth	Iron	Iron	Fire
Luck	Iron	Fire	Wood	Water	Iron
Soul	Wood	Fire	Earth	Earth	Fire

Year	1935	1936	1937	1938	1939
Element	Wood	Fire	Fire	Earth	Earth
Zodiac	Pig	Mouse	Ox	Tiger	Hare
Mewa	2 Black	1 White	9 Maroon	8 White	7 Red
Life Force	Water	Water	Earth	Wood	Wood
Health	Wood	Fire	Fire	Earth	Earth
Power	Fire	Water	Water	Earth	Earth
Luck	Fire	Wood	Water	Iron	Fire
Soul	Iron	Iron	Fire	Water	Water

Year	1940	1941	1942	1943	1944
Element	Iron	Iron	Water	Water	Wood
Zodiac	Dragon	Snake	Horse	Sheep	Monkey
Mewa	6 White	5 Yellow	4 Green	3 Indigo	2 Black
Life Force	Earth	Fire	Fire	Earth	Iron
Health	Iron	Iron	Water	Water	Wood
Power	Iron	Iron	Wood	Wood	Water
Luck	Wood	Water	Iron	Fire	Wood
Soul	Fire	Wood	Wood	Fire	Earth

Year	1945	1946	1947	1948	1949
Element	Wood	Fire	Fire	Earth	Earth
Zodiac	Bird	Dog	Pig	Mouse	Ox
Mewa	1 White	9 Maroon	8 White	7 Red	6 White
Life Force	Iron	Earth	Water	Water	Earth
Health	Wood	Fire	Fire	Earth	Earth
Power	Water	Earth	Earth	Fire	Fire
Luck	Water	Iron	Fire	Wood	Water
Soul	Earth	Fire	Iron	Iron	Fire

Tibetan Astrology

Year	1950	1951	1952	1953	1954
Element	Iron	Iron	Water	Water	Wood
Zodiac	Tiger	Hare	Dragon	Snake	Horse
Mewa	5 Yellow	4 Green	3 Indigo	2 Black	1 White
Life Force	Wood	Wood	Earth	Fire	Fire
Health	Iron	Iron	Water	Water	Wood
Power	Wood	Wood	Water	Water	Iron
Luck	Iron	Fire	Wood	Water	Iron
Soul	Water	Water	Fire	Wood	Wood

Year	1955	1956	1957	1958	1959
Element	Wood	Fire	Fire	Earth	Earth
Zodiac	Sheep	Monkey	Bird	Dog	Pig
Mewa	9 Maroon	8 White	7 Red	6 White	5 Yellow
Life Force	Earth	Iron	Iron	Earth	Water
Health	Wood	Fire	Fire	Earth	Earth
Power	Iron	Fire	Fire	Wood	Wood
Luck	Fire	Wood	Water	Iron	Fire
Soul	Fire	Earth	Earth	Fire	Iron

Year	1960	1961	1962	1963	1964
Element	Iron	Iron	Water	Water	Wood
Zodiac	Mouse	Ox	Tiger	Hare	Dragon
Mewa	4 Green	3 Indigo	2 Black	1 White	9 Maroon
Life Force	Water	Earth	Wood	Wood	Earth
Health	Iron	Iron	Water	Water	Wood
Power	Earth	Earth	Iron	Iron	Fire
Luck	Wood	Water	Iron	Fire	Wood
Soul	Iron	Fire	Water	Water	Fire

Year	1965	1966	1967	1968	1969
Element	Wood	Fire	Fire	Earth	Earth
Zodiac	Snake	Horse	Sheep	Monkey	Bird
Mewa	8 White	7 Red	6 White	5 Yellow	4 Green
Life Force	Fire	Fire	Earth	Iron	Iron
Health	Wood	Fire	Fire	Earth	Earth
Power	Fire	Water	Water	Earth	Earth
Luck	Water	Iron	Fire	Wood	Water
Soul	Wood	Wood	Fire	Earth	Earth

Year	1970	1971	1972	1973	1974
Element	Iron	Iron	Water	Water	Wood
Zodiac	Dog	Pig	Mouse	Ox	Tiger
Mewa	3 Indigo	2 Black	1 White	9 Maroon	8 White
Life Force	Earth	Water	Water	Earth	Wood
Health	Iron	Iron	Water	Water	Wood
Power	Iron	Iron	Wood	Wood	Water
Luck	Iron	Fire	Wood	Water	Iron
Soul	Fire	Iron	Iron	Fire	Water

Tibetan Astrology

Year	1975	1976	1977	1978	1979
Element	Wood	Fire	Fire	Earth	Earth
Zodiac	Hare	Dragon	Snake	Horse	Sheep
Mewa	7 Red	6 White	5 Yellow	4 Green	3 Indigo
Life Force	Wood	Earth	Fire	Fire	Earth
Health	Wood	Fire	Fire	Earth	Earth
Power	Water	Earth	Earth	Fire	Fire
Luck	Fire	Wood	Water	Iron	Fire
Soul	Water	Fire	Wood	Wood	Fire

Year	1980	1981	1982	1983	1984
Element	Iron	Iron	Water	Water	Wood
Zodiac	Monkey	Bird	Dog	Pig	Mouse
Mewa	2 Black	1 White	9 Maroon	8 White	7 Red
Life Force	Iron	Iron	Earth	Water	Water
Health	Iron	Iron	Water	Water	Wood
Power	Wood	Wood	Water	Water	Iron
Luck	Wood	Water	Iron	Fire	Wood
Soul	Earth	Earth	Fire	Iron	Iron

Year	1985	1986	1987	1988	1989
Element	Wood	Fire	Fire	Earth	Earth
Zodiac	Ox	Tiger	Hare	Dragon	Snake
Mewa	6 White	5 Yellow	4 Green	3 Indigo	2 Black
Life Force	Earth	Wood	Wood	Earth	Fire
Health	Wood	Fire	Fire	Earth	Earth
Power	Iron	Fire	Fire	Wood	Wood
Luck	Water	Iron	Fire	Wood	Water
Soul	Fire	Water	Water	Fire	Wood

Year	1990	1991	1992	1993	1994
Element	Iron	Iron	Water	Water	Wood
Zodiac	Horse	Sheep	Monkey	Bird	Dog
Mewa	1 White	9 Maroon	8 White	7 Red	6 White
Life Force	Fire	Earth	Iron	Iron	Earth
Health	Iron	Iron	Water	Water	Wood
Power	Earth	Earth	Iron	Iron	Fire
Luck	Iron	Fire	Wood	Water	Iron
Soul	Wood	Fire	Earth	Earth	Fire

Year	1995	1996	1997	1998	1999
Element	Wood	Fire	Fire	Earth	Earth
Zodiac	Pig	Mouse	Ox	Tiger	Hare
Mewa	5 Yellow	4 Green	3 Indigo	2 Black	1 White
Life Force	Water	Water	Earth	Wood	Wood
Health	Wood	Fire	Fire	Earth	Earth
Power	Fire	Water	Water	Earth	Earth
Luck	Fire	Wood	Water	Iron	Fire
Soul	Iron	Iron	Fire	Water	Water

Tibetan Astrology

Year	2000	2001	2002	2003	2004
Element	Iron	Iron	Water	Water	Wood
Zodiac	Dragon	Snake	Horse	Sheep	Monkey
Mewa	9 Maroon	8 White	7 Red	6 White	5 Yellow
Life Force	Earth	Fire	Fire	Earth	Iron
Health	Iron	Iron	Water	Water	Wood
Power	Iron	Iron	Wood	Wood	Water
Luck	Wood	Water	Iron	Fire	Wood
Soul	Fire	Wood	Wood	Fire	Earth

Year	2005	2006	2007	2008	2009
Element	Wood	Fire	Fire	Earth	Earth
Zodiac	Bird	Dog	Pig	Mouse	Ox
Mewa	4 Green	3 Indigo	2 Black	1 White	9 Maroon
Life Force	Iron	Earth	Water	Water	Earth
Health	Wood	Fire	Fire	Earth	Earth
Power	Water	Earth	Earth	Fire	Fire
Luck	Water	Iron	Fire	Wood	Water
Soul	Earth	Fire	Iron	Iron	Fire

Year	2010	2011	2012	2013	2014
Element	Iron	Iron	Water	Water	Wood
Zodiac	Tiger	Hare	Dragon	Snake	Horse
Mewa	8 White	7 Red	6 White	5 Yellow	4 Green
Life Force	Wood	Wood	Earth	Fire	Fire
Health	Iron	Iron	Water	Water	Wood
Power	Wood	Wood	Water	Water	Iron
Luck	Iron	Fire	Wood	Water	Iron
Soul	Water	Water	Fire	Wood	Wood

Year	2015	2016	2017	2018	2019
Element	Wood	Fire	Fire	Earth	Earth
Zodiac	Sheep	Monkey	Bird	Dog	Pig
Mewa	3 Indigo	2 Black	1 White	9 Maroon	8 White
Life Force	Earth	Iron	Iron	Earth	Water
Health	Wood	Fire	Fire	Earth	Earth
Power	Iron	Fire	Fire	Wood	Wood
Luck	Fire	Wood	Water	Iron	Fire
Soul	Fire	Earth	Earth	Fire	Iron

Year	2020	2021	2022	2023	2024
Element	Iron	Iron	Water	Water	Wood
Zodiac	Mouse	Ox	Tiger	Hare	Dragon
Mewa	7 Red	6 White	5 Yellow	4 Green	3 Indigo
Life Force	Water	Earth	Wood	Wood	Earth
Health	Iron	Iron	Water	Water	Wood
Power	Earth	Earth	Iron	Iron	Fire
Luck	Wood	Water	Iron	Fire	Wood
Soul	Iron	Fire	Water	Water	Fire

Tibetan Astrology

Year	2025	2026	2027	2028	2029
Element	Wood	Fire	Fire	Earth	Earth
Zodiac	Snake	Horse	Sheep	Monkey	Bird
Mewa	2 Black	1 White	9 Maroon	8 White	7 Red
Life Force	Fire	Fire	Earth	Iron	Iron
Health	Wood	Fire	Fire	Earth	Earth
Power	Fire	Water	Water	Earth	Earth
Luck	Water	Iron	Fire	Wood	Water
Soul	Wood	Wood	Fire	Earth	Earth

Year	2030	2031	2032	2033	2034
Element	Iron	Iron	Water	Water	Wood
Zodiac	Dog	Pig	Mouse	Ox	Tiger
Mewa	6 White	5 Yellow	4 Green	3 Indigo	2 Black
Life Force	Earth	Water	Water	Earth	Wood
Health	Iron	Iron	Water	Water	Wood
Power	Iron	Iron	Wood	Wood	Water
Luck	Iron	Fire	Wood	Water	Iron
Soul	Fire	Iron	Iron	Fire	Water

Year	2035	2036	2037	2038	2039
Element	Wood	Fire	Fire	Earth	Earth
Zodiac	Hare	Dragon	Snake	Horse	Sheep
Mewa	1 White	9 Maroon	8 White	7 Red	6 White
Life Force	Wood	Earth	Fire	Fire	Earth
Health	Wood	Fire	Fire	Earth	Earth
Power	Water	Earth	Earth	Fire	Fire
Luck	Fire	Wood	Water	Iron	Fire
Soul	Water	Fire	Wood	Wood	Fire

Year	2040	2041	2042	2043	2044
Element	Iron	Iron	Water	Water	Wood
Zodiac	Monkey	Bird	Dog	Pig	Mouse
Mewa	5 Yellow	4 Green	3 Indigo	2 Black	1 White
Life Force	Iron	Iron	Earth	Water	Water
Health	Iron	Iron	Water	Water	Wood
Power	Wood	Wood	Water	Water	Iron
Luck	Wood	Water	Iron	Fire	Wood
Soul	Earth	Earth	Fire	Iron	Iron

Year	2045	2046	2047	2048	2049
Element	Wood	Fire	Fire	Earth	Earth
Zodiac	Ox	Tiger	Hare	Dragon	Snake
Mewa	9 Maroon	8 White	7 Red	6 White	5 Yellow
Life Force	Earth	Wood	Wood	Earth	Fire
Health	Wood	Fire	Fire	Earth	Earth
Power	Iron	Fire	Fire	Wood	Wood
Luck	Water	Iron	Fire	Wood	Water
Soul	Fire	Water	Water	Fire	Wood

Tibetan Astrology

Year	2050	2051	2052	2053	2054
Element	Iron	Iron	Water	Water	Wood
Zodiac	Horse	Sheep	Monkey	Bird	Dog
Mewa	4 Green	3 Indigo	2 Black	1 White	9 Maroon
Life Force	Fire	Earth	Iron	Iron	Earth
Health	Iron	Iron	Water	Water	Wood
Power	Earth	Earth	Iron	Iron	Fire
Luck	Iron	Fire	Wood	Water	Iron
Soul	Wood	Fire	Earth	Earth	Fire

Year	2055	2056	2057	2058	2059
Element	Wood	Fire	Fire	Earth	Earth
Zodiac	Pig	Mouse	Ox	Tiger	Hare
Mewa	8 White	7 Red	6 White	5 Yellow	4 Green
Life Force	Water	Water	Earth	Wood	Wood
Health	Wood	Fire	Fire	Earth	Earth
Power	Fire	Water	Water	Earth	Earth
Luck	Fire	Wood	Water	Iron	Fire
Soul	Iron	Iron	Fire	Water	Water

Year	2060	2061	2062	2063	2064
Element	Iron	Iron	Water	Water	Wood
Zodiac	Dragon	Snake	Horse	Sheep	Monkey
Mewa	3 Indigo	2 Black	1 White	9 Maroon	8 White
Life Force	Earth	Fire	Fire	Earth	Iron
Health	Iron	Iron	Water	Water	Wood
Power	Iron	Iron	Wood	Wood	Water
Luck	Wood	Water	Iron	Fire	Wood
Soul	Fire	Wood	Wood	Fire	Earth

Year	2065	2066	2067	2068	2069
Element	Wood	Fire	Fire	Earth	Earth
Zodiac	Bird	Dog	Pig	Mouse	Ox
Mewa	7 Red	6 White	5 Yellow	4 Green	3 Indigo
Life Force	Iron	Earth	Water	Water	Earth
Health	Wood	Fire	Fire	Earth	Earth
Power	Water	Earth	Earth	Fire	Fire
Luck	Water	Iron	Fire	Wood	Water
Soul	Earth	Fire	Iron	Iron	Fire

Year	2070	2071	2072	2073	2074
Element	Iron	Iron	Water	Water	Wood
Zodiac	Tiger	Hare	Dragon	Snake	Horse
Mewa	2 Black	1 White	9 Maroon	8 White	7 Red
Life Force	Wood	Wood	Earth	Fire	Fire
Health	Iron	Iron	Water	Water	Wood
Power	Wood	Wood	Water	Water	Iron
Luck	Iron	Fire	Wood	Water	Iron
Soul	Water	Water	Fire	Wood	Wood

Tibetan Astrology

Year	2075	2076	2077	2078	2079
Element	Wood	Fire	Fire	Earth	Earth
Zodiac	Sheep	Monkey	Bird	Dog	Pig
Mewa	6 White	5 Yellow	4 Green	3 Indigo	2 Black
Life Force	Earth	Iron	Iron	Earth	Water
Health	Wood	Fire	Fire	Earth	Earth
Power	Iron	Fire	Fire	Wood	Wood
Luck	Fire	Wood	Water	Iron	Fire
Soul	Fire	Earth	Earth	Fire	Iron

Year	2080	2081	2082	2083	2084
Element	Iron	Iron	Water	Water	Wood
Zodiac	Mouse	Ox	Tiger	Hare	Dragon
Mewa	1 White	9 Maroon	8 White	7 Red	6 White
Life Force	Water	Earth	Wood	Wood	Earth
Health	Iron	Iron	Water	Water	Wood
Power	Earth	Earth	Iron	Iron	Fire
Luck	Wood	Water	Iron	Fire	Wood
Soul	Iron	Fire	Water	Water	Fire

Year	2085	2086	2087	2088	2089
Element	Wood	Fire	Fire	Earth	Earth
Zodiac	Snake	Horse	Sheep	Monkey	Bird
Mewa	5 Yellow	4 Green	3 Indigo	2 Black	1 White
Life Force	Fire	Fire	Earth	Iron	Iron
Health	Wood	Fire	Fire	Earth	Earth
Power	Fire	Water	Water	Earth	Earth
Luck	Water	Iron	Fire	Wood	Water
Soul	Wood	Wood	Fire	Earth	Earth

Year	2090	2091	2092	2093	2094
Element	Iron	Iron	Water	Water	Wood
Zodiac	Dog	Pig	Mouse	Ox	Tiger
Mewa	9 Maroon	8 White	7 Red	6 White	5 Yellow
Life Force	Earth	Water	Water	Earth	Wood
Health	Iron	Iron	Water	Water	Wood
Power	Iron	Iron	Wood	Wood	Water
Luck	Iron	Fire	Wood	Water	Iron
Soul	Fire	Iron	Iron	Fire	Water

Year	2095	2096	2097	2098	2099
Element	Wood	Fire	Fire	Earth	Earth
Zodiac	Hare	Dragon	Snake	Horse	Sheep
Mewa	4 Green	3 Indigo	2 Black	1 White	9 Maroon
Life Force	Wood	Earth	Fire	Fire	Earth
Health	Wood	Fire	Fire	Earth	Earth
Power	Water	Earth	Earth	Fire	Fire
Luck	Fire	Wood	Water	Iron	Fire
Soul	Water	Fire	Wood	Wood	Fire

Worked Example

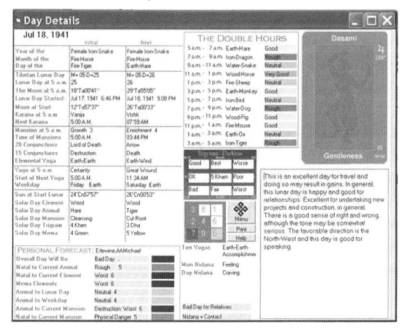

Not a Workbook

This is not a "How-to" book, but a "What's It All About" book, so there will be no in-depth, step-by-step presentation for each Tibetan astrological technique. However, I will give one output example here that may help. Also, where possible throughout the book, I have explained how some of the techniques are calculated. With others, it is just too complex and with still others, those of us studying this are still trying to figure out what's what.

For those of you who don't like to figure all this out or who fear the many possibilities for error in doing so, I have written a Tibetan Astrology program for the PC that does all of what is in this book an more. You can read more about it by following the links on StarTypes.com. Above: sample program screen.

Tibetan Astrology

Calculations for July 18, 1941

Here are the proper calculations for my own birth on July 18, 1941 at 5:03 PM EDT (Eastern Daylight Time) in Lancaster, Pa. First I will list the results, and then describe what each entry presents. Keep in mind that there are different methods in use in the Tibetan astrology community, so another lineage or style may give different results. I have mostly followed the Tsurphu tradition.

(00) July 18, 1941 5:03 EDT, Lancaster, PA

## Features	Start of Day	Next Value
(01) Tibetan Year:	Female Iron-Snake	
(02) Month	Fire-Horse	Fire-Horse
(03) Day	Fire Tiger	Earth-Hare
(04) Lunar Month/Day	5th Month, 25th Day	5th M, 26th Day
(05) Lunar Day 5 A.M.	25th Day	26th Day
(06) Long. Moon 5 A.M.	18°Taurus00'41"	29°Taurus55'05"
(07) 25th Day Starts	July 17, 1941 6:46 PM	July 18 - 9:08 P.M.
(08) Long Moon Start	12°Taurus57'37"	26°Taurus00'33"
(09) Karana 5 A.M.	Vanija	Vishti
(10) Next Karana	5:00 A.M.	07:59 A.M.
(11) Ten-Yogas	Earth-Earth (Accomplishment)	
(12) Mewa	4 Green	
(13) Trigram	5 Kham	
(14) Mansion 5 A.M.	Growth #3	Enrichment #4
(15) Time of Mansions	5:00 A.M.	03:44 PM
(16) 28 Conjunctions	Lord of Death	Arrow
(17) 15 Conjunctures	Destruction	Death
(18) Elemental Yoga	Earth-Earth	Earth-Wind
(19) Yoga at 5 A.M.	Certainty	Great Wound
(20) Next Yoga	5:00 A.M.	11:34 P.M.
(21) Weekday	Friday-Earth	Saturday-Earth
(22) Sun Start L.D.	24°Cancer57'57"	26°Cancer00'537
(23) Solar Day Element	Wood	Wood
(24) Solar Day Animal	Hare	Tiger
(25) Solar Day Mansion	Cleansing	Cut Root
(26) Solar Day Trigram	4 Khen	3 Dha
(27) Solar Day Mewa	4 Green	5 Yellow
(28) Monthly Nidana	Feeling	
(29) Day Nidana	Craving	

Tibetan Astrology

(30) The Double Hours
5 A.M. - 7 A.M.	Earth-Hare
7 A.M. - 9 A.M.	Iron-Dragon
9 A.M. – 11 A.M.	Water-Snake
11 A.M. - 1 P.M.	Wood-Horse
1 P.M. - 3 P.M.	Fire-Sheep
3 P.M. - 5 P.M.	Earth-Monkey
5 P.M. - 7 P.M.	Iron-Bird
7 P.M. - 9 P.M.	Water-Dog
9 P.M. - 11 P.M.	Wood-Pig
11 P.M. - 1 A.M.	Fire-Mouse
1 A.M. - 3 A.M.	Earth-Ox
3 A.M. - 5 A.M.	Iron-Tiger

(00) July 18, 1941 5:03 EDT, Lancaster, PA
This is the birth information.

(01) Tibetan Year
This is the polarity-element-animal combination for the current year, as taken from the sixty-year sexagenary table. The female-Iron-Snake year.

(02) Month
This is the 5th lunar month, starting with Losar (Tibetan New Year), the month of the Fire-Horse. Notice that the next month's element animal combination is given to the right.

(03) Day
This is the day of the Fire-Tiger. The next day is also provide, that of the Earth-Hare.

(04) Lunar Month/Day
The 5th lunar month, and the 25th Tithie or lunar day at 5 A.M. of the calendar date. The following day is also provided.

(05) Lunar Day 5 A.M.
This indicates that a 5 A.M. on July 18th, the 25th lunar day was in progress. The next would be, of course, the 26th lunar day.

(06) Long. Moon 5 A.M.
This is the longitude of the Moon in the tropical zodiac at 5 A.M. of the day. Also shown is the longitude for 5 A.M. of the following day.

(07) 25th Day Starts

This is the date and time when the 25th lunar day started. Notice it was during the previous day. Also shown, is the date/time when the 26th lunar day began, which was in the evening of the July 18th.

(08) Long Moon Start
This is the longitude of the Moon in the tropical zodiac at the start of the 25th lunar day. Also shown is the longitude of the Moon in the tropical zodiac at the start of the 26th day.

(09) Karana 5 A.M.
This is the half-lunar day or Karana in progress at 5 A.M. of July 18th. Also given is the name of the following Karana.

(10) Next Karana
This gives the time for the initial Karana, which always will be that in progress at 5 A.M., and the time that the next Karana begins, in this case 7:59 A.M. of July 18th.

(11) Ten-Yogas
This is a repeat of what is listed in #18 below, which see for details. Here the quality of the combination is given.

(12) Mewa
This is the Mewa or Magic-Square number for the current day.

(13) Trigram
This is the Trigram for the current day.

(14) Lunar Mansion 5 A.M.
This is the number and name of the Lunar Mansion or Nakshatra at 5 A.M. of the date. The next mansion and number are also indicated.

(15) Time of Mansions
The time of the initial Lunar Mansion will always be 5
A.M., but the time that the following Lunar Mansion
begins is notated to the right.

(16) 28 Conjunctions
This is the conjunction in progress at 5 A.M. of the
current day as well as the next conjunction, which will
follow it.

(17) 15 Conjunctures
The Conjuncture for 5 A.M. is shown, along with the
following one.

(18) Elemental Yoga
This is probably the most-used astrological factor, used
by lay people as much (or more) than clergy. It
represents the combination of the particular planet day
of the week's element with the element of the current
Nakshatra or Lunar Mansion.

(19) Yoga at 5 A.M.
The Yoga or Jorwa at 5 A.M. is given, along with the
next yoga in order.

(20) Next Yoga
The time of the yoga is 5 A.M., but to the right is the
time of day that the next yoga will begin.

(21) Weekday
The day of the week is listed, which itself represents a
planet, along with the weekday element.

(22) Sun Start L.D.

Tibetan Astrology

The position of the Sun at the start of the lunar day in progress at 5 A.M. is given in the tropical zodiac, along with the Sun position at the beginning of the next lunar day in order.

(23) Solar Day Element
The solar-day element for the day.

(24) Solar Day Animal
The solar-day animal for the day.

(25) Solar Day Mansion
The solar-day Lunar Mansion for the day.

(26) Solar Day Trigram
The solar-day Trigram for the day.

(27) Solar Day Mewa
The solar-day Mewa for the day.

(28) Monthly Nidana
The Nidana for the month is shown.

(29) Day Nidana
The Nidana for the current day is shown.

(30) The Double Hours
This is a table of the double hours for the current day.

616

Tidal Force

In the last 20 years or so, scientists too have become more aware of lunar effects on the earth and its inhabitants. In general, much of this research may be summed up and is expressed in the combined solunar gravitational force. This unique measure includes both terrestrial and solar gravitational influence in a single indicator, incorporating the effects of the accelerated orbital motion of the Moon and the closeness of the separation-interval at perigee-syzygy, the consequence of a coincident Sun/Moon alignment in celestial latitude or declination, and the perturbed motion of perigee subject to increased solar gravitational force when perigee-syzygy occurs near the time of perihelion.

In brief, this is the most accurate single indicator for lunar gravitational forces that we have been able to locate. This tidal force indicator may be helpful in indicating the relative strength of any lunar day from a geophysical point of view. The indicator is listed as a percentage of the force, ranging from zero to 100%, with 100% being the strongest tidal force. There is not room here to include tables of the Tidal-Force factor, but it is available as part of the PC program "Tibetan Astrology," available on StarTypes.com.

References

Some material in this book is the result of personal discussions with a number of very distinguished lamas in the Karma Kagyu Lineage, including His Holiness Ogyen Trinley Dorje, the 17th Gyalwa Karmapa, H.E. Tai Situ Rinpoche, H.E. Jamgon Kongtrul Rinpoche, H.E. Gyaltsap Rinpoche, H.E. Shamar Rinpoche, Ven. Thrangu Rinpoche, Ven. Khenpo Tsultrim Gyatso Rinpoche, Ven. Bardor Tulku Rinpoche, Khenpo Ugyen Tenzin, and, in particular, Ven. Khenpo Karthar, Rinpoche.

Most of the information used to create this program came from four Buddhist practitioners or scholars, each with a wide knowledge. In order of my meeting them, they are:

Tibetan Astrology

John M. Reynolds

A remarkable student of the dharma, Reynolds is as much a yogi as he is a scholar. We met in the early 1980s and Reynolds gave a 2-day seminar on Tibetan Astrology at the Heart Center, here in Big Rapids, Michigan. He provided background information on the history of Tibetan astrology as well as the techniques. In 1978, John Reynolds published a detailed Tibetan astrological calendar, perhaps the first document (in English) of its kind. As John puts it, he soon became more interested in the Tibetan Buddhism than in the astrology, per se.

Tibetan Astrology

Sange Wangchuk

I met Sange wangchuk at Karma Triyana Dharmachakra (KTD) Monastery in upstate New York in the middle 1980s. With the permission of Khenpo Karthar, Rinpoche, abbot of KTD, I invited Wangchuk to come and reside with us in Big Rapids, Michigan, where he spend over 2 1/2 years. During that time, we worked to translate and understand the basics of Tibetan astrology, both that inherited from India (Kar-Tsi) and that from China (Jung-Tsi). Sange Wangchuk was a rare individual, with a knowledge of not only Tibetan, but also Sanskrit, Nepalese, Bhutanese, Hindi, and several other languages. He also was an expert graphic artist and calligrapher, not to mention his vocal skills in the songs of Milarepa, Tibet's greatest yogi. Wangchuk put on a workship at our center on Tibetan astrology and worked with me to document the basic elements of their astrology.

Tibetan Astrology

Dr. Drubgyud Tendar

In 1997, at the prompting of the Ven. Dzogchen Ponlop, Rinpoche, We invited Dr. Drubgyud to come to our center for an extended stay. The purpose was to attempt to document the basic algorithms of Tibetan astrology used by the Karma Kagyu Lineage, in particular the Tsurphu tradition initiated by the 3rd Karmpa, Rangjung Dorje. The Tsurphu tradition was in danger of being lost because very few practitioners remain, after the Chinese forced many Tibetans to flee for their lives, when they occupied Tibet.

Although there was quite a language barrier, I worked with Dr. Drubgyud to document and recreate the algorithms necessary to represent the tradition as it has existed for centuries. We were successful in recreating the basic algorithms, so that they compare to written existing records to a high degree of accuracy. This was our main work and it is included in this program. In addition, Dr. Drubgyud was kind enough to assist in finishing and commenting on some of the Jung-Tsi material that was started with John Reynolds and Sange Wangchuk.

Tibetan Astrology

Edward Henning

Edward Henning is a practitioner, translator, and scholar of Tibetan astrology, in particular the Kalachakra or Wheel of Time. Henning was kind enough to translate the names and descriptions of the various Earth Lords and to answer a great number of questions from your editor. His excellent site HTTP://www.Kalachakra.org contains much information of interest to those interested in Tibetan astrology. He also has a book in the works on the Kalachaka that may be available by the time your read this: "Kalachakra and the Tibetan Calendar." It is available on Amazon.com.

Tibetan Astrology

Other References:

N.P. Subramania Iyer, Kalaprakasika, Ranjan Publications, 1982

Ven. Khenpo Karthar, Rinpoche. From a teaching on Buddhist Festivals, given Big Rapids, MI, 1980s

D. Bahadur L.D. Swamikannuu Pillai, Panchang and Horoscope, Asian Educational Services, 1985.

Michael Erlewine, "The Vision of the Eclipse," AFA/Circle Books Calendar, 1980s

Michael Erlewine, "Lunar Gaps," Matrix Journal, 1990

Michael Erlewine, "Science and the Lunation Cycle," Matrix Journal, 1990

Michael Erlewine, Yearly Lunar Practice Calendar, from KTD Dharma Goods, 315 Marion Avenue, Big Rapids, MI 49307

D. Bahadur L.D. Swamikannuu Pillai, Indian Chronology, Asian Educational Services, 1982.

Swami Prakashananda, personal communication.

Shyam Sundar Das, personal communication.

Sange Wangchug, personal communication, teaching, and translation of Tibetan texts.

Dr. Drubgyud Tendar, personal communication. Dr. Tendar is a skilled Tibetan astrology, who contributed much information on the Tsurphu calendar system and other related items.

John Reynolds, from personal discussions, seminars, calendar, papers.

Reynolds, John (aka Acharya Vajranatha) Tibetan Astrology, article

Tibetan Astrology

Reynolds, John, Tibetan Astrology, NCGR Newsletter

John Reynolds, 1978 Tibetan Astrological Calendar & Almanac, Kalachakra Publications, Katmandu, Nepal

Cornu, Philipps, "Tibetan Astrology," Shambhala Publications, 1997, An excellent book that has only recently been published.

Michael Erlewine can be reached at: Michael@Erlewine.net

About the Author

Michael Erlewine

Internationally known astrologer and author Noel Tyl (author of 34 books on astrology) has this to say about Michael Erlewine:

"Michael Erlewine is the giant influence whose creativity is forever imprinted on all astrologers' work since the beginning of the Computer era! He is the man who single-handedly applied computer technology to astrological measurement, research, and interpretation, and has been the formative and leading light of astrology's modern growth. Erlewine humanized it all, adding perception and incisive practical analyses to modern, computerized astrology. Now, for a second generation of astrologers and their public, Erlewine's genius continues with StarTypes ... and it's simply amazing!"

A Brief Bio of Michael Erlewine

Michael Erlewine has studied and practiced astrology for over 40 years, as an author, teacher, lecturer, personal consultant, programmer, and conference producer.

Tibetan Astrology

Erlewine was the first astrologer to program astrology, on microcomputers and make those programs available to his fellow astrologers. This was in 1977. He founded Matrix Astrology in 1978, and his company, along with Microsoft, are the two oldest software companies still on the Internet.

Michael, soon joined by his astrologer-brother Stephen Erlewine, went on to revolutionize astrology by producing, for the new microcomputers, the first written astrological reports, first research system, first high resolution chart wheels, geographic and star maps, and on and on.

Along the way Matrix produced programs that spoke astrology (audio), personal astrological videos, infomercials, and many other pioneering feats.

Michael Erlewine has received major awards from UAC (United Astrological Conferences), AFA (American Federation of Astrologers), and the PIA (Professional Astrologers Incorporated), and scores of online awards.

Michael and Stephen Erlewine have published a yearly calendar for almost 30 years, since 1969. Michael Erlewine has produced and put on more than 36 conferences in the areas of astrology and Buddhism.

Tibetan Astrology

Example Astro*Image Card

Aside from his current work as a consultant for NBC's iVillage and Astrology.com, Erlewine has personally designed over 6,000 tarot-like astrology cards, making authentic astrology available to people with little or no experience in the topic. These Astro*Image™ cards are available through a variety of small astrological programs and in eBooks. Some examples can be found at WWW.StarTypes.com, where there is also a link to his astrological software.

Tibetan Astrology

Michael Erlewine has been doing personal astrology readings for almost forty years and enjoys sharing his knowledge with others. However, his busy schedule makes it difficult to honor all requests. However, feel free to email (Michael@Erlewine.net) him if you wish a personal chart reading. He will let you know if his current schedule will allow him to work with you.

The sections that follow will give you more details about Michael Erlewine and his very active center.

The Heart Center House

In 1972, Michael and Margaret Erlewine established the Heart Center, a center for community studies. Today, the Heart Center continues to be a center for astrological and spiritual work. Over the years, hundreds of invited guests have stayed at the Heart Center, some for just a night, others for many years. Astrologers, authors, musicians, Sanskrit scholars, swamis - you name it, the Heart Center has been a home for a wide group of individuals, all united by their interest in spiritual or cultural ideas.

Heart Center Library

Erlewine also founded and directs The Heart Center Astrological Library, the largest astrological library in the United States, and probably the world, that is open to researchers. Meticulously catalogued, the current library project is the scanning of the Table of Contents for all major books and periodicals on astrology.

The library does not have regular hours, so contact ahead of time if you wish to visit. Michael@erlewine.net.

The All-Music Guide / All-Movie Guide

Michael Erlewine's devotion to studying and playing the music of Black Americans, in particular blues, led to his traveling to small blues clubs of Chicago and hearing live, blues greats like Little Walter, Magic Sam, Big Walter Horton, and many others. He went on to interview many dozens of performers. Much of this interviewing took place at the Ann Arbor Blues Festivals, in 1969 and 1970, the first electric blues festivals of any size ever held in North America, and than later at the Ann Arbor Blues & Jazz Festivals.

With their extensive knowledge of the blues music, Erlewine and his brother Daniel were asked to play host to the score or so of professional blues musicians and their bands. They were in charge of serving them food and (of course) drink. Michael went on to interview most of the performers in these early festivals, with an audio recorder, and later on with video.
The interviewing led to more study and ultimately resulted in Michael founding and developing AMG, the

All-Music Guide, today the largest single database of music reviews and documentation on the planet.

Erlewine started from a one-room office, and the reviewers and music aficionados of the time laughed at his attempt to cover all music. But he persisted, and the all-Music Guide appeared as a Gopher Site, before the World Wide Web even existed-a database of popular music for all music lovers.

Over the years AMG grew, and the All-Movie Guide and All Game Guide were born, and also flourished. Later, Erlewine would create ClassicPosters.com, devoted to the history and documentation of rock n' roll posters, some 35,000 of them.

These guides changed the way music was reviewed and rated. Previous to AMG, review guides like the "Rolling Stones Record Guide" were run by a few sophisticated reviewers, and the emphasis was on the expertise of the reviewer, and their point of view. Erlewine insisted on treating all artists equally, and not comparing artist to artist, what can be important, Michael points out, is to find the best music any artist has produced, not if the artist is better or worse than Jimmie Hendrix or Bob Dylan.

Erlewine sold AMG in 1996, at which time he had 150 fulltime employees, and 500 free-lance writers. He had edited and published any number of books and CD-ROMs on music and film. During the time he owned and ran AMG, there were no advertisements on the site and nothing for sale. As Erlewine writes, "All of us deserve to have access to our own popular culture. That is what AMG and ClassicPosters.com are all about." Today, AMG reviews can be found everywhere across the Internet. Erlewine's music collection is housed in an AMG warehouse, numbering almost 500,000 CDs.

Tibetan Astrology

Heart Center Meditation Room

Michael Erlewine has been active in Buddhism since the 1950s. Here are his own words:

"Back in the late 1950s, and early 1960, Buddhism was one of many ideas we stayed up late, smoked cigarettes, drank lots of coffee, and talked about, along with existentialism, poetry, and the like.

"It was not until I met the Tibetan lama, Chogyam Trungpa Rinpoche, in 1974 that I understood Buddhism as not just Philosophy, but also as path, a way to get through life. Having been raised Catholic, serving as an altar boy, learning church Latin, and all that, I had not been given any kind of a path, other than the path of faith. I hung onto that faith as long as I could, but it told me very little about how to live and work in this world.,

"I had been trying to learn the basics of Tibetan Buddhism before I met Trungpa Rinpoche, but the spark that welded all of that together was missing.

Trungpa provided that spark. I got to be his chauffer for a weekend, and to design a poster for his public talk.

"More important, only about an hour after we met, Trungpa took me into a small room for a couple of hours and taught me to meditate. I didn't even understand what I was learning. All that I know was that I was learning about myself.

"After that meeting, I begin to understand a lot more of what I had read, but it was almost ten years later that I met my teacher, Khenpo Karthar, Rinpoche, the abbot of Karma Triyana Dharmachakra Monstery, in the mountains above Woodstock, NY. Meeting Rinpoche was life-changing.

Heart Center Symbol

"It was not long after that we started the Heart Center Meditation Center here in Big Rapids, which is still going today. My wife and I became more and more involved with the monastery in New York, and we ended up serving on several boards, and even as fundraisers for the monastery. We helped to raise the funds to build a

3-year retreat in upstate New York, one for men and one for women.

"We also established KTD Dharma Goods, a mail-order dharma goods business that helped practitioners find the meditation materials they might need. We published many sadhanas, the traditional Buddhist practice texts, plus other teachings, in print and on audio tape.

Years have gone by, and I am still working with Khenpo, Rinpoche and the sangha at the Woodstock monastery. Some years ago, Rinpoche surprised my wife and I by telling us we should go to Tibet and meet His Holiness the 17th Karmapa, and that we should go right away, that summer, and I hate to leave the house!

That trip, and a second trip that followed some years later, turned out to be pilgrimages that were also life changing. Our center in Big Rapids has a separate building as a shrine room and even a small Stupa; pictures are shown below.

I can never repay the kindness that Khenpo Rinpoche and the other rinpoches that I have taken teachings from have shown me.

Music Career

Tibetan Astrology

c 1967

Michael Erlewine's career in music started early on, when he dropped out of high school and hitchhiked to Venice West, in Santa Monica, California, in an attempt to catch a ride on the tail end of the Beatnik era. This was 1960, and he was a little late for that, but right on time for the folk music revival that was just beginning to bloom at that time. Like many other people his age, Erlewine traveled from college center to center across the nation: Ann Arbor, Berkeley, Cambridge, and Greenwich Village. There was a well-beaten track on which traveled the young folk musicians of the future.

Erlewine, who also played folk guitar, hitchhiked for a stint with a young Bob Dylan, and then more extensively with guitar virtuoso and instrumentalist Perry Lederman. Erlewine helped to put on Dylan's first concert in Ann Arbor. He hung out with people like Ramblin' Jack Elliot, Joan Baez, The New Lost City Ramblers, and the County Gentlemen.

In 1965, the same year that the Grateful Dead were forming, Michael Erlewine, his brother Daniel, and a few others formed the first new-style band in the Midwest, the Prime Movers Blues Band. Iggy Pop was their drummer, and his stint in the band was how he got the name Iggy. This was the beginning of the hippie era. Michael was the band's lead singer, and played amplified Chicago-style blues harmonica. He still plays.

Erlewine was also the manager of the band, and personally designed and silkscreened the band's posters, one of which is shown below.

The Prime Movers became a seminal band throughout the Midwest, and even traveled as far as the West Coast, where the band spent 1967, the "summer of Love," playing at all of the famous clubs, for example, opening for Eric Clapton and Cream, at the Fillmore Auditorium.

As the 60s wound down, and bands began to break up, Erlewine was still studying the music of American Blacks, in particular blues. Because of their knowledge of blues and the players, Michael and his brother Dan were invited to help host the first major electric blues festival in the United States, the 1969 Ann Arbor Blues Festival. They got to wine and dine the performers, and generally look after them.

Michael interviewed (audio and video) most of the players at the first two Ann Arbor Blues Festivals, they included: Big Joe Turner, Luther Allison, Carey Bell, Bobby Bland, Clifton Chenier, James Cotton, Pee Wee Crayton, Arthur, Crudup, Jimmy Dawkins, Doctor Ross, Sleepy John Estes, Lowell Fulson, Buddy Guy, John Lee hooker, Howlin' wolf, J.B. Hutto, Albert King, B.B King, Freddie king, Sam Lay, Light-nin' Hopkins, Manse Lipscomb, Robert Lockwood, Magic Sam, Fred Mcdowell, Muddy Waters, Charlie Musslewhite, Louis Myers , Junior Parker, Brewer Phillips, Otis rush, Johnnie Shines, George Smith, Son House, Victoria

Tibetan Astrology

Spivey, Hubert Sumlin, Sunnyland Slim, Roosevelt Sykes, Eddie Taylor, Hound Dog Taylor, Big mama Thornton, Eddie Vinson, Sippie Wallace, Junior Wells, Big Joe Williams, Robert Pete Williams, Johnny Young, and Mighty Joe Young.

Email:

Michael Erlewine can be reached at
Michael@Erlewine.net